About the Authors

For five decades, award-winning writer **Brad Steiger** has been devoted to exploring and examining unusual, hidden, secret, and otherwise strange occurrences. A former high school teacher and college instructor, Brad published his first articles on the unexplained in 1956. Since then he has written more than 2,000 articles with paranormal themes. He is author or coauthor of more than 170 titles, including *Real Ghosts, Restless Spirits, and Haunted Places; The Werewolf Book; Mysteries of Time and Space;* and *Revelation: The Divine Fire.*

An expert on health and healing, spirituality, and the paranormal, **Sherry Steiger** has numerous magazine articles to her credit and has authored or coauthored more than 40 books, including *Conspiracies and Secret Societies* and the best-selling "Miracles" series. An ordained minister, Sherry has served as a counselor to troubled youth, the homeless, migrant workers, and families in need of crisis intervention. With her background in nursing and theology, Sherry began researching alternative health issues and mysteries of the unknown in the 1960s, and she cofounded and produced the highly acclaimed *Celebrate Life,* a multimedia experiential presentation and workshop program.

Visible Ink Press®
43311 Joy Rd., #414
Canton, MI 48187-2075

Visible Ink Press is a registered trademark of Visible Ink Press LLC.

Project Manager: Kevin Hile
Art Director: Mary Claire Krzewinski
Typesetting: Marco Di Vita
Proofreader: Sarah Hermsen
Indexer: Lawrence W. Baker

All photos: iStock.com

ISBN 978-1-57859-214-2

Library of Congress Cataloging-in-Publication Data has been applied for.

Printed in the United States of America

REAL MIRACLES DIVINE INTERVENTION AND FEATS OF INCREDIBLE SURVIVAL

BRAD STEIGER
and
SHERRY HANSEN STEIGER

VISIBLE
INK
PRESS

Detroit

CONTENTS

INTRODUCTION

Jon Butler, a Yale University professor of American history, defined miracles as physical events that defy the laws of nature. "Most miracles have some physical manifestation that is evident not only to the individuals involved, but may be evident to the people around them," he said. "The catch is, how do you explain it?"

Many choose to explain miracles as religious experiences. Miracle stories are found in all the world's religions whose traditions include historical accounts of wonder-working saints and sages. The ancient acts of divine intervention in human affairs are celebrated regularly by the faithful who gather in churches, synagogues, and mosques throughout the world. Both the Old and New Testaments of the Bible are filled with miracles and wonders performed by prophets, angels, and God. So, too, does the Qur'an contain accounts of countless miracles, thus enabling the contemporary followers of Islam to expect such occurrences as proof of the validity of their faith. Islamic theologians have established two basic kinds of miracles: the *mu'jizat* (prophetic miracles) and the *karamat* (those wonders performed by holy people and saints).

Contemporary Jews, Buddhists, Christians, Hindus, and Muslims still pray for and expect miraculous occurrences in their own lives today, as demonstrated in several surveys. For example, on November 29, 2007, the Harris Poll released the findings of a survey of U.S. adults conducted between November 7 and 13, 2007. The poll found that 82 percent believed in God; 74 percent believed in angels; and 79 percent believed in miracles.

But the belief in miracles is not necessarily limited to those who adhere to a specific religion. The May 1, 2000, issue of *Newsweek* carried the result of a poll that stated that 84 percent of American adults believe that God performs miracles, and 48 percent claim to have witnessed one. Interestingly, 43 percent of those polled belonged to no religious body at all, but they admitted that they had on occasion prayed for God's intervention. In another example, from May through August 2007, Pew's Religious Landscape Survey questioned 35,000 Americans, nearly 30 percent of whom professed no denominational religious identity. This major survey, released in June 2008, found that U.S. adults believe overwhelmingly in God (92 percent), and 58 percent stated that they prayed at least once a day.

Despite such popular faith in miracles, the Roman Catholic Church does not treat claims about miracles lightly. Contrary to those skeptics who suggest that the Church is likely to accept nearly all claims of miracles as genuine, many careful steps are taken by various committees to authenticate a miracle. Father Frederick Jelly, a professor of systematic theology at Mount Saint Mary's Seminary in Emmitsburg, Maryland, has served on miracles committees. He listed the questions typically asked by the Church before it authenticates a miracle:

1. What is the psychological state of the person claiming the miracle?

2. Is there a profit motive behind the miracle claim?

3. What is the character of the person who is claiming the miracle?

4. Does the miracle contain any elements contrary to scripture or faith?

5. What are the spiritual fruits of the miracle; i.e., does it attract people to prayer or to acts of greater charity?

Once these questions have been determined and reviewed, the committee makes its decision as to whether or not the event was heaven-inspired. If the committee decides the event is miraculous and its implications have national or international effect, the case may be referred to the Vatican's Sacred Congregation for the Doctrine of the Faith in Rome. The Sacred Congregation has the authority to institute a new investigation and make its own ruling and recommendation to the Pope, who is the final arbiter of miracles.

By no means do Roman Catholics have a monopoly on religious visions and miracles. In October 2000, a Lutheran minister and a sociologist in Minnesota released their study that more than 30 percent of 2000 Protestant Christians surveyed said that they had had dramatic visions, heard heavenly voices, or experienced prophetic dreams.

In April 2001, details of research conducted at the University of Wales detected a common core to religious experiences that crosses boundaries of culture and faith. An analysis of 6,000 such experiences revealed that Christians may describe a religious experience as an encounter with Jesus, Mary, or an angel; Muslims also often interpret the phenomenon as the presence of an angel; and Jews describe the event as a sign of insight or an experience of God.

As one might imagine, the scientific community has also studied claims about religious experiences and other miracles. Philadelphia scientist Andrew Newberg, author of *Why God Won't Go Away*, said that the human brain is set up in such a way as to be receptive of spiritual and religious experiences. Matthew Alper, who penned *The God Part of the Brain*, which is about the neuroscience of belief, went so far as to declare that dogmatic religious beliefs that insist that particular faiths are unique, rather than the results of universal brain chemistry, are irrational and dangerous.

Other scientists assert that although objective observation and experimentation may not be able to prove that miracles exist, this does not invalidate them. In his book *The Faith of Biology and the Biology of Faith,* Robert Pollack, a professor of biological sciences at Columbia University, conceded that religious experience may seem irrational to a materialistic scientist, but he argued that irrational experiences are not necessarily unreal. In fact, they can be just as real—just as much a part of being human—as those realities that have been defined through reason. Daniel Batson, a University of Kansas psychologist who studies the effects of such experiences as miracles on people, added that the brain is merely the hardware through which religion is experienced. "To say that the brain produces religion is like saying a piano produces music," he commented.

Lorenzo Albacete, a Roman Catholic priest and professor of theology at St. Joseph's Seminary in Yonkers, wrote in the *New York Times Magazine* (December 18, 2000) that he was somewhat nervous about the new efforts of science to explain human spirituality: "If the religious experience is an authentic contact with a transcendent Mystery, it not only will but should exceed the grasp of science. Otherwise, what about it would be transcendent?" Father James Wiseman, associate professor of theology at Catholic University, said that there are always going to be some people "who see immediately the hand of God in every coincidence, and those who are going to be skeptical of everything. And there is a great in-between."

Others in the religious and theological community have been similarly diplomatic in explaining miracles. For instance, Philip Hefner, a professor of systematic theology at the Lutheran School of Theology at Chicago, stated in an essay in *Newsweek* (May 1, 2000) that he would rather talk about blessings: "We receive blessings, often quite unexpectedly, and we want to praise God for them. We know we cannot claim the credit for these blessings. Even though we cannot predict their arrival, nor understand why so much of human life involves sorrow and evil, we can be grateful and render praise."

Real Miracles, Divine Intervention, and Feats of Incredible Survival is a book that will provide an antidote to all those who suffer from doubt, disbelief, cynicism, and a fear that they walk unnoticed and alone on their life path. In these remarkable stories of endurance, survival, heroism, and achievement, the indomitable human spirit shines forth in its full splendor and is uplifted to a glory beyond imagining.

Real Miracles is about ordinary men and women who have survived natural disasters, horrific accidents, strange encounters, and medical emergencies. Many of the stories of divine intervention, miraculous healings, near-death-experiences, and inspirational spiritual manifestations come from the Steiger Questionnaire of Mystical and Paranormal Experiences, which was begun in 1968. More than 30,000 respondents drawn from readers of our books, lecture audiences, and media appearances have shared their accounts of personal interaction with angels, spirit guides, or benevolent beings who have been responsible for real miracles in their lives. In the accounts of those who somehow managed to hang on to life by a thread in the face of incredible odds, the reader will come to admire those who bore the unexpected threats to their life with courage.

It has often been noted that one's strength increases in proportion to the obstacles imposed upon it. Perhaps nowhere is the wonder of the human soul more profound than when it allies itself with the Infinite in awesome medical miracles of amazing births, awakenings from long comas, or from emerging from risky surgeries with a life that has been renewed.

Real Miracles is loosely organized into six chapters, though the reader may notice that some concepts crossing over from chapter to chapter. An index is provided in the back of this book to help the reader locate tales on specific topics of interest.

This a book for everyone: for those who believe that the human being is itself a miracle and for those who believe that the unquenchable human spirit, when forced to do so, will find a way to create its own miracles. *Real Miracles* is a book for those who believe that a miracle is an event that occurs contrary to the established course of nature and for those who are content to marvel at the strength, abilities, and courage of their fellow humans who found a way to beat the odds.

NATURAL DISASTERS

Cold, Snow, and Ice

✴

Frozen Like a Block of Ice, Two-Year-Old Karlee Was Revived

When Robert Kosolofski left for his job at the dairy at 2:30 A.M. the morning of February 23, 1994, he had no idea that his two-year-old daughter, Karlee, had tried to follow him out to the garage. If he had caught sight of the toddler in her pajamas and diapers leaving the house, he surely would have stopped and carried her back to bed. There was a wind-chill factor of 40 degrees below zero that morning.

Unknown to Robert, little Karlee had pulled on a coat and a pair of boots over her pajamas and set out to go with her daddy to work at the local dairy in Roleau, Saskatchewan. When she pushed open the door to go outside, it slammed shut behind her and locked automatically. Doctors later estimated that Karlee had frozen within only a few minutes of exposure to the 40-below temperature.

When Karlee's mother, Karrie, awakened around 8:00 A.M., she was startled to discover that the two-year-old was not in her bed. After searching the house without finding Karlee—and noticing that her coat and boots were missing—Karrie began to fear the worst. It seemed impossible that Karlee would have gone outside, but when Karrie opened the door, she found their only child frozen stiff on the doorstep.

By the time the ambulance got Karrie and her daughter to the hospital little Karlee had no pulse and no heartbeat. Dr. John Burgess, a cardiovascular and thoracic surgeon at Plains Health Center in Regina, told reporters that Karlee had literally been frozen like a block of ice. Her body temperature had dropped from a normal 98.6 to 57.2 degrees. From the descriptions given by the attending physicians at the Health Center, one can visualize poor little Karlee's tiny legs so frozen and rigid, so delicately fragile, that they appeared as though they could easily snap right off, like icicles.

A dedicated medical team began working desperately to bring the two-year-old girl back to life. Doctors connected her to a heart and lung machine which, for nearly five hours, slowly withdrew Karlee's blood, warmed it, then recirculated it into her body.

Her heart began to beat again when her body temperature reached 77 degrees. Doctors shocked Karlee's heart twice to keep it beating until her tiny body gradually warmed up to 98.6 degrees.

Remarkably, since she had frozen so quickly, none of Karlee's vital organs, including her brain, were damaged. The only lasting damage sustained by the little girl was the loss of the lower part of her left leg due to frostbite.

Dr. Joy Dobson, an anesthesiologist at Plains Health Center, declared that they had all witnessed a miracle when a baby frozen like a block of ice had been brought back to life.

According to *The Guinness Book of Records*, Karlee Kosolofski's icy temperature of 57.2 degrees was seven degrees lower than the lowest body temperature that anyone had ever survived.

As He Kept Moving on Frozen Feet, He Stayed Connected to His Wife by Prayer

On a bitterly cold winter's day in 1995, the tugboat making its way across the freezing North Atlantic near the Canadian shoreline ran into a shoal that gashed its bottom. Within a few moments, the boat over-turned and threw its four-man crew into the icy waters.

David Barnes later recalled that the swirling vortex caused by the sinking boat was so strong that the suction pulled him under the water and pulled off his boots. When he rose back to the surface, he discovered that his three friends were gone.

> *He knew that somehow he must keep moving or he would freeze to death.*

The icy water was bone-numbing, and Barnes desperately clung to a small flotation tank that had popped to the surface. He estimated that he was about two miles from shore, and even though he was already half-frozen, he began to paddle toward land.

Night had fallen by the time he reached some ice-covered rocks on the desolate shore. With what seemed his final gasps of life, he pulled himself out of the water.

Barnes was now on land, but the windy, ten-degree cold was turning his soaked clothing into ice. Although he was exhausted, he knew that somehow he must keep moving or he would freeze to death.

Barnes tried to stand up and walk, but his numb feet would not support him. For a time it seemed easier to give up the struggle, but he kept his mind focused on his wife, Carolann, and their son, Dwayne. He prayed that God would allow him to survive to be with them once again.

As painful as it was to endure, Barnes managed to stand erect and lean beside a large block of ice until his feet and ankles froze into a solid mass, thereby providing enough

Babies have proven to be remarkably resilient, surviving the worst weather extremes in remarkable ways.

stability to enable him to walk. For seven hours he kept moving until he came upon a cabin that was used by quarry workers. Giving thanks to God, Barnes was able to get a fire started and begin to thaw out his frozen limbs.

Meanwhile, in the Barnes home, Carolann had been notified by Search and Rescue that David and his crewmates had been killed when their tugboat had keeled over and thrown them into the freezing North Atlantic. When Carolann protested that she knew David would somehow survive, she was told that no one would be able to remain alive in the terrible cold of the ocean. A few hours later, in prayer, Maryann felt a strong mental connection with her husband, assuring her that he was alive.

The next morning quarry workers found a nearly frozen man in their cabin and rushed David Barnes to a hospital. An astonished Dr. Fred Brushett said that it was a miracle that anyone could survive what Barnes had endured. To add yet another miraculous outcome to the story of the man who literally became a human ice cube, Barnes's feet did not have to be amputated and only his toes suffered nerve damage.

Three-Year-Old Eager to See His Mom and New Sister
Started Out in a Snowstorm in His Little Electric Car

It seemed wonderfully appropriate to Naiomi Johnson that she would give birth to her daughter on Valentine's Day, February 14, 1993. And while she was recuperating in the hospital, her husband, Darryl, and their three-year-old son, Donald, were at home

Electric cars for kids can be great fun on a sunny day, but one child decided to drive his in a blizzard!

in Midland, Ontario, surrounded by snowdrifts, eagerly anticipating the return of mother and brand new baby sister.

Little Donald was eager to see his mommy and his baby sister. He really missed Mommy and couldn't wait to see what a sister would look like.

Daddy told him that he had to wait a while to see Mommy and little sister. It was very cold outside, and there were snow drifts as high as mountains. It was impossible to go to town to get them. They would just have to wait until the roads were cleared.

But Donald couldn't imagine that there were any snow banks that could stop his little electric toy car. He could see no reason why he couldn't just get into his own little car and drive off to the hospital and visit his mom and sister. If Daddy didn't want to go, well, he could just wait at home.

Just in case Daddy might really object to his setting out to visit Mommy and baby sister, Donald got up really early while Daddy was still sleeping and set out in his electric car to drive to the hospital.

It didn't take long for the car's battery to run down, and pretty soon it wouldn't move at all.

Not to worry. It couldn't be that far to the hospital. He would walk the rest of the way.

Once he started walking, it didn't take Donald very long to realize that Daddy was right. It really was very, very cold. And the snow drifts were as high as mountains.

And he was lost. He had no idea where he was.

Constable Kirk Wood of the Ontario Provincial Police theorized that at this point little Donald Johnston was probably less than thirty minutes from death. The three-year-old boy had no real protection from the cold, blowing wind.

But Donald apparently had two guardian angels on duty that cold morning in Ontario—one from heaven and another from a nearby farm.

The Johnson's neighbor, Brian Holmes, was outside his farmhouse doing chores with Samantha, his six-year-old German shepherd, when he noticed that the big dog was acting strangely, as if she sensed something was wrong. All of a sudden, she lifted her head, sniffed the air, and ran toward the woods.

Although Samantha's actions were somewhat peculiar, Holmes finally concluded that she had picked up the scent of a rabbit or some other animal, and he went on with his morning chores.

If Samantha had been able to explain her motives to her master, she might have informed him that she had far more serious concerns on that frigid morning than chasing rabbits through the snow. A sense beyond her physical sensory abilities had told her that somewhere a small human child was in a desperate situation.

Samantha found the three-year-old sitting under a tree, cold and crying. She licked his face and nudged him to his feet. She knew that the little human must not rest in any one place for very long or he would freeze to death. She kept him on his feet and continued to push him in the direction of the farmhouse.

To Donald's eyes, Samantha must have seemed like a big, furry angel. He threw his arms around her neck and allowed her to guide him where she felt was the best path. To his three-old mindset, the trees bending and moaning in the cold wind and the eight-foot-high snowdrifts must have seemed like a frantic frozen nightmare. Somehow he knew that this big dog would bring him back to warmth and life.

Brian Holmes had just begun to wonder about his dog when he spotted her coming down the road with a small boy hanging on to her for dear life. He immediately brought Donald inside the farmhouse, fed him, and let him get nice and warm.

Samantha had been able to sense that there was a little lost boy somewhere out there among the snowdrifts and the freezing cold. She had found Donald, and in that marvelous expression of symbiotic relationship between humans and canines, she brought him to their home so her master could keep him warm and preserve his spark of life.

She Thought Her Baby Was Killed
When the Snow-covered Roof Caved In

When the roof of the community center in Bardufoss, Norway, collapsed under the weight of heavy snows on March 11, 2000, Hilde Kristin Stensen became frantic. Her 13-month-old daughter, Sunniva, had been playing in the room where the roof and outer walls had caved in.

Hilde Kristin had been in the community center's kitchen when the disaster occurred. She and Sunniva had traveled to the town about 750 miles north of Oslo to be with her soldier husband as he participated in the Joint Winter 2000 exercise that was being conducted by twelve nations. The Norwegian troops were using the community center in Bardufoss as their headquarters during the exercise, and military personnel from the United States, Britain, Germany, and other European nations had their own headquarters elsewhere. All had been peaceful and normal—until without warning the roof and walls had collapsed on the soldiers and their families.

Hilde Kristin rushed to room where she had last seen Sunniva playing and panicked further when she could not budge the door. She called Sunniva's name, but she could not hear a sound from her to indicate that she was alive.

There were groans and moans from inside the room, telling Hilde Kristin that many people were injured. Perhaps others had been killed by the crush of the snow and the debris from the roof and ceiling.

The distraught mother felt certain that her baby was dead. Somehow she had to find her husband in all the confusion and destruction, and together they would search for the body of Sunniva under all the snow and rubble.

Just when she was about to be swallowed up by despair and grief, Hilde Kristin heard familiar cries. She turned to see Sunniva in the arms of 2nd. Lt. Niels Edie. Her baby was alive, and although very shaken up, seemingly not a great deal worse for the terrible ordeal.

Edie told Hilde Kristin that he had been in the same room with little Sunniva when the roof and walls collapsed. He had seen the baby suddenly covered with snow and rubble. As soon as he could get to his feet, he had begun digging to free her from beneath the pile of hard-packed snow and debris.

Hilde Kristin praised Edie for his quick action and declared him the Stensen family hero and angel of the day.

Tragically, while a fast-acting, quick-thinking officer had saved a 13-month-old baby girl from death that day, three soldiers were killed and 10 others injured by the unexpected collapse of the community center's roof.

His Dog Provided His Only Heat as He Lay Freezing

When Desmond Pemberton, 58, lay unable to move in the cold of Kaimanawa Forest Park on the North Island of New Zealand, he had only his puppy, "B," to keep him from freezing to death.

Pemberton, wearing only a pair of polar fleece pants, a polypropylene singlet, a T-shirt, and a bush shirt, set out on August 8, 2001, in his Suzuki four-wheel drive SUV accompanied with "B," his Labrador/Blue Heeler mix, for what was to be a brief outing in the park. Pemberton, who was in remission from lung cancer and also suffers from emphysema, perhaps over-exerted himself on the drive and collapsed at the steering wheel, sending the Suzuki and its passengers crashing into a ravine.

For five days and nights, Pemberton lay in and out of consciousness. Temperatures fell to minus four degrees and on three nights icy rain fell to further decrease his chances of survival. The only thing that kept Pemberton from freezing was "B," his faithful companion, who snuggled up against him to share his body warmth.

On Monday, August 13, a forest survey helicopter spotted a crashed Suziki SUV near Sika Lodge, about 36 miles southeast of Taupo. Upon investigating, they found the nearly-dead Pemberton, who had been missing since Wednesday, August 8th. At his side in the wreckage in the ravine was Pemberton's faithful "B".

The *New Zealand Herald* reported that Pemberton was frozen and unable to speak when his rescuers located him. One of the men told reporters that Pemberton was so cold that he was "actually stiff and couldn't even open his mouth." Senior Constable Barry Shepherd added that the man was suffering from hypothermia and would almost certainly have died if he had suffered such exposure to the cold for one more night. Medical authorities said that Pemberton had been kept alive by the warmth of his dog, who slept by his side at night when temperatures plunged.

Although "B" could have struck out any time on his own to reach shelter and food within two or three days, he chose to remain by his owner's side and place his survival above his own.

Found Outside in Subzero Weather Clad in Only a Diaper, Erik's Body Temperature Had Dropped to 60.8

On February 24, 2001, 13-month-old Erika, clad only in her diaper, wandered away from the home where she had been sleeping with her mother, Leyla Nordby, and her two-year-old sister. Awaking during the night at 3:00 A.M., Leyla was shocked to find her baby outside in subzero weather.

Paramedics found the infant's toes frozen together and her mouth frozen shut, thereby preventing them from inserting a breathing tube into her throat.

> *The baby's heart had stopped beating and ... her body temperature was 60.8 degrees.*

Leyla had no idea how her 13-month-old daughter could have managed to walk outside on a night when the temperature dipped to 20 below zero. She and her two daughters had been overnight guests at a friend's house. Leyla and her friend had hired a baby-sitter to look after their children, and the two women had gone out socializing. They returned home around 10:30 P.M., paid and released the baby-sitter, and everybody had gone to bed.

At around 3:00 A.M., Leyla awakened and discovered that her baby was not in bed with her. After searching the house and still not finding the infant, someone noticed that the door appeared not to have latched properly when the baby-sitter left. A few minutes later, a frantic Leyla found Erika face down in the snow, her little hands curled beneath her body, with only a diaper to provide any kind of covering against the subzero weather.

Doctors at Stollery Children's Hospital in Edmonton, Alberta, said that when she was brought in for attention the baby's heart had stopped beating and that her body temperature was 60.8 degrees. A medical team set up a heart and lung machine to begin warming the little girl's body, but before they could begin the procedure, her heart began beating on its own.

Dr. Alf Conradi, director of the pediatric intensive care unit at Stollery Children's Hospital, told the press on February 26 that the 13-month old baby was doing well. While her frostbite injuries were considerable, she appeared not to have suffered any permanent organ or brain damage.

Dr. Allen De Caen, a pediatric intensive care specialist at the hospital, said that he felt humbled by the little girl's incredible recovery. He expressed his opinion that one could fairly use the word "miracle" in describing the baby's dramatic survival.

French Olympic Hockey Star Loses Feet to Frostbite after Wandering in Deep Snow for Eight Days

Eric Lemarque, 34, was certainly no stranger to cold and ice. Born in France, he played hockey for the French national team in the 1994 Winter Olympics. He also represented France in the 1994 and 1995 International Ice Hockey Federation World Championships. In 2004, Lemarque lived in the West Hill section of Los Angeles and worked as a hockey coach.

Always willing to attempt new adventures on snow and ice, Lemarque was trying the relatively new winter sport of snowboarding at Mammoth Mountain ski resort on February 6, 2004, when he left the boundaries of a run and became disoriented. Unfortunately, Lemarque had gone to the resort by himself, so no one was aware that he was wandering around the mountain's western slopes in snow that reached 15 feet in depth.

Lemarque continued to walk aimlessly for days. Completely unprepared for survival in the mountains in February, he had only the clothing that he was wearing to snowboard—and the snowboard. He had some sticks of bubblegum to chew, and he discovered that he could survive on pine nuts and tree bark. At night, he slept on pine branches to keep himself dry.

Although he was in good physical condition and was used to cold temperatures, he knew that his feet had suffered frostbite early in his ordeal. When he examined them, he found them red and purple and ice cold. For days he walked with one foot in a boot and no socks on either foot.

Lemarque was probably saved because his parents, unable to reach him by telephone, called the resort, inquiring if he might still be staying there.

On February 14, a helicopter spotted his body on a mountain slope. When rescue workers approached him, they could see that he was conscious, but barely able to move.

Lemarque had suffered such severe frostbite that circulation to his feet had been cut off and gangrene had set in. Surgeons had no choice other than to amputate his feet from the ankles down.

Many people have found themselves unexpectedly lost in the woods just by wandering a little ways off the beaten trail.

On March 3, an optimistic Lemarque was looking forward to a follow-up surgical procedure that would close the wounds from the amputation. Doctors had informed him that in six to eight weeks he would be fitted with prosthetics.

Eric Lemarque appraised his experience as a positive one: His divorced parents had at least temporarily united to initiate a search for him. He had felt the presence of God acting to save him from dying alone in the mountains. And he was already looking forward to snowboarding in the next winter.

For 13 Days in the Cold Oregon Woods, 76-Year-Old Woman Had Nothing but Prayers to Sustain Her

For 13 days, Doris Anderson, 76, wandered in the Oregon woods, equipped with nothing other than prayer, hope, and the will to survive.

Mrs. Anderson's ordeal began on Saturday, August 25, 2007, when her husband Harold, 75, convinced her to go bow hunting with him in the Wallowa Mountains of eastern Oregon. Less than enthusiastic to begin with, she became even more down on the whole project when their SUV got stuck on an old, little-used dirt road the very next day.

Harold said that they had to walk back to the main road and try to flag down someone to give them a ride into the nearest town. Doris hiked a ways, then complained that she was too tired to make it to the main road. Harold told her to go back to the SUV where she would be comfortable and wait for him to come back with help.

Harold proved not to be the best individual to send for help. During the journey, he hurt his leg, sprained his wrist, and wasn't rescued until Monday, August 27, when some hunters found him and gave him a ride into town.

Sheriff's deputies went out to bring Doris back to civilization after her two-day wait in the SUV, but when they arrived to retrieve her, she wasn't there. The officers looked around for some kind of sign that would tell them where Mrs. Anderson might be, but after searching the area, they concluded that she had wandered off on her own.

For four days, search parties, including helicopters using thermal imaging equipment, combed the woods looking for the 76-year-old woman.

> *For thirteen days, she drank water from a small creek, ate berries from some bushes.*

After that investment of time and people power, the search was called off. Night-time temperatures were dipping near the freezing mark. Doris Anderson was reported as being dressed only in light clothing. At her age, she was unlikely to survive.

And now the investigation took a new twist. Harold Anderson was accused of deliberately dumping his wife alone in the woods to wander and die. After days of hard interrogation, the law officers decided that Harold was not a murderer.

But the couple's two adult daughters made another decision when their mother had been missing for over a week. They assumed along with the authorities that she was dead and they began to plan a memorial service.

Deputy Travis Ash and Oregon State Trooper Chris Hawkins may have given Harold Anderson a bad time for a few days, all in the line of duty, but they had ended up completely believing that he had not harmed his wife, so on September 6, on their day off, they decided to see if they could find Doris.

Traveling through the woods on their ATVs, they spotted a number of ravens circling over a particular area. Curious, they found the birds hovering over a ravine. Down in the ravine, they found Doris Anderson where she had been all along, unable to climb out by herself. For 13 days, she drank water from a small creek, ate berries from some bushes, and nearly froze to death at night without any covering or fire. She had also lost her shoes when she had tumbled down in the ravine, and the officers could see that her toes were frostbitten. They also noted that she was dehydrated and disoriented. When they got her to a hospital, her internal temperature was only 90 degrees.

After several weeks of rehabilitation, Doris Anderson said that all the while that she was in the ravine she maintained her faith in God and in the power of prayer. She never stopped believing that God would create a miracle and she would be found.

Rescue of Six Mountain Climbers from Mount Cook Described as "Miraculous"

The six Sydney, Australia, mountain climbers who spent several days buried in their tent under heavy snow and avalanches in the New Zealand Alps described their rescue on August 16, 2008, as "miraculous."

The group were all members of Sydney's Coast and Mountain Walkers of New South Wales, and most of them were amateurs when it came to challenging difficult mountain peaks. However, Terry Cole, 37, Jenni Landon, 37, Stephen Dolphin, 53, David Freeland, 55, Gerald Osman, 32, and Melissa Clerke, who celebrated her 27th birthday on the climb, set out on the morning of August 9 for Mount Cook, from Mueller Hut via the Annette Plateau. Almost immediately they were beset by unexpected heavy snowfalls that, for some of the climbers, soon became neck-deep.

Things didn't get better. Battling blizzards, avalanches, and treacherous crevasses—all the while carrying 30-pound backpacks—soon had members fighting exhaustion and hypothermia. They sought refuge in their tent, but because of the heavy snowfall, they had to keep shoveling to prevent being buried alive and suffocated. Even when someone else took his or her turn shoveling, sleep was almost impossible for those whose turn it was to rest.

Late on the night of Thursday, August 14, Stephen Dolphin set off the EPIRB (emergency beacon). The members of the group all realized that they were in a situation from which it was impossible for them to survive without assistance.

The six climbers decided to make an effort to trek to Mueller Hut on Friday, but once again neck-deep snow tested their failing endurance and they retreated back to their tent.

New Zealand's Rescue Coordination Centre attempted a search and rescue mission on Friday night, but the helicopter found it extremely difficult to battle the heavy snow and winds. The aircraft also set off avalanches which might further bury the climbers or even bring down the chopper.

At dawn on Saturday, eight mountaineers and two dogs set out on their own expedition to attempt to find the stranded group. They, too, found the passage to Mount Cook impossible to navigate.

On that same morning, a rescue helicopter set out for the spot where the emergency beacon still called, but a blizzard forced it to turn back.

Then, at 9:20 A.M., the sky suddenly cleared, and the rescue chopper returned to make another attempt—this time a successful one.

The six members of Sydney's Coast and Mountain Walkers had all survived and were flown to Christchurch, where they were able to enjoy something to eat other than chocolate and Vita-Wheats™. While no show of hands was taken to see how many of the group might return to challenge Mount Cook, all of the members declared their survival a miracle.

Earthquakes

Woman Survives 63 Days in Cramped Space after Kashmir Quake

After Dr. Abdul Hamid had examined Naqsha Bibi, 40, a woman who had been buried alive for 63 days in the earthquake that struck in 2005, he could only shrug and suggest that while some medical scientists may deny such things, there are miracles in this world. Naqsha Bibi had surely been the recipient of such a miracle.

Naqsha Bibi was found still alive in the ruins of a collapsed house on December 10, 2005, two months after the October 8 earthquake that devastated large parts of Indian- and Pakistan-administered Kashmir and the northern areas of Pakistan. One of her cousins, Faiz Din, admitted that none of the family had even been looking for Naqsha. Everyone assumed that she had been killed when the disaster first struck. Her father had both of his legs broken by the quake and his brother had accompanied him to Islamabad as an attendant.

Naqsha had been trapped in her kitchen when the house collapsed around her. The space in which she was found was so small that she was forced to assume a fetal or crouching position. Over the 63 days in which she was entombed, her muscles actually froze in this embryonic position.

On December 10, when Faiz Din and others began clearing the debris from Naqsha's house, they found her body in her tiny cocoon-like space. Assuming that she was dead, Faiz Din and the others were surprised when she opened her eyes.

When they considered her emaciated condition, her relatives believed that although she had somehow miraculously survived over two months trapped in the debris of the earthquake, she was surely on the verge of death. Out of respect, they placed Naqsha in a tent where others could not gawk at her and continued with the business of cleaning up the widespread results of the earthquake.

Two days later, a team of German doctors visiting the Kashmir camp discovered Naqsha still alive and contacted the Pakistan Islamic Medical Association (PIMA), who arranged to have the miracle woman brought to Muzaffarabad. Once secured in a PIMA camp, Dr. Mariam Bashir, a Danish doctor of Pakistani origin, found Naqsha in a state of shock, but remarkably physically stable.

After 63 days in her coffin of collapsed stone, Naqsha weighed about 70 pounds, half the weight of a normal woman her size. Because Naqsha could not yet take solid food, the doctor ordered intravenous feeding, moving within a few hours to a liquid diet.

The next morning, Naqsha smiled at the doctor and appeared to be making rapid progress. Although she was yet too weak to speak, her smile indicated her awareness that she was being helped by skilled individuals to be restored to health.

When inquiries were made concerning just how a woman could survive 63 days cramped up in a small cavity under piles of debris in what had been her kitchen, Faiz Din told investigators that he found traces of rotting food when he uncovered his cousin. He was amazed that the air in the tiny space seemed fresh, leading him to believe that somehow an airway must have remained open through the heaps of debris.

A number of violent earthquakes have shaken China in recent years.

In addition, there was a trickle of water on one side of the small cavity that must have come from one of several small streams in the area.

Although her limbs remained stiff and would require a great deal of therapy to restore them to their former flexibility, doctors saw no reason why Naqsha Bibi should not be restored to a normal life.

Massive 2008 Quake in China Produces Many Miracles, Including a Miracle Couple Who Beat Incredible Odds

On May 12, 2008, the worst natural disaster to strike China in 30 years occurred when an earthquake, variously reported as 7.9 or 8.0 on the Richter scale, struck the nation of 1.3 billion people and claimed an estimated 80,000 lives. Amidst the death and destruction, there were miracles.

On May 16, Jiao was rescued from under a heap of debris in Dujianyang. The young woman said that she had spent her twentieth birthday buried alive and that the greatest gift she could have received was being rescued after spending four days trapped beneath a collapsed building.

It seemed as though 16-year-old schoolgirl Li Anning and some other girls had summoned their miracle. Trapped in the rubble of Beichuan, the girls sang to keep up their spirits. The last line of one of the songs that they sang over and over declared that "blessing and happiness" comes always at the ending.

On May 19, 61-year-old Li Ningcui was discovered still alive under a pile of rubble at a marketplace in Beichuan after seven days.

On that same date in Sichuan province, where the quake was centered, two women were found buried alive in a collapsed building.

In Mianyang, a married couple, both physicians, were declared China's miracle couple after enduring a 139-hour ordeal trapped in the ruins of their state-owned apartment on the hospital grounds. Dr. Xie Shou Ju said that she was the fortunate one, buried for a total of 72 hours. Her husband, Dr. Tang Xiong, was trapped in the rubble for six days.

On the evening of May 11, Dr. Xie, 30, a gynecologist, had worked the night shift at Beichuan's People Hospital. She was home, taking a nap on the sofa of their first floor apartment. Her husband of three years, Dr. Tang, was just getting ready to leave for his shift at 2:30 P.M.

Before Dr. Tang left for the hospital, the apartment began to rock and the windows burst. In the next few moments, three floors of living quarters crashed through their ceiling, trapping Dr. Xie under a small slab of cement propped up at one end by the sofa and burying Dr. Tang in rubble in another part of their apartment.

Xie was awakened by the ceiling lamp swaying and the room rocking. She was tossed from the sofa, and she was at first perplexed why everything was dark. Then she realized that she was lying in a very small angular space beneath a slab of ceiling. Once she became aware of what had occurred, she later said that she had thoughts of the massive earthquake in Tangshan City in 1976 that had killed as many as 650,000 people.

Xie found that she had enough room to slightly turn her body, and she discovered a small crack above her where air and light could enter. She could now determine that it was day, but since she had been sleeping when the earthquake struck, she had no idea what time it might be. She had confidence, however, that her husband was at work and would soon be home to extricate her from her tiny dungeon.

A few moments later, when she called out for help, she heard a male voice answer her. It was Tang. He, too, was trapped in the rubble of the floors that had smashed through the ceiling of their apartment. For the next several days, the two would continue to shout words of encouragement to one another.

Xie managed to reach a small tin of snacks that had crashed along with the rubble into their apartment. The tin contained some tofu, which she estimated could last her for quite a few days if she rationed it carefully. She used the container to collect her urine if the necessity should arise that she would have to drink it in order to survive.

After it seemed that help would be slow in coming to them, Xie and Tang made the decision to cease shouting to one another in order to conserve their strength. Xie did hear sounds of digging above her, so although she knew it would take time to reach them, she did become encouraged that they would be saved. She denied herself all negative thoughts and focused only on being rescued and living in the future.

After 72 hours spent trapped in her little cement "tent," Dr. Xie was rescued by a team from Hainan province. She suffered only slight dehydration, and she began at once to work with the team to acquire the heavy equipment that would be required to save her husband.

For two days, she stood by as the rescue workers extricated the huge pieces of the three floors that had crashed through the ceiling of their apartment and still held her husband captive. Just as they were about to break through the final barriers to Dr. Tang's freedom, they received word from the authorities that they must evacuate the area at once. A major dam was about to burst and would flood that area of Beichuan.

All the rescue workers began to run to escape the deluge. Dr. Xie had no choice but to flee with them, tears burning her eyes as she thought of the horror of her husband drowning in the small cement cage that held him prisoner.

Dr. Xie felt at her lowest emotional point since the earthquake occurred. It seemed as if all hopes of her husband surviving were now completely dashed. The small space allowed them in their destroyed apartment now seemed to be places of refuge compared to the aspect of the entire area being engulfed by several feet of water.

By that evening, word came that the dam appeared to be holding fast, and the anticipated flooding would not occur. But now it was too dark to resume the work with the heavy digging equipment.

> *Dr. Xie ... attributed their survival to the positive attitude that she and her husband always tried to maintain.*

Although the area was not flooded by water from the dam bursting, thundershowers began, thus renewing the possibility of Tang being drowned in his prison. As if the storms were not enough, a heavy aftershock shook the region, and all Dr. Xie could think of during the night was her husband alone in the dark, trying to remain confident and positive.

The dedicated rescue workers began their efforts to free Dr. Tang promptly at 6:00 A.M. the next morning. The rescuers had fashioned a tunnel and were almost ready to extricate Tang when another aftershock shook the area and a geologist arrived to order them to stop their efforts and leave at once.

Fortunately, the shock did not last long and did not seem to collapse the rescuers' tunnel. Dr. Tang was pulled to freedom shortly after 9:00 A.M.

Remarkably, other than dehydration and hunger, the physician had suffered no serious injuries apart from extensive bruising and the possibility of amputation for his right foot. He had lost no blood, broken no bones, and received no head injuries.

Doctors Tang and Xie expressed their gratitude to the army, the rescue team, and the government for their persistence in retrieving them from the massive pile of rubble that had cascaded down on them in their apartment.

Dr. Xie also attributed their survival to the positive attitude that she and her husband always tried to maintain in every aspect of their lives.

Destiny, fate, whatever one wishes to call it, may also have played a role in the lives of the two physicians. Dr. Xie had left the night shift, and Dr. Tang was about to leave for his shift at the hospital. Of the 150 doctors, nurses, and hospital staff present at the Beichuan's People Hospital when the earthquake struck, only four survived.

Four-Year-Old Turkish Boy Emerges Alive
after 140 hours in 18-Inch Hole

When a devastating earthquake struck Turkey in August 1999, one of the last victims to be pulled alive from the destruction was Ismail Cimen, a four-year-old boy. Ismail had been trapped in a gap just 18 inches high for 140 hours.

On August 23, Sait Cimen, Ismail's uncle, continued to search for any of his relatives who might have survived the terrible effects of the earthquake. As he pulled rubble aside, steeling himself to find the dead, hoping to find the living, Sait moved the beam of his flashlight into a small hole. There, he was overjoyed to see little Ismail squinting back at him. Sait called for help, and within minutes Bulgarian and Turkish rescue workers were hard at work to free the boy.

The Cimen family lived in an apartment in Cinarcik, about 45 miles south of Istanbul. When the earthquake struck, Ismail had been playing with his toy truck—and then he remembered falling.

After the pile of rubble under which he lay stopped shaking, Ismail began to cry out for his parents and his sisters. There was no reply from anyone.

Although Ismail could see nothing in the darkness that had descended upon him, it was probably best that he was not aware that the body of one of his sisters lay crushed to death just inches from him.

One can only imagine the terror that would seize a four-year-old boy who was playing with his truck one moment and then the next is plunged into darkness and is trapped in a tiny crawl space under tons of rubble. Ismail began clawing at the debris surrounding him, desperately fighting for his life.

Perhaps it was the whisper of an angel in Sait's ear that directed him to a particular heap of debris ...

Ismail's mother, Serife, had been pulled from the collapsed building and taken to a hospital in Bursa. The bodies of his father, Fatih, and three sisters had been found, crushed by the collapse of their apartment building.

Nearly six days had passed since the earthquake struck, and the surviving members of the Cimen family had already prepared a grave for little Ismail, whose body was still missing.

Perhaps it was some inner guidance that led Sait Cimen to return once more to the rubble and seek the body of his nephew so Ismail might receive a proper burial.

Perhaps it was the whisper of an angel in Sait's ear that directed him to a particular heap of debris and caused him to shine his flashlight down the small opening and to discover Ismail's face squinting back at him.

Whatever the guiding force, Sait Cimen proclaimed the discovery of his nephew after being buried for 140 hours to be other nothing short of a miracle of God.

Dehydrated, emaciated from lack of water and food, Ismail Cimen was taken to an Istanbul hospital where he recovered from his ordeal.

While Ismail Cimen had been trapped for 140 hours, French rescue workers freed a paraplegic woman from under a collapsed building in Golcuk 130 hours after the earthquake shattered the area. Mrs. Adalet Cetinol, 57, was found by the rescue team after they had employed highly sensitive listening devices to detect any sounds of survival in the rubble. Mrs. Cetinol, suffering from kidney problems, was taken immediately to a hospital.

The French rescue workers also managed to extricate Melahat Sarsan in Cinarcik after she had endured 138 hours trapped in the rubble from her apartment. Mrs. Sarsan was flown to a military hospital in Istanbul.

Tiffany Becomes Symbol of Hope after Northridge, California, Earthquake

On March 3, 1994, 41 days after the Northridge, California, earthquake, Tiffany, a 10-year-old Persian mix, was found alive in the closet in which she had sought sanctuary when the ground began to move under her feet on January 17.

Laurie Booth, Tiffany's owner, had searched everywhere for her beloved cat. She had posted signs, taken out newspaper ads, and asked her neighbors in Saugus if they could remember seeing the cat before or after the quake.

Ironically, Tiffany had only been a few feet away from her desperate owner. Apparently, she had fled for safety to a neighbor's storage closet and had been accidentally locked in.

When she was finally found, Tiffany was dehydrated, nearly starved, and only fleetingly conscious. She had not eaten for 41 days and had only a little rainwater to drink.

Veterinarian Sandy Sanford, who treated Tiffany at the Animal Clinic of Santa Clarita, put her on intravenous vitamin, sugar, and electrolyte solutions. Tiffany was fed orally every hour or so through a syringe because she was far too weak to feed herself.

Laurie Booth said that she still could not believe that Tiffany was alive. When she first picked her up Tiffany was just like a piece of tissue paper—frail and stiff and very cold.

Veterinarian John Burkhartsmeyer, owner of the Santa Clarita clinic, expressed his opinion that Tiffany had just barely made it. Bones and skin was all that was left of her.

Tiffany's inspiring story of survival and indomitable will to live touched hearts as far away as Europe. Veterinarians decreed her survival as highly unusual, if not downright miraculous. Tiffany had become a symbol of hope to all those citizens of California who sought to rebuild their lives after the devastating effects of the quake of January 17.

On Friday, March 5, just as CBS News was at the Santa Clarita clinic preparing to telecast a live report on Tiffany's fight for survival, the valiant cat went into cardiac and respiratory arrest. Veterinarian Sanford spent 20 minutes attempting to revive her with cardiopulmonary resuscitation, oxygen and drug therapy, but Tiffany, who had lost about 60 percent of her body weight during her 41-day ordeal, was unable to respond.

Laurie Booth was distraught over her pet's death. How could she not have heard Tiffany crying for her when she was so close in a neighbor's storage closet? Why could she not have found her sooner so that her life would have been saved?

But Laurie remained thankful that she had been able to find Tiffany when she was still alive and that she didn't die alone in a cold place. She knew she was loved, Laurie said. Tiffany definitely was a little fighter.

Floods

Saved from Drowning for a Destined Purpose Several Years Later

When Tropical Storm Allison struck Houston, Texas, in 2001, Minnie Hightower was on the telephone in her bedroom. At the same time, lightning struck an external electrical box, which zapped her electrical oven in the kitchen and knocked out all the telephones in her home.

The lightning bolt nearly knocked Minnie out of this world. As she held her bedroom phone, a blue spark issued from the receiver and sent her flying across the room. She said later that she remembers looking down and seeing her toenails blow off.

After she had recovered what she deemed an acceptable level of equilibrium, she decided that she should be examined by a medical doctor. She got into her car to drive herself to the hospital, but she had only traveled about five blocks when she lapsed into unconsciousness behind the wheel.

As she sat unconscious and helpless, the floodwaters unleashed by Allison rushed through the city streets and began to engulf her car.

She dimly recalls the floodwaters moving up to her chest and her head bobbing up and down as the water rushed in. In her fleeting moments of awareness, it seemed that she would surely drown.

But an angel in the form of a fireman broke through her car window and carried her to safety.

Minnie Hightower was in the hospital for three days. She was quite aware that she had been the recipient of a miracle, and she was also very much aware that she had been spared for a reason.

On April 25, 2006, she donated one of her kidneys to her sister-in-law, thoroughly convinced that the Lord had been looking out for both of them and had melded their destinies into one.

The Miracle Survival of a Family Washed Away from Their Home by a Billion Gallons of Water from a Burst Reservoir

On December 14, 2005, a reservoir broke at Ameren UE's Taum Sauk hydroelectric plant in southeast Missouri.

Completed in 1963, the dam had concrete walls 90 feet tall. A fail-safe mechanism had been installed which would prevent too much water from being pumped into the

Living by a lake, river, or sea is a dream for many people, but more and more are finding that this highly prized real estate can come at an unfortunate cost.

reservoir. On the cold, snowy night of December 14, the backup set of instruments malfunctioned, thereby causing millions of gallons beyond its capacity to flow into the reservoir and cause it to rupture. As a consequence, about a billion gallons of water burst free, destroying everything in its path, including an entire hardwood forest. Directly in its savage course of watery annihilation was the three-bedroom brick, ranch-style home of the Toops family.

Jerry and Lisa Toops and their three children—Tanner, five; Tara, three; and seven-month-old Tucker—lived in a forested valley in Johnson's Shut-Ins State Park, where Jerry, 42, was superintendent. For those unfamiliar with the term "Shut-Ins," it should be explained that perhaps millions of years ago, the area that is now southeast Missouri was one of great volcanic activity. Sometime during this prehistoric era, the volcanoes trapped or "shut-in" the Black River. Over the centuries, the confined water carved incredible gorges, natural water slides, and potholes in hard rock. In the summertime, Jerry, as the park superintendent, was kept busy with visitors who found the Shut-Ins a favorite place for swimming, camping, and hiking. But now, in the weeks before Christmas, the park was almost always devoid of any visitors.

Jerry Toops loved the outdoor lifestyle, and although he took pride in being what others called self-reliant, he recognized the handiwork of God in nature. Both Jerry and Lisa, 38, were practicing Christians and disciples of the work ethic that advised early-to-bed, early-to-rise made for a productive life.

The Toops were all in bed sleeping by 9:00 P.M. that terrible night when the reservoir burst, but about 4:00 A.M. Tucker awoke, crying to be fed. Lisa lifted the baby from his crib and left the master bedroom to nurse him in the living room.

Lisa had fallen asleep with Tucker on a couch, and she was awakened around 5:00 A.M. by a strange, powerful roaring sound. Although she had no idea what was happening, the only thought that came to her was that a tornado was bearing down on them. She yelled at Jerry to wake up and get the kids.

Lisa grabbed baby Tucker and ran to Tanner's room. She figured that if it was a tornado, the family's best hope would be to retreat to the basement.

She had just made it to Tanner's bedside when cold water began filling the room. She told Tanner to hold his breath.

> *A strong swimmer, Jerry had made it to the roof, but a high rush of water over 30 feet high soon swept him away.*

She only had a few moments more to ask for the help of Jesus before the full force of the flood waters struck their house. Later, she would estimate that it took only 10 seconds to fill the bedroom with frigid water from the reservoir.

Jerry, 42, heard his wife scream and awakened to what he described as hearing the sound of a squadron of F-14 jets combined with the roar of several trains. Before he could make a move to save his family, a solid wall of water exploded the back bedroom wall and hit him full force. In the next instant, the opposite wall blew out and plunged him underwater.

Lisa managed to retain her hold on the baby, as the flood carried them outside, but Tanner was washed away from her. She could hear him calling for his mommy. She prayed that he would remember his swimming lessons and try to swim. At last she managed to locate him in the cold, wet darkness of the night and keep Tanner with her and the baby.

A strong swimmer, Jerry had made it to the roof, but a high rush of water over 30 feet high soon swept him away. He tried to resist the incredible power of the flood by attempting to grab on to anything that he could. He tried desperately to swim toward a line of cedar trees.

At last he was able to clutch the branches of a tree and maintain his hold against the rushing flood.

And there he perched, exhausted, dressed only in his undershorts, freezing in the 32-degree night that was swirling snow around him.

Neither parent had had any time to alert little Tara of the danger, but the doggie paddle lessons she had received that summer served her well. Washed out of her bed by the flood in a matter of seconds, the three-year-old paddled through the water until she reached a patch of higher ground and took refuge under some cedar boughs.

Captain Ryan Wadlow of the Lesterville volunteer fire department lived near the state park so he was first on the scene. He had just been leaving for his job as a heavy-equipment operator when the emergency pager went off. He had no idea that the Toops family had been washed from their home and that they had been exposed to the cold and snow for at least 45 minutes before he arrived.

After struggling through the mud and avoiding the piles of debris and the uprooted trees, Wadlow found Jerry Toops clinging to the upper limbs of a cedar tree. As he helped Jerry down, Wadlow saw that he was bleeding and appeared to be in shock.

Wadlow walked Toops to the ambulance that had arrived, then returned to look for other survivors. Toops could identify himself as the park superintendent, but he seemed unable to answer coherently any other question put to him.

Other rescue workers arrived, and Lisa Toops was found wearing only a nightshirt at the edge of the destructive path that the floodwaters had taken. She, too, was incoherent, but she still held her baby Tucker in her arms.

Tanner lay across his mother's legs, and at first the rescuers assumed that he was dead. Even when someone picked up the five-year-old and wrapped him in a coat, no pulse could be detected in the boy.

As they carried Lisa, Tucker, and Tanner to another ambulance, Lisa was able to tell her rescuers that she had three children.

That meant one was still missing.

Wadlow found three-year-old Tara beneath the broken boughs of a cedar tree, covered with silt and debris, wearing muddy pajamas. Her blue eyes were wide open, but she was breathing in short, shallow gasps.

When Jerry Toops was told that all members of his family had been found alive, he wept and said that they had experienced a miracle.

The Toops family was taken by ambulance to a local medical center, then transferred to Cardinal Glennon Hospital in St. Louis. They were all treated for hypothermia. Each of them was covered with cuts and bruises—except for Tara, who had escaped without a scratch. Tanner fared the worst. He had suffered cardiac arrest and was hospitalized for two weeks.

Although the Toops had survived a nightmare of cascading flood waters that had completely demolished their home, the reservoir break had occurred in a sparsely populated section of Reynolds County, Missouri, and the Toops' home was the only one destroyed.

The citizens of nearby Lesterville held a fund-raiser for the Toops family, and a parsonage at a church was converted into a temporary home for them. One may assume that the Toops' Christmas observance that year was truly one of great thankfulness.

They Sailed Away on Their Floating House but Survived with Minor Scratches

On August 18, 2007, Roger Oldham, 65, didn't know that there was a flood on the way to his little town of 803 people until his sister called him and told him that she had heard on the news that Stockton, Minnesota, was being evacuated. Oldham was certainly aware that the entire southeastern Minnesota and southwestern Wisconsin region had been hit by one storm after another that summer, but he didn't think any kind of order to get out of Stockton would be given.

After he hung up the telephone, he looked out the window and saw another violent storm slamming into their small town. Even worse, he saw flood waters rushing down the street and pouring out of the drainage ditch that ran alongside their house.

Turning to his wife, Bonnie, and his mother-in-law, he told them that he thought the three of them should head for the roof of their one-story house.

Bonnie, 52, picked up some blankets to protect them from the storm. The two women tried to get up on the roof by standing on a glass patio table, but that broke, so Roger ran in the house and dragged out a desk for them to stand on while they crawled up to the roof.

The three had been where they considered the safest place to seek refuge for only a few minutes when they were startled by the sound of an explosion. Raging flood waters from the drainage ditch had destroyed the west wall of their cinder block basement and torn the house loose from its foundation. With a violent lurch, their home began floating down the streets of Stockton.

As Oldham, Bonnie, and his mother-in-law held on to the roof for dear life, they began to shout for help. As if they were riding in an out-of-control boat, they moved across their neighbors' yards, a good many of whom had climbed onto the roofs of their own homes.

Roger Oldham later said that, as they floated away, they were most concerned that their house would tip over and dump them in the raging flood waters. He felt as though they might not make it and that all they could do to help themselves was to pray.

The Oldham house was carried over 1,000 feet until it hit the railroad tracks. The combination of the storms and the flood had twisted and raised the tracks to the point that they were able to keep the Oldham's home from floating any farther.

The three of them shouted for help intermittently for five hours, but the roar of the storm and the sound of the flood waters were so loud that no one could hear their cries.

Around 5:00 A.M., a firefighter spotted the house sitting on the railroad tracks and sent a boat to rescue them. The three were taken to Winona Community Hospital where they were able to warm up before they were released. Fortunately, none of them had suffered more than a few scratches.

One of the Oldhams' neighbors who watched them being carried away by the flood waters said that it was a miracle that they had survived. The Oldhams were also aware that others were not so fortunate.

The August storms that shook southeastern Minnesota and southwestern Wisconsin were held accountable for at least four deaths. Two were killed in their vehicle near Stockton, and two others died in another vehicle near Witoka, Minnesota.

Weela—the Pit Bull that Became a One-Dog Rescue Squad

In January 1993 unusually heavy rains in southern California caused a dam to break miles upstream on the Tijuana River. At its best, under normal conditions, the river is

Pit bulls have a bad reputation in the United States for being vicious dogs, but most are actually loyal, heroic, and loving pets.

a very narrow, three-foot-wide flow of water. Under the unusual circumstances, the collapse of the dam transformed the customary trickle of the river into a raging wall of water that isolated both people and animals for almost three months.

Nearly every disaster has its hero. One individual who rises out of the crowd to perform acts of courage and very often life-threatening feats to save the lives of others. In the case of the 1993 floods, the hero was Weela, a 65-pound pit bull.

Pit bulls generally hold bad reputations in the media. There is no denying that some careless and irresponsible dog owners have allowed their pit bulls unrestrained and uncurbed freedom that, in turn, have given the breed some bad press as vicious and aggressive animals.

Such is not the case with responsible owners such as Lori Watkins of Imperial Beach, California, who found Weela as a puppy left to die in a back alley along with the rest of an abandoned litter. Lori took all ten puppies with her back to the Watkins ranch where the pups were treated with kindness and taught basic obedience and good manners, rather than aggressive tactics and fighting skills.

As the puppies grew older, Lori Watkins found a good home for each of them—with the exception of Weela, who had become attached to her son Gary.

On one occasion, Lori thought for a few minutes that she may have made the wrong choice of dogs. Gary, 11, was in the pursuit of lizards when Weela suddenly sent him sprawling with a full body slam.

Lori experienced a moment of disappointment in Weela's behavior, because she had always been so gentle in her play.

Then when a coiled rattlesnake struck Weela in the face, she saw that the faithful pit bull had blocked Gary from the snake's strike and taken the hit herself.

Fortunately for many victims of the 1993 flood, Weela survived the rattlesnake's venom.

> *The 65-pound, four-legged superhero had saved the lives of 30 humans, 29 dogs, 13 horses, and one cat.*

When the dam first broke in January, Lori and her husband, Dan, together with Weela, worked for six hours struggling against driving rain, strong river current, and floating debris to save a neighbor's 12 dogs. Both Lori and Dan were surprised at the way in which Weela always took the lead and seemed to have an uncanny ability to avoid quicksand, treacherous drop-offs, and mud bogs.

On one occasion Lori sank into mud up to her waist. At first Weela tried to dig her out, then she just grabbed her owner by her coat and pulled her free.

When the floods finally subsided, grateful residents of the area tabulated that the 65-pound, four-legged superhero had saved the lives of 30 humans, 29 dogs, 13 horses, and one cat. Weela was subsequently named the winner of the Ken-L Ration Dog Hero of the Year award.

Lori Watkins spoke with great pride of her rugged female pit bull. She pointed out that Weela had never been trained in any rescue techniques. It was as if she simply knew what to do.

Among Weela's heroic deeds were such courageous acts as the following:

She waded across a raging river to carry a 50-pound backpack of food to a number of dogs stranded on an island.

She guided a rescue team around quicksand, thereby enabling them to rescue starving horses.

She sensed a deadly undertow at the edge of the Tijuana River and prevented 30 Mexican men, women, and children from entering the water to cross at that point. By constantly barking at the group, she led them upstream to a shallow spot where they could cross safely.

She located frightened dogs and guided them to high ground.

She dragged human rescuers free of mud when they were stuck and unable to move.

Barney the Bull's Wild 60-Mile Ride on Floodwaters

On Sunday, January 6, 2008, Don Baxter of Tweed Valley, New South Wales, Australia, thought that he had seen the last of his 12-month Brahman bull calf, Barney, when a raging flood swept through the valley. One minute Barney was warily keeping an eye on the storm from the safety of Baxter's Limpinwood property; the next, a wall of water from the Hopping Dick Creek washed him away.

Helpless to save his young bull, Baxter made the sad assumption that the animal would either drown outright in the turbulent water or that Barney would become tangled in barbed wire or tree branches and be held under until he was dead.

Seven hours later, Don Baxter was shaking his head in disbelief. Barney had been sighted near the mouth of the Tweed River, over 60 miles downstream. A passer-by had spotted what appeared to be an exhausted bull floating toward the sea at the Fingal ocean entrance. Thankfully, the passer-by happened to be an animal lover and alerted park rangers who managed to pull Barney ashore.

When Baxter received his bull back onto his property, he said that it had to be a miracle that Barney had been able to pass over all the flooded bridges and causeways and whatever other obstacles he had to overcome.

Hurricanes and Tsunamis

A Voice within Saved Her from Perishing at Sea

In October 1983, Tami Ashcraft, 23, and her boyfriend, Richard Sharp, both of whom were accomplished sailors and California residents, accepted the job of delivering a yacht from Tahiti to San Diego. The yacht was a luxurious 44-footer named *Hazana*, and the two were having a splendid time sailing east through calm seas.

A week into their seafaring, the *Hazana*'s radio picked up reports of a tropical depression off Central America. Ashcraft and Sharp made the decision to run north of the storm and avoid encountering violent seas.

Before they could make the detour, they suddenly found themselves in the heart of a Category 4 hurricane that the stateside weather observers had named Raymond. Fifty-foot waves were soon crashing down on the 44-foot yacht, which now offered little more security against the hurricane than a rowboat.

Sharp sent Tami below deck and fastened himself to a lifeline. Within a very few moments, the *Hazana* had rolled over, then, astonishingly, flipped end to end.

Later, Tami estimated that she may have been unconscious for as long as 27 hours. Her head was covered in blood, probably as a result of bouncing off the walls below deck as the yacht was tossed about by the hurricane.

When she managed to stagger deckside, the storm was over, but she was devastated to find that Richard's broken lifeline was being dragged behind the yacht. The merciless, pounding, crashing sea had claimed another stalwart seaman's life.

Stunned by the death of her boyfriend, Tami was able to turn away from her grief long enough to take stock of her situation. The masts had been torn from the *Hazana*; the cabin was almost completely flooded; the engine and the electronic equipment were nonfunctional.

Grieving for Sharp and weak from loss of blood, Tami Ashcraft sat in a kind of trance for two days. She did nothing but drift in her consciousness just as the yacht was adrift in the ocean.

Then, she recalled in her book *Red Sky in Mourning*, she heard a voice in her head demanding that she snap out of it and get to work. For two days, she had sat on the verge of a mental breakdown, not even bothering to eat. Now, a voice was challenging her to survive.

Tami took inventory of the stores on board and found that she had enough food and water to sustain her.

Next, following the direction of the voice within, she began working with a sextant to solve the great question of exactly where she was. The voice reminded Tami that she was a good sailor and completely capable of accomplishing such a task.

Within two days of working with the sextant, she had determined her position and where the most propitious currents lay. She rigged a sail to help bring the yacht to the currents, and after 42 days of accomplished seamanship, Tami Ashcraft sailed into Hawaii's Hilo Harbor.

Hurricane Rita Hurled Two Trees into Her Bed

When the 116-mile-per-hour winds of Hurricane Rita began to roar through Jasper, Texas, on September 26, 2005, Sandra Sheffield decided that she had better get Mildred, her 80-year-old mother-in-law, out of bed and down to the den floor.

Sandra's husband, a minister at the county jail, was working, so, becoming more frightened at being alone by the minute, she told Mildred that the winds were becoming too strong to remain safely in her bedroom. Sandra helped her mother-in-law leave the room just seconds before two trees crashed into the room and landed on the bed where she had been sleeping.

Mildred was momentarily awestruck with the realization that if she had remained in bed, the two invading trees would undoubtedly have killed her.

Shaken by the close call, the two women braved the strong winds to run to their neighbors' house and wait out the storm in their company.

A Scruffy Little Dog Saved a Boy from the Violent Tsunami

Early in the morning of December 26, 2004, a 9.3 earthquake shook the ocean floor off northwestern Sumatra, forcing billions of tons of seawater upward. Massive waves raged toward the beaches of Sumatra, Thailand, and Sri Lanka, cascading downward on thousands of unsuspecting villagers, holiday celebrants, and foreign tourists. The great tsunami then continued its destructive course until it exhausted the last of its energy on the beaches of Kenya.

On the fateful morning of December 26, 2004, R. Ramakrishnana, a fisherman from a village outside of Chinnakalapet, India, had just returned to shore, his boat filled with a successful catch. As he was walking home, he heard a strange noise coming from the ocean, and he climbed to the rooftop of the two-story community center to investigate. Horrified, he saw mammoth waves coming toward the village.

His wife, Sangeeta, did not question his orders to leave their hut immediately and to run for the top of the hill with their children. She knew that he was an experienced seaman who could quickly identify an ocean that had suddenly turned dangerous, destructive, and deadly. Sangeeta's terrible dilemma lay in the harsh reality that she had three sons, but only two arms with which to carry them to safety.

She picked up the two youngest, and shouted for seven-year-old Dinakaran to follow her. Faced with the prospect of outrunning the deadly tsunami crashing toward shore, the desperate mother felt that her oldest son had the greatest chance of gaining the safety of higher ground.

But then she saw that the frightened and confused Dinakaran was not following her up the hill. He had decided to seek refuge in the small family hut 40 yards from the shore.

Texas has been hit by many hurricanes in its history, including Hurricanes Rita and Katrina.

Sangeeta shouted once again for Dinakaran to run up the hill. Then, as the waves were lapping at her feet, she turned her back on him. With her younger sons in her arms, she exerted what little strength she had remaining to reach safety. With a great cry of anguish, she steeled herself to the thought that she would never again see her Dinakaran alive.

But she had not counted on their little scruffy yellow puppy, Selvakumar, who followed the boy into the hut. Selvakumar grabbed the seven-year-old by the collar of his shirt and dragged him out of the hut. Once they were out in the open, the waves crashing around their legs, the pup kept nipping and nudging Dinakaran up the hill to safety.

Sangeeta had collapsed in grief as soon as she had crossed the main road at the top of the hill. Others from the village told her that they had seen the Ramakrishnan home collapse and be carried away by the tremendous force of the waves. She knew that her husband was safe on the rooftop of the community center. She had her two younger sons clutched to her trembling sides, but Dinakaran was lost to her forever.

Her cries of sorrow were suddenly replaced with shouts of joy when she saw Dinakaran coming toward her, Selvakumar still steadfastly at her son's side.

While other villagers proclaimed the dog's rescue of Dinakaran a miracle, Sangeeta believes that some very special spirit inhabits the body of the little yellow dog. Perhaps, she suggests, it is the spirit of her deceased brother-in-law, who used Selvakumar to save his nephew's life from the deadly tsunami that would claim as many as 300,000 lives in Sumatra, Thailand, Sri Lanka, and India on that fateful Sunday morning.

20-Day-Old Baby Remained Afloat on Her Air Mattress

A. Suppiah and his wife owned a restaurant near the beach in the holiday resort of Penang, Malaysia. On December 26, 2004, it was pretty much business as usual until the huge waves of the tsunami slammed into the resort.

Suppiah and his wife were given no warning. One minute they were serving customers breakfast. The next they were swept out of their place of business by the angry waters that had invaded the shore.

When the two of them bobbed to the surface and their wits had returned to them, they both screamed that their 20-day-old daughter, Tulasi, had been sleeping in a backroom when the tsunami struck. Had she been carried out to sea? Had she been drowned in the backroom when it had filled with water?

The parents had to find their daughter at all costs. Somehow, exerting almost superhuman strength, they managed to fight their way back into the ruins of their restaurant.

When they anxiously opened the door to the backroom, they were blessed with the sight of a miracle. The tiny 20-day-old baby was alive, floating on an air mattress in five feet of water.

Suppiah and his wife were assured of Tulasi's well-being when she began to cry loudly for her feeding.

They Survived the Deadly Tsunami by Scuba Diving

Remarkably, Faye Linda Wachs, 35, a sociology professor, and Eugene J. Kim, 34, a transportation consultant, from Santa Monica, California, survived the December 26 tsunami by scuba diving under the monster waves. While others suffered a veritable hell above them, they were enjoying the beauty and wonder of a wide variety of sea life.

The couple was diving at a depth of 120 feet off the island of Ko Phi Phi in Thailand when the tsunami struck. They became aware of a sudden powerful current and of diminishing visibility in the water, but they had no idea of the destruction being wreaked above them.

After they had surfaced and began heading toward shore, they were shocked to see dead bodies floating in the water. Many of the corpses had their clothes ripped off. All around them, people were attempting to drag bodies back to shore.

When they reached the beach, it seemed to them as if they had somehow surfaced into an alternate reality where some terrible war was being waged. Piles of dead bodies were being separated with Thais in some, tourists in others. People were lying about with broken arms and legs and awful wounds.

They found their cabana leveled, and all their possessions washed away. All they had were their bathing suits, their flip-flops, and, fortunately, their wallets. But as they

As one couple discovered, a clever way of surviving a tsunami is to remain underwater.

looked around the scenes of devastation, they realized how fortunate they were. Somehow, they had been present at a natural catastrophe of biblical proportions, yet they had freakishly survived.

Being Caught by a Tsunami Is Like Being in a Washing Machine

John Krueger, 34, of Winter Park, Colorado, was vacationing with his wife, Romina Canton, 26, an Argentine, enjoying the luxury of their bungalow on the beach north of Phuket. They had absolutely no warning when the sea suddenly rushed into their bungalow.

Krueger remembered how the water had rushed under the floor and raised them to the ceiling. Next it blew out their doors, the windows, and the back concrete wall.

He was terrified when he saw Romina being swept away with the back wall.

Pressed against the roof, Krueger broke his way out of his helpless position only to be pulled under 10 feet of water.

When he surfaced and looked around for his wife, he was forced to conclude that she had been carried out to sea.

Many men and women were swept out to sea and their bodies were never reclaimed from the ocean depths. Romina was one of the fortunate ones.

She fought to survive in the raging sea for more than an hour before some miracle brought her back to shore with a broken nose, a fractured foot, and scrapes over most of her body. Romina was naked when Krueger found her on the beach because she had just finished showering when the tsunami carried her out to sea.

Krueger later described the experience of being caught by a tsunami as being very much like white water rafting without the raft or like being thrown into a washing machine.

Saved by the Strap of Her New Swimming Suit

Caroline Franklin and Peter Greenwood of London were spending a portion of their holiday on a remote island north of Phuket before continuing on to Melbourne. On December 26, 2004, they were enjoying the beach, oblivious to the death and destruction that was headed their way.

Peter suddenly shouted that they must leave the beach at once. He had just begun to explain something about a huge wall of water coming toward them. He had grabbed her arm and the two had begun to run for higher ground when they were torn apart by the incoming sea.

Caroline was knocked unconscious by the wave. She was picked up and carried away from the beach, but the strap of her swimsuit snagged in the branches of a tree.

When she regained consciousness, she saw that she had been saved from being dragged out to sea by the strap of the new Missoni Italian swimsuit that she had bought especially for the trip.

Some people were shouting that the highest point on the island was a water tower, so after the water stopped coming into shore, Caroline Franklin disengaged her swimsuit from the tree branch and began to head for the tower.

Peter Greenwood had also managed to find refuge in a tree. He had no idea if Caroline was alive or if she had been carried out to sea, so he got down from the tree and walked to the water tower.

It was there they found that their lives had been spared by the powerful tsunami, but of the 40 people on the island, at least 11 had been taken by the merciless waves. Many of those who had found their way to the tower were severely injured.

The two visitors from London had lost everything they had with them, but they had retained their lives. Caroline Franklin remarked that she didn't even have the Missoni swimsuit, because she and Peter had used it as a sling for a woman with a broken arm.

Miracle Dolphins Symbolize Rebirth after Hurricane Katrina

On August 29, 2005, a lot of people had to make some important decisions before Hurricane Katrina swept down on them. As the massive hurricane drew nearer, the staff of the Gulfport, Mississippi, Oceanarium that saw to the care of the "Miracle 16 Dolphins" had to decide what to do with the dolphins in the pool.

Eight of the dolphins were evacuated to hotel pools on higher ground.

The remaining eight had to stay behind to face Katrina on their own.

No one is really certain how they managed to escape, but two weeks later, they were sighted in the ocean, alive and together, including two mothers and their babies.

Many of the eight dolphins that had survived Katrina were in rather physically stressed condition. Some had suffered puncture wounds. They were all dehydrated and looked as if they could use a good meal.

There are many tales about friendly dolphins who save people from drowning, from sharks, or from storms.

The directors of the Atlantis Paradise island resort in the Bahamas learned of the tragic plight of the eight dolphins and offered them all a new home.

Teri Corbett of the Marine Mammal Operation at the Atlantis hotel had pieced together a number of accounts of how the dolphins had managed to make their way to the ocean after Katrina struck. According to the stories of some who claimed to be eyewitnesses, a massive wave had demolished their show pool at the Oceanarium and drew them out to sea.

After a great deal of effort, the hotel directors managed to reunite the "Miracle 16" in the dolphin pool at the Atlantis Paradise island resort.

In August 2006, the hotel invited 17 families who had survived Hurricane Katrina to visit Atlantis and go for a swim with fellow survivors.

Although many of the dolphins still bore scars from the wounds they received from being tossed from their pool at the Gulfport Oceanarium and dragged out to sea, they remained as playful as ever with their human companions. In a very real sense, as many have observed, the "Miracle Dolphins" have become a symbol of survival against all odds—including a hurricane.

Lightning Strikes

Somehow He Got on Thor's Bad List

Brad Willard may never know why Thor, the Norse god of thunder and lightning, had it in for him, but for some reason in May 1993 the south Florida man seemed to attract lightning bolts.

The Orlando insurance salesman was determined to keep right on playing golf when thunder clouds started to roll in. His friends ran for the clubhouse, but Willard persisted to position his nine-iron for one more hole.

Willard felt a bizarre tingling throughout his entire body, and there was a blinding flash of light. The next thing the stunned golfer knew was that the golf club had been knocked from his hands and he was flat on his back.

> *As he staggered to his feet to climb into the golf cart, another bolt zapped him and threw him back on the green.*

As he staggered to his feet to climb into the golf cart, another bolt zapped him and threw him back on the green.

Once more, as Willard lay helplessly on the ground, another lightning bolt pounded him for a third time.

Willard's startled friends had been watching him get pummeled by Thor's missives from the safety of the clubhouse and had called 911.

Brad Willard believes that one more zap and he would have been fried. He did not escape future demonstrations of Thor's wrath. Later, a lightning strike destroyed his computer and split a massive oak tree on his lawn, causing it to crash through his roof.

Lightning Disrupts Fourth of July Fireworks by Knocking Down 38 Spectators

Of all times and places, in 1995 a lightning storm flashed and rumbled along with the fireworks display during a Fourth of July celebration in Castalia, North Carolina. The added noise and light show might have been more appreciated if a massive bolt of lightning hadn't touched down near an American flag held proudly aloft by a 100-foot construction crane. The powerful jolt of electricity traveled down the length of the steel crane and enveloped 38 people standing or sitting near the machine, including 11 members of one family.

By some miracle granted the celebrants of Independence Day, all of the individuals lived—even though they were all knocked down and many of them were unconscious for hours.

Sixteen-year-old Daniel Cole appeared to be dead, but someone in the crowd who had been standing some distance away from the crane knew CPR and managed to revive him. A short time later, Cole again expired, but was revived once again, this time in one of the ambulances that had arrived on the scene.

A bolt of lightning can easily kill a person by, in effect, shorting out the nervous system and stopping the heart; remarkably, many people have survived not just one, but several lightning strokes.

Katherine Strange, 33, said that her legs were left paralyzed for eight hours after the powerful current tore through the victims. Ms. Strange happened to be looking at the crane when the bolt struck it. She later described it as a vivid blue streak that seemed to dance along the crane and reach out for the people standing nearest it.

Some of the individuals struck by the dancing blue current said that they thought they were dying—or had already been knocked down dead. As they regained consciousness and looked around them, they were afraid everyone around them was dead.

Bill Freeman, a member of the Castalia Volunteer Fire and Rescue Squad, said that it was a million-to-one miracle that everyone lived and that no one was critically injured.

Interestingly, because the huge construction crane had rubber tires, the operator, who was watching the fireworks from the cab, felt nothing from the tremendous bolt of lightning.

On the other hand, teenaged Daniel Cole only remembered reaching up to adjust his cap—and nothing else until he woke up the next morning in the hospital.

Days later, a number of the victims described the sensation of being struck by the lightning bolt as the worst pain that they had ever known.

Everyone agreed that their guardian angels were watching over them that Fourth of July.

Father and Son Survive Terrible Bolt that Bounced across the Lake

John Reimer and his son Josh were walking the trail around Omaha, Nebraska's Lake Zorinsky on May 29, 2004, when a lightning bolt struck John in the foot and stopped his heart.

An off-duty firefighter was at the lake and saw John Reimer fall. He immediately ran over to the victim, and when he could feel no pulse, he began emergency procedures.

John Reimer's body was smoldering from the force of the powerful electrical jolt. His face had turned purple in color, and there was blood coming from his nose and mouth.

Josh had also been struck. His nose had been crushed, but he was breathing.

Rescue workers actually had to cut John's shoes off his feet. On the trail, John had left a burned footprint in the asphalt.

In the hospital, neither man could remember anything about the lightning strike. A few clouds had been gathering, but nothing that would indicate that a violent storm would soon strike. If they had suspected an electrical storm, they would not have been out walking by the lake.

In John's opinion, the bolt must have bounced across the water, for they saw no lightning flashes in the sky above them. Rescue workers agreed that this might have been so, for lightning can move along the ground or on the surface of a lake—and it can also strike as far as 10 miles from where an actual storm may be occurring.

Josh's maxilla, the part of the skull around the nose and cheek, was crushed, and surgeons installed steel plates in his face to repair the injury.

John was left with a hole in his left eardrum, and the sensation from time to time as if small electrical shocks were moving through his body. Also, on occasion, his feet and legs go numb.

Whenever John walks around the lake and sees the spot where lightning struck him and his son, he gives a prayer of thanks for the miracle of their being spared death.

Sport, the Electrified Beagle

On Wednesday, April 24, 2002, Sally Andis, who lives in rural Washington, Indiana, stepped inside just as a thunderstorm was beginning to pelt down rain. Sport, her little beagle, was just outside the back door, chained to a nearby tree.

There was the sound of thunder, the flash of lightning. Sally heard Sport let out a yelp—and then she couldn't see anything. All the lights in the house went out. Every appliance in the house had its cord blown away from the electrical outlets.

She had been standing near the backdoor when a bolt of lightning struck nearby, and the loud sound had deafened her in her right ear. She stumbled about for a few moments, disoriented. Later, she would remember that everything looked as if it were in some kind of strange fog.

After a few more moments of confusion, Sally's mind cleared and she became filled with concern for her little beagle, chained to the tree where the lightning bolt had struck. She became desperate with fear when she saw that the heat of the lightning strike had left a charred ring around the tree and melted through Sport's chain. Bits of the chain were on the ground, but there was no beagle in sight.

Thinking she heard sounds coming from the nearby creek, Sally ran to investigate and found her little Sport trying to soak up as much water as possible. His fur was singed, and he was bleeding from one paw. When she picked him up, his body felt hot and he was panting, as if he couldn't get enough air. Later, Sport seemed to regain his equilibrium, and after a detailed examination, the veterinarian proclaimed him unharmed. The singed hair would grow back, and the beagle would be none the worse for having undergone such an "enlightening experience."

The *Washington Times-Herald* carried a story of the miracle beagle who survived being struck by lightning. It was apparent that a lightning bolt had hit the tree in the Andises' back yard, traveled through Sport's chain, melted the links that bound him to the tree, then continued its jolting pathway

One of the most popular canine breeds in America is the beagle. These scrappy dogs have proven themselves to be heroes on many occasions.

through the dog and into the foundation of the house, blasting bricks 30 to 40 feet away.

Although the electrified beagle seemed sound of body, Sally Andis told reporters that he now preferred staying in the house, rather than romping outdoors in the back yard.

Struck while Leading His Students on a Charity Walk, Teacher Says He Survived Because of His Large Head

On September 30, 2006, teacher Charlie Sutton was leading a number of his pupils from King Alfred's School in Wantage, Oxfordshire, on an eight-mile charity walk to raise money for school equipment when a sudden bolt of lightning struck him directly on the head.

Sutton's students watched in terror and awe as their teacher was knocked flat, then struggled to get back on his feet. He was obviously—and understandably—confused. It seemed apparent that he was unable to see—and then he seemed to collapse in a kind of seizure.

Sutton regained consciousness on the way to the hospital, and though he was still dazed, he said that he remembered his students shouting and screaming when he was struck by the lightning. He described the sensation as similar to being struck with a baseball bat.

At the John Radcliffe Hospital, Sutton found himself surrounded by staff members who wanted a closer look at the miracle man who had cheated death by surviving a direct lightning strike.

Surely, it had to be a miracle, for once the temporary state of blindness passed, Charlie Sutton was left only with a minor burn to the back of his head. In addition to declaring Sutton's survival as miraculous, the doctors were puzzled because although they could see clearly the entry burn, they could not find any place on his body where the powerful electrical charge had exited.

Blessed with remarkable good fortune, Sutton also had a good sense of humor. He told people that his rugby teammates had agreed that he had survived because of his thick head. Charlie said that his mates told him that they knew his big, thick head would come in handy one day.

✳

Saved by Her Thick-soled Shoes

Terri Hoag, 37, of Debary, Florida, was walking with her younger son, Logan, 2, to a neighbor's house for an ice cream party on May 26, 2006, when a fast-approaching rain storm began to sprinkle on them. Terri picked up Logan, and they started to run for cover at their neighbors' place, where her older son, Luke, was waiting for them to arrive.

After running only a few steps, Terri was struck by lightning.

Dale Stevens heard Logan crying and looked outside to see his neighbor lying face down on the ground. Stevens ran to her side and determined that she was not breathing. Logan, however, appeared to be frightened, but uninjured.

Fortunately for Terri Hoag, Stevens was a firefighter and a paramedic, and another neighbor, Carlos Camara, had been trained in CPR in the Army.

The two men carried her into the Stevens' home and conducted emergency procedures on her until an ambulance arrived. Once at the hospital, she was placed on a ventilator and listed in serious condition.

Rob, Terri's husband, was thankful that she was wearing sneakers with very thick rubber soles, which helped ground her. Because she was carrying Logan, those same heavy rubber soles spared the two-year-old from harm because Terri served as a "ground" and the lightning passed right through him.

By the next morning, Terri was doing well enough that the ventilator could be removed and she was released from the hospital without any residual damage from the lightning bolt.

Electrical Charge Misses Girl by Inches

When Melanie Holland, 36, returned from her night shift at a supermarket on July 26, 2006, she was horrified to discover that her home had been struck by lightning. An electrical storm had lifted the roof and wreaked devastation on the upstairs of their four-bedroom home. As she stepped into the house, she could see the sky through torn away sections of the roof.

She could deal with the destruction of her house. A house was only bricks and mortar. But what about her children, Emily and Luke, and her husband, John?

Thankfully, they were all safe, but what remarkable experiences they had shared.

John Holland, 40, was sound asleep when six-foot pieces of the ceiling in the bedroom came crashing down on him. Jolted awake, he ran to look after Emily and Luke.

After the Hollands had pieced the entire story together with some help from their neighbors, they decided that little Emily was one of the luckiest seven-year-old children in the world.

During the violent electrical storm that had jolted Locks Heath, Southampton, that night, lightning struck an antenna on the Holland's roof. A teenaged neighbor saw what he described as a fireball hitting the chimney of the Holland home. According to a spokesman for the Hampshire Fire and Rescue Service, the strike created a massive power surge that caused the light switches to explode and blow off the walls.

Witnesses saw the roof collapse, but what they could not see was debris and the fireball that descended on Emily's bedroom.

The electrical charge trashed her bedroom, missed her head by inches, scorched her bed sheets and mattress, and singed the stomach area and arm of her pajamas. Miraculously, Emily suffered only a small burn mark on her arm.

He Must Beware July 30

Sixty-eight-year-old Don Frick was enjoying a festival in Pennsylvania in July 2007 when he heard people talking about a storm rapidly moving in over the area. He moved inside a shed with a group of others to be safe.

Moments later, lightning struck the ground nearby, and Frick and four others were shocked by the bolt. Frick was thrown up against a wall and knocked unconscious.

When he regained consciousness and found himself uninjured, he proclaimed himself a very fortunate man. Twenty-seven years ago to the very day—on July 30, 1980—Frick had been struck by lightning while driving a tractor-trailer. At that time, the bolt had struck the antenna on the outside of the cab and followed the connection to injure Frick's left side.

Lightning Strike Stops Her Heart, Places Her in Coma for Three Weeks

On October 1, 2007, Lara Eusterman, 39, her two youngest sons, and her mother, Kathy Larsen, were walking atop a ridge and discussing where, on the Idaho countryside, the Eusterman family might build a house. As they walked they noticed a single black storm cloud that appeared to be approaching them and moving very swiftly across the sky.

Lara decided that the cloud might be bringing rain and that they should return to their car until the potential storm blew over.

Lara was in the lead when a loud, deafening crack of thunder sounded, and a bolt of lighting knocked all four of them off their feet.

> *Leaving Lara and calling 911 was the action that probably saved Lara's life.*

Kathy Larsen and her grandsons got back up almost immediately, but Lara Eusterman remained on the ground. When Kathy went to check on her daughter, she was startled to see that her eyes were open but that she was turning blue.

Aware that her daughter had not only been knocked unconscious by the lightning, but that her system was not getting enough oxygen, Kathy began CPR as quickly as possible.

By now, the two boys were becoming very concerned about their mother and frightened that something was terribly wrong with her. Grandmother Kathy calmed them as best she could and sent them to a group of houses nearby to ask for help.

Although it was a difficult decision, Kathy left Lara lying on the ground while she walked the distance to get her cell phone from their car. Leaving Lara and calling 911 was the action that probably saved Lara's life.

When rescue workers arrived, it was quickly determined that the lightning strike had briefly stopped Lara's heart and placed her in a coma.

She would remain in that coma for three weeks.

When Lara's husband, John, an attorney, arrived at the hospital in Boise, his young sons were crying and screaming that their mother was dead. The doctors informed John Eusterman that his wife was not dead, but that she was in the deepest coma a person could enter—a 3 on a scale of 15.

Lara had also suffered burn wounds to her scalp and both legs from the fury of the lightning strike.

Three weeks later, Lara Eusterman awakened from the coma with no knowledge of the lightning strike nor any events of the month before they spotted that single dark and explosive storm cloud while walking on the ridge. She continued outpatient rehabilitation for several weeks before her recovery.

Lightning Strikes Her Feet, Exits through Her Nose Ring

Jessica Lafreniere, 21, of Antrim, New Hampshire, was struck by lightning while walking through the family garage on July 9, 2008. The bolt came through a window, struck her feet, and came out through her nose ring.

Jessica and her mother, Danielle Taylor, had been outside when they saw a storm brewing. After they had been inside for a few minutes, Jessica remembered that they had left a hose running on the lawn, so she decided to go out through the garage and turn it off.

Danielle said that she saw a bright light come in through a window in the garage and strike her daughter. Next, a brilliant red flash came up from Jessica's feet, lit up her face, and threw her into her mother's arms.

According to her mother, Jessica's skin turned blue and purple and she felt stiff as a board.

Jessica showed up for work on her overnight shift apparently none the worse for her electrifying experience. Her only complaint was numbness on the top of her lip and the tip of her nose.

Lightning Bolt Strikes Three Workers at Once

On April 21, 2008, three construction workers from Schafter Contracting were working just north of Concourse E at Twin Cities International Airport when it began to rain. At 10:20 P.M., one of the men was setting out orange construction cones when lightning struck him in the head.

Incredibly, the lightning bolt then passed through the two workers nearest him, jolting their hands and arms. One of the men later remarked it was like holding onto an electric fence.

The worker who was struck in the head was knocked unconscious and woke up a few moments later, asking what had happened. He was treated for minor injuries, but his coworkers were unharmed.

Tornadoes

A Mother's Mental Radar Saves Family from Sudden Tornado

While on a vacation to Florida in 1972, Sherry Hansen, her husband, Paul, their two children, Erik and Melissa, and two teenaged friends, Jan and Jimmy, escaped a sudden and terrible death only by heeding the warning that was transmitted to them through Sherry's special maternal radar.

Driving straight through from Columbus, Ohio, in an oversized van that had been customized for sleeping and storing camp gear, they arrived at their campsite tired, yet

Tornadoes can level buildings and toss trucks dozens of feet across a field, yet some people have been sucked up into funnel clouds and survived to tell their tales.

enthusiastic enough to set up the tents that night. For the next two days, they enjoyed beach walks, building sand castles, collecting shells, and burying each other in the sand.

On the third night at the campsite, all parties were zipped into their sleeping bags and had been sound asleep for many hours when all of a sudden, Sherry bolted out of her sleeping bag and screamed, "We've got to get out of here—now!"

Nearly in a trance state, Sherry repeated herself until all were awake. By this time Sherry's family and friends had learned not to question her instincts when they came from that depth of feeling, as there had been sufficient experiences to prove them valid.

Wiping the sleep from his eyes, Paul had an understandably annoying edge to his voice when he asked, "I don't understand. Why do we have to leave now? The sky is clear; all the stars are brightly shining; all else in the campground is completely quiet. What possibly could be wrong?"

Somewhat puzzled herself, Sherry answered, "I honestly have no idea. I just *know* that if we don't leave now something terrible is going to happen."

Jan and Jimmy already had Erik and Melissa in their arms and were awaiting instructions outside the tent. When Sherry went out and saw the clear night air and observed the extreme quiet and peace that seemed to be all around the campground area she acknowledged that she, too, felt it was weird, but *necessary*.

Coming up with a constructive idea of where to go and what to do was the next item of business. Sherry thought of an idea that must have sounded insane at four o'clock in the morning—to take all their dirty laundry to the closest Laundromat, which happened to be in the next town. Then at least they would be doing something constructive during their getaway. So they hurriedly gathered up the dirty laundry, grabbing damp, sandy towels and beach blankets to be washed as well.

In Sherry's mind there was no time to take anything else except a couple of food items, so they could eat an early breakfast at the laundromat.

During the approximately 45-minute drive, they had monitored the radio for any storm warning or an alert that had been issued of some such danger, but there was no indication of any sort of disaster.

What could they do but make the best of it? They all sang songs until they reached the laundromat, then everyone pitched in to do the many loads of wash.

By now the first hues of dawn were coloring the sky, and with clean, dry, fresh-smelling towels and beach clothes (and clean diapers for one-year-old Melissa), the group loaded up the van and turned to Sherry for the sign to return to camp.

Singing all the way back to the campground, they had all but forgotten the reason they had left—until they couldn't find their tents.

Driving into the campground, they saw a vacant lot where their camp had been set up. There were some scattered cans from the food boxes and some clothes tossed here and there, as if they had been thrown about by some incredible force.

They got out of the van and stood in a complete daze.

Just then a park ranger drove up and excitedly bolted out of his truck. "Oh, my God! Thank heavens you are all safe," he said. "We have been conducting a search for your family. We thought you all must have been killed!

"We have just had the most incredible freak occurrence of nature I've ever seen in my over 35 years as a park ranger. Somewhere around 4:30 A.M. or so, out of nowhere—and I mean out of nowhere—came this waterspout from the ocean—out of a clear sky!

"It swept onto the campground with no warning and with absolutely no time for anyone to act or to warn others. It tossed your tents in the air like they were kites. It picked them up, spun them around, and tossed them in all different directions. We are still finding things from your camp area scattered *everywhere!*"

The park ranger explained that a waterspout is like a "mini-tornado" or small hurricane that comes in off the ocean with incredible force and then either dissipates or goes back out to sea.

He suddenly looked Sherry square in the eyes and asked, "Excuse my language, but how in the hell did you get the kids and all out in time? What happened? Where did you go at this time of the morning?

"You can't believe how worried we have been," he continued. "There is no conceivable way that you would have escaped unhurt. More than likely, if you had all been asleep in your tents—as we assumed you were—you would have all been in pieces around the area with the rest of your belongings. You really must have angels surrounding you guys!"

> *The park ranger explained that a waterspout is like a "mini-tornado" or small hurricane that comes in off the ocean with incredible force.*

After explaining Sherry's sudden feeling that their lives were endangered, the ranger simply looked at them and shook his head, saying, "Boy, this is sure one for the books! Come, let me show you where your tents ended up."

They followed the ranger to view the twisted, mangled tents with the stakes piercing the fabric at various points.

Sherry and her family stood in awe. After taking a few pictures of the carnage as a lasting reminder of their narrow escape, they all shed tears and offered many prayers of thanks that their lives had been spared on such a night of unsuspected violence!

A Tornado Lifted His Truck off a Bridge and Dumped It into the River—with Him in It

The weather had turned terrible on April 26, 1994, in Port Charlotte, Florida. Robert Riccio sat in his pickup truck, trying his best to be patient as he waited in the long line of backed-up traffic on the bridge. He had his windshield wipers going full power as the rain poured down on the traffic line. And then it started to lightning. A real storm was in the making.

Suddenly, Robert felt his 3,400-pound truck start to move sideways. A tornado had moved over the bridge. Within seconds, Robert and his truck were picked up and thrown over the guard rail. He was falling upside down toward the river below.

When he hit the river and the water closed over him, every window in the cab exploded as the truck sank 22 feet to the bottom.

Robert struggled to get out of the crushed window on the driver's side, and he finally reached the surface, gasping for air.

From what he could determine, he was alone. His was the only vehicle that had been thrown by the tornado into the river.

Robert knew his only hope was to get to one of the pillars of the bridge and hold on for dear life.

Easier thought than done. The water, wiped up by the storm, created large waves that kept him away from a pillar.

After several exhaustive efforts, Robert realized that he might have a better chance if he drifted with the current to another bridge nearly a quarter of a mile downriver.

Within a few minutes, he managed to wrap his arms around a barnacle-encrusted pillar. Although the barnacles ripped at his flesh, Robert would not release his grip. He kept thinking of his beloved wife and daughter and that he must stay alive to join them.

After nearly 30 minutes of clutching to the pillar, rescue workers pulled him into a boat and soon had him in an ambulance.

Robert Riccio was treated for water in his lungs, cuts, and bruises, but he suffered no serious injuries. Somehow, Riccio said, he knew God was looking after him.

Woman and Her Two Infant Sons Taken for a Ride on a Mattress

Chanta Adams said that she felt like Dorothy in the *Wizard of Oz* after a tornado lifted her and her two infant sons from their home and deposited them on some tree branches 50 feet away.

The tornado had been spun out of Hurricane Bertha and on July 13, 1996, it devastated the tiny town of Edwardsville, Virginia, near Chesapeake Bay. Twenty-two-year-old mother Chanta Adams was lying on their queen-sized bed, sleeping between her sons, Javonte, two, and Trevaughn, 15 months, when she was suddenly awakened by a loud roaring sound, as if a freight train were bearing down on them. Chanta screamed for her 16-year-old cousin, Khalif, to run into their bedroom, but just then the side of their mobile room blew out and he was blown away like a dried leaf and carried toward the woods.

Chanta instinctively wrapped her arms around her sons as the violent twister lifted the queen-sized bed with them on it and spun it around and around until they were three stories high, spinning crazily in the center of the howling winds.

Chanta said later that the three of them were being tossed around as if they were rubber balls, and she kept praying for God to let them down, *gently, please, gently.*

And then her prayer was granted. They landed among the broken branches and rain-drenched trees 50 feet from the spot where their home had once been. Amazingly, all three of them were still on the mattress, a son on either side of his mother.

Captain Thomas Neale of the Northumberland (Virginia) County Sheriff's Department declared Chanta Adams and her children among the luckiest people in the world to survive being carried aloft by a tornado. Although they didn't escape without a scratch—Chanta required 26 stitches in her scalp; two-year-old Javonte had a broken collar bone, a fractured skull, and a broken eye socket bone; 15-month-old Trevaughn had minor scrapes and bruises—the Adams family readily agrees that they experienced a miracle. God was indeed looking out for them.

> *They landed among the broken branches and rain-drenched trees 50 feet from the spot where their home had once been.*

And what about cousin Khalif, who was blown out of the side of the mobile home as if he were a dried leaf in the wind? He escaped with only a cut on his back, so he, too, must have had a guardian angel on his shoulder.

Miracle Baby Rides a Tornado for Quarter of a Mile

Shortly before midnight on November 11, 1995, a driving rainstorm pounding Des Arc, Arkansas, was transformed into a deadly F2 tornado. Keith and Donna Walls felt secure in their substantial, solid wood frame home, but the 200-mile-per-hour twister struck their house so violently that rescue workers who came upon the scene later declared that there was not enough wood left to build a doghouse. Law enforcement officers said that they had never seen anything like the destruction visited upon the Walls home. Nothing remained. Even such heavy items as refrigerators, sinks, and bathtubs had been carried away.

Fighting stinging rains and attempting to pierce the darkness with their flashlights, rescue workers began a grim search of the surrounding rice fields, desperately seeking some sign of the Walls family, which included Joshua, a seven-month-old baby boy. About a quarter of a mile from the demolished home, a deputy sheriff managed to hear the sound of a baby crying over the roar of the 50-mile-per-hour wind.

Incredibly, Joshua was still alive, lying face down in the mud, his lower body submerged in a puddle of water. The baby was dressed only in a diaper and nightshirt, and his body was turning blue from the cold.

Rescue workers felt his tiny arms and legs, and in the illumination from their flashlights determined after a cursory examination that little Joshua suffered only a scratch on one cheek and a small bruise on one leg.

Tragically, the bodies of his parents were found nearby. Neither of them had survived the awful wrath of the tornado.

One of the rescue workers declared that little Joshua had been granted two miracles. First, he had been carried at least a quarter of a mile by a deadly tornado that had completed demolished their home. Second, he had been set down in such a manner that only the lower part of his body was below water. If he had been lowered to the ground headfirst into the puddle of water, Joshua would surely have drowned.

Later, a spokesperson for the Emergency Management Coordinator of Prairie County, Arkansas, observed how unbelievable it was that a tornado could take an entire house right down to its concrete foundation and throw a baby boy some 300 yards into a field where he would survive with only a few bruises.

Little Joshua, the miracle baby, was turned over to the care of his grandparents.

Family Survives Being Sucked Out of Their Home by a Twister

The tornadoes that struck Oklahoma in the first days of May 1999 left death and destruction in their wake. The early reports issued on May 6 declared 41 deaths, 55 people missing, and nearly 700 individuals injured. The account of the miracle that occurred to 10-month-old Aleah and her mother and father was one story that lifted the hearts of those who had been so brutalized by the monstrous power of the twisters.

Deputy Robert Jolley was chasing one of the twisters across the mangled landscape of Grady County when he spotted a man wandering down a road, apparently in a state of shock. When Deputy Jolley stopped to question him, Robert Williams told the officer that the tornado had sucked his daughter, son-in-law, and 10-month-old baby granddaughter out of closet where they had taken shelter.

The survivor of the frightening experience described how his wife had died in his arms when a trailer had crashed into the remaining walls of the closet. Williams was able only to hold her head in his hands and tell her good-bye as the tears rolled down her cheeks. She had been unable to speak a word before she died.

Deputy Jolley set out in search of the three victims who had been pulled from the home by the terrible suction of the twister. Perhaps by some miracle they had been spared.

About 100 feet from what remained of the Williams' home, the officer saw what at first he thought was a rag doll in a pile of debris caught at the base of a tree. Gently, Deputy Jolley picked up the "doll," which upon closer examination, proved to be a baby girl whose eyes and ears were packed with mud. As he carefully wiped the mud from her face, little Aleah began to cry.

The sound of that baby crying made the deputy feel a wonderful surge of joy.

Deputy Jolley rushed little Aleah to the hospital where she was reunited with her mother Amy, who by some miracle had suffered only bruises and scratches. Amy's husband, Ben Molton, had received more serious injuries, but incredibly, they had managed to survive the ordeal of having been sucked out of their home and carried away by an historic F5 tornado. A tornado is considered formidable if its damage ranks F2 or higher on the Fujita scale.

Surviving the initial tornado strike is sometimes only the first challenge; escaping from the rubble is the next.

Firefighter Discovers One of the "Dolls" in the Field Is a Baby

Eleven-month-old Kyson Stowell is another miracle baby.

Firefighter David Harmon, 31, was walking through a field that was littered with plastic dolls after the tornado that had struck Castalain, Tennessee, in February 2008. The dolls had all belonged to an avid collector whose house had been completely demolished by the twister.

As it grew dark, Harmon took out his flashlight and continued to search among the debris that was scattered all over the field.

At first he couldn't believe his eyes, but one of the dolls appeared to be moving. Walking cautiously closer to the doll, Harmon saw that it was lying face down in the mud. But that was when he saw its little buttock cheeks moving, and he knew that he had not found an animated doll, but a real baby.

Harmon rushed over to the baby shivering in the cold and lifted him out of the mud. The little boy was wearing only a T-shirt and a diaper that had slipped down to his legs. He took a deep breath of air and started crying.

> **It didn't take long for the authorities to identify little Kyson Stowell, who had been carried over 100 yards by the force of the tornado.**

It didn't take long for the authorities to identify little Kyson Stowell, who had been carried over 100 yards by the force of the tornado and ironically dropped amidst a scattered collection of dolls.

Tragically, his mother, Kerrie, 23, had been killed by the monster storm that had destroyed Castalain.

Kyson's grandfather, Doug Stowell, 45, said that it was a miracle that his little grandson wasn't killed along with his mother. Stowell said that their home had been completely demolished and to be able to find Kyson 300 feet from the site, lying face down in the mud and alive, was truly a blessing from God.

Missouri Teenager Survives Record Ride on a Tornado

Nineteen-year-old Matt Suter had often remarked to his friends that he would like one day to see a tornado. He never said that he wanted to be in one.

On March 12, 2006, Matt was just relaxing in his boxer shorts, watching the television news with his uncle Robert Dewhirst and grandmother Linda Kelley in their mobile home outside of Fordland, Missouri. They began to notice a terrible roar approaching the mobile home court, a roar that got louder and louder, as if some jet airplanes were bearing down on them.

Matt got up to shut a window, but before he was successful, both the window and the door were sucked right out of the trailer. He remembers seeing that the walls, roof, and floor were moving. Later, he would learn that winds in excess of 150 miles per hour were turning the mobile home upside down.

And then those powerful winds just pulled him out of the trailer and took off with him into the night.

A heavy glass lamp knocked him unconscious, and when he awakened, he was lying in some soft grass in an open field.

Matt had no doubt that a tornado had swept down on them. He could see no lights in the direction of the trailer court, and he had no idea if his grandmother and his uncle were alive or dead.

He set off running toward the court and saw debris from the homes everywhere. He assumed that neither of them had survived that kind of destruction, so he ran to the home of his best friend.

Although Linda Kelley and Robert Dewhirst were buried in the wreckage of their mobile home, they both survived. Mrs. Kelley wanted to go searching for her grandson, and she prayed that she wouldn't find him dead.

Matt Suter arrived at the Cornelison home, bleeding from the wound to his head and limping from his cut and bruised bare feet. After a few hours, the family was reunited and thankful that they were all alive.

Later, a meteorologist with a global positioning satellite device used by the National Weather Service measured the distance that Matt Suter had been carried from the mobile home to the pasture as 1,307 feet. Tom Grazulis, an author and tornado researcher, said that distance is the farthest that anyone had ever been carried by a tornado and lived.

Dr. Ron Buening placed five surgical staples in Suter's head wound and said that the teenager's lack of other serious injuries corroborated his account. The doctor, pronouncing Matt the luckiest man on Earth, stated that if Suter had been blown across the mobile home court into the field, he would have received many more cuts, bruises, and body surface wounds than he did. Dr. Buening said that there was no question in his mind that Matt Suter had survived the longest trip on a twister on record.

ACCIDENTS

Airline Crashes

She Fell Two Miles and Walked 10 Days through the Rainforest to Survive

On Christmas Eve, December 24, 1971, 17-year-old Juliane Margaret Koepcke was traveling with her mother, highly respected Peruvian ornithologist Maria Koepcke, from Lima to meet with her father, noted biologist Hans-Wilhelm Koepcke, in Pucallpa so they might spend the holiday together. Juliane, a senior at the German High School in Lima, had been studying to become a zoologist and follow in the scientific path established by her parents.

LANSA (Lineas Aereas Nacionales Airlines) 508 departed Lima's Jorge Chavez International Airport just a few minutes before noon. The flight carried 93 passengers aboard a Lockheed Electra OB-R 941 commercial airliner. About a half hour after takeoff with the aircraft at 21,000 feet, the Electra entered a region of violent thunderstorms and heavy turbulence.

According to some accounts, the crew urged the pilot to turn back, but because it was Christmas Eve and he knew the passengers were eager to enjoy the holiday with friends and relatives, he decided to continue battling the increasingly violent weather. Most of the passengers were young Peruvians returning home from school, and the pilot felt that he could evade the effects of the storm.

The official report of the tragedy states that after flying for 20 minutes in a zone of strong turbulence and lightning, lightning struck the Electra, causing a fire and the separation of the right wing. Although the crew attempted to maintain control, the heavy turbulence soon caused the separation of a part of the left wing and the aircraft crashed in flames into mountainous terrain in the Amazon rainforest.

A lightning stroke set fire to the right wing of the plane in which Juliane Koepcke was a passenger.

As the teenager looked out the window and saw the right wing in flames, she turned to her mother who glanced out at the wing separating from the aircraft and said that it was now the end of everything that they had known.

Within the next few moments, Juliane was dimly aware that she was whirling about in midair.

When she awakened three hours later, she was in the Amazon rainforest, still strapped to her seat. Although she had sustained an injury that left her without sight in one eye, Juliane had fallen two miles and survived.

As she rose from the seat, Juliane felt the pain of a fractured collarbone and a gash on her right arm, but she could walk.

Her first thought was to locate her mother. Perhaps she, too, had somehow survived the crash.

Juliane found some wreckage and a number of empty seats, but she could find no trace of her mother.

After she found a row of three seats still holding the bodies of three young school-girls, Juliane decided that everyone who had been on the flight was probably dead and that she should begin to walk through the jungle to get some help.

Although she was dazed and in shock, Juliane remembered the words of her biologist father who had told her many times that if she were ever lost in the jungle to begin walking downhill. Moving downhill in the rainforest would lead to water and water would eventually lead to civilization.

Dressed only in a blouse, miniskirt, and one sandal, Juliane had little protection against the vicious attacks of insects, but she pressed on, until she found a stream. Once again, she heard the words of her father, who had advised her on their many trips into the rainforest to follow the water. She stepped into the knee-high stream and began walking.

Juliane stayed in the stream for nine days, fighting nasty swarms of insects when she rested on land and scraping off leeches when she re-entered the water.

On the ninth day of her trek, she found a canoe and a small house that she assumed belonged to lumbermen. She knew that they would be coming back to the shelter, so she made herself as comfortable as possible and waited.

It was nearly nightfall when the lumbermen returned and found Juliane waiting for them. It was too late to begin a canoe trip to civilization, but they did tend to the many insect infestations on her body. One of the men poured gasoline on the lumps on her skin which indicated the places where insects had burrowed and laid eggs. Some of them were beginning to hatch, and Juliane later said that she counted 35 worms that crawled out of her arms.

The next day, two of the men took Juliane on a seven-hour canoe trip to a lumber station where she was airlifted to a hospital.

Rescue crews had searched in vain for the wreckage of the LANSA Electra. It had taken Juliane nearly 10 days of steady walking to reach the camp of the lumbermen. Perhaps there may have been other passengers who possessed her survival skills and were still alive. When officials interviewed Juliane in the hospital, she was able to provide them with enough information to enable rescue workers to find the wreckage of Flight 508.

When they reached the site in the rainforest, the rescue team found evidence that as many as 14 passengers had managed to survive the initial crash but had died awaiting help. Unfortunately, none of them had been tutored in jungle survival by a father and a mother who had taken them along on numerous expeditions to the rainforest.

Now that the wreckage had been found, the tragic results totaled 91 dead—all six crew members and 86 of the 87 passengers. The sole survivor was 17-year-old Juliane Margaret Koepcke, who had fallen two miles strapped to her seat and who had walked for 10 days through the jungle until she was rescued by lumbermen.

The remarkable feat of Juliane, who became a biologist in Germany, has been dramatized in an Italian film entitled *The Story of Juliane Koepcke* (also known as *Miracles Still Happen*) in 1974. In 1999, the famed director Werner Herzog made a documentary treatment of Juliane Koepcke's ordeal called *Wings of Hope*.

His New Airplane Nearly Cost Him His Life
but a Positive Attitude Helped Him to Survive

High school history teacher Dennis Steinbock of Klamath Falls, Oregon, had his pilot's license for 18 years when he bought a homebuilt Zodiac airplane from an aviation enthusiast in Alabama. On June 18, 2007, Steinbock planned to fly to Alabama, pick up the plane, then make a stop near Branson, Missouri. He climbed into the VW Beetle-sized cabin of his new aircraft and took off with expectations of a pleasant flight.

Somewhere over Mississippi, Steinbock's plane experienced unexpected engine trouble. Below him was a thickly wooded area. He spotted a clearing and tried to steer the falling airplane toward it. Tall trees prevented his reaching the open area, and his plane slammed into a thick tree trunk and flipped over on its top, pinning Steinbock underneath.

> *Steinbock grabbed one of the Altoid tins and tried to use it as a mirror to signal that he was still alive.*

Hanging upside down, Steinbock could barely move in the tiny cabin, but he continued to struggle until he was upright. It was painful for him to move, so he assumed that he had broken some bones during the crash. He tried pushing with all of his strength in an effort to free himself from the wreckage, but he couldn't budge the plane.

Although the area seemed more wilderness than a rural environment, he shouted for help in the hope that someone might have a residence nearby. After a half hour or so of shouting, he gave up and decided that he must begin to concentrate on how he might survive until he was found.

It was a hot and humid summer's day, and Steinbock soon drank the two bottles of water that he had with him in the cabin.

He was grateful for the thunderstorm that poured down rain that first night, but he only had a couple Altoid containers with which he was able to catch and retain the water.

For the next two days, Steinbock sucked water from wet maps and grabbed some leaves to chew to provide him with moisture and some nourishment.

Fifty-four hours after his ordeal began, he heard planes flying overhead. Within a short time, a helicopter appeared to be hovering directly over the wreckage.

Steinbock grabbed one of the Altoid tins and tried to use it as a mirror to signal that he was still alive.

It took only a few more minutes before rescue workers arrived on the ground with the Jaws of Life. Working swiftly and expertly, they soon had Steinbock extricated from the wreckage and placed on a spine board.

The grateful survivor was informed that the Civil Air Patrol had detected an emergency signal from his aircraft, but they were only able to trace it within a mile radius. A rescue team had been searching for him in the forested area, which Steinbock learned was about 15 miles from Oxford, Mississippi.

Steinbock was taken to a Memphis hospital where he was treated for a punctured lung, broken ribs, muscle trauma, and dehydration. After staying a week, he was advised to consult a physical therapist and a podiatrist to treat his legs, feet, shoulder, and back.

Steinbock's son, Stephen, drove to Memphis to bring him home to Klamath Falls because the punctured lung made it impossible for him to fly in a pressurized cabin.

Dennis Steinbock was greeted by many friends and well-wishers in Klamath Falls who told him that they had been praying for his safe return. Many declared that his survival was a miracle.

The men in the cockpit were dead, but little Kate, strapped in her car seat, survived the Cessna crash.

Steinbock acknowledged that he was well aware that he could die while awaiting rescue, but he had prayed and maintained a positive attitude throughout the ordeal.

Being Strapped in Car Seat Saved Granddaughter

Allen D. Williams, 65, the CEO and founder of an Edmonton, Alberta, engineering firm, was known as a visionary and a leader in the engineering consulting industry. Williams also loved to fly, and according to family and friends, he had logged more hours in the air than many airline captains had achieved.

In late October 2007, Williams and Steven T. Sutton, the company's chief financial advisor, had flown in Williams' Cessna 172 to Golden, British Columbia, for a business retreat. On the flight back to Edmonton, the two men were joined by Williams' granddaughter, three-year-old Kate Williams.

Williams strapped Kate into a child's car seat and saw that she was snuggly secure before taking off from the airport in Golden at 1:00 P.M. on Sunday, October 28.

Shortly after takeoff, the Cessna 172 found itself in low clouds, heavy snow, and poor visibility. About an hour after leaving the airport, the small plane crashed in the

rugged mountains of British Columbia. The Cessna flipped over in icy water and landed nose down at the edge of a riverbank.

Members of the rescue squad that set out to locate the crash said that they were
slowed in their efforts by bad weather and nightfall. After five hours of searching, they
located the Cessna's twisted, snow-filled wreckage.

Digging through snow and debris, they found the two men dead, but when they discovered little Kate still alive and hanging upside down in the aircraft, they felt that
they had witnessed a miracle.

The rescuers said that the three-year-old had survived the crash because of the care
that her grandfather had applied in strapping her into a car seat in addition to the
plane's safety belt. That extra protection, a representative from the Royal Canadian
Mounted Police agreed, was what had saved Kate's life.

As one of the rescuers handed Kate to another, the three-year-old cried out that she
was not leaving without Pablo, her teddy bear.

The rescuer inside the wreckage felt around in the debris and retrieved the teddy,
brushing Pablo free of snow before handing it back to Kate. He said that she seemed
very upset that her beloved little bear had nearly been lost in the snow bank that had
drifted into the aircraft.

Kate was taken to the Alberta Children's Hospital in Calgary for overnight observation where she was found to have suffered non-life threatening head injuries. She
was reunited with her parents and returned to her home in Golden.

He May Have Survived the Plane Crash
Because He Took the Wrong Seat

In a tragic commuter plane crash that killed 13 people flying en route from St. Louis
to Kirksville, Missouri, on October 19, 2004, one of two miracle survivors may have
been saved because he did not sit in his assigned seat.

Dr. John Krogh, 68, was the last passenger to board the Corporate Airlines flight for
Kirksville, where most of those on the plane were on their way to attend a conference
on humanism in medicine at the Kirksville College of Osteopathic Medicine. Dr. Krogh
spotted a seat by a window that appeared to have plenty of leg room, so he took it.

Wendy Bonham, 44, his assistant, turned around to inform him that he was not sitting in his seat, but Krogh, of Wallsburg, Utah, a part-time faculty member at Provo
College, protested that he was unaware that they had been assigned seats.

Then the Jetstream 32, a twin-engine turboprop, was beginning its takeoff, so Dr.
Krogh made no effort to discover which seat was truly his.

The skies were overcast, and thunderstorms were in the area, but no one expected
the horror that suddenly attacked the flight.

The next thing Krogh knew, they had crashed and fire seemed to be all around the
passengers. He looked out his window and saw that the wing had been torn off. As far

as his own condition, he could readily diagnose that he had a broken hip. With such an injury, he knew that he would be unable to do anything other than pull himself out and fall to the ground eight feet below him.

After he had managed to roll free of the aircraft, he could hear the scream of the other passengers. He was left feeling helpless, wondering if there was anything that he could do.

He saw someone else pulling themselves out the same window from which he had escaped the inferno, and he was certain that it was his secretary, Wendy Bonham. She dropped to the ground in the same spot where Dr. Krogh had landed, but that place seemed now to be in flames. Krogh thought that he would never again see his assistant alive.

When rescuers arrived at the scene, the terrible sight that greeted them of a turboprop with a broken wing engulfed in flames seemed to negate the hope finding any survivors. However, both Dr. Krogh and Wendy Bonham were found alive.

When the two were examined at the Northeast Regional Medical Center, Dr. Charles Zeman, director of trauma services, declared the condition of both survivors to be truly a miracle. Dr. Zeman commented that they saw patients who had been in car accidents coming in with much worse injuries. To survive such a deadly airplane crash and escape with little more than a few broken bones seemed totally inexplicable.

> *The skies were overcast, and thunderstorms were in the area, but no one expected the horror that suddenly attacked the flight.*

Twelve-Year-Old Girl, the Sole Survivor, Saved by Falling Luggage

It had been such a wonderful holiday. Francesca "Frankie" Lewis, 12, had been invited to join her best friend Talia Klein, 13, and Talia's father Michael, 37, a prominent Santa Barbara businessman, on a vacation at Klein's eco-resort on the Panamanian island of Islas Secas. The plan was to arrive on December 20, then, after a few days, return to Santa Barbara for Christmas Eve. But as poets, priests, and philosophers of the human condition have noted for centuries, in the midst of the happiest of occasions, tragedy may strike.

On Sunday, December 23, 2007, Talia and Michael Klein, Frankie, and their pilot, Edwin Lasso, 23, took off in a Cessna 172 with the flight plan of heading for the town of Volcan for a bit of sightseeing. Although the Panamanian region had experienced storms and heavy rains since Friday, Klein did not assess the weather disturbances as severe enough to warrant postponing their plans. Before takeoff, Michael Klein instructed the pilot that he wished to take aerial photos of the Baru volcano.

As the Cessna drew nearer to the volcano, the pilot complained that the winds in the mountains around Baru were too strong for light aircraft.

Within only a few minutes of takeoff, the plane crashed into the side of a mountain near the Baru volcano, about 270 miles west of Panama City.

Talia, Michael, and the pilot were killed instantly.

During the cartwheeling descent, Frankie was spun upside down and the luggage cascaded on top of her. Being pinned under the luggage was probably what saved her life as the Cessna hit a tree high up on the mountain, sheared off a wing, and caromed across the thick jungle growth until it landed upside down in a tree.

A local trout farmer called the crisis management office in the nearby town of Boquete to report his sighting of a small aircraft struggling against high winds near Baru. The office in Boquete was hardly equipped for such an emergency. It did not even have radios or first-aid kits. And the area described by the trout farmer would involve a possible search of more than 200 square miles of jungle.

At first light on Christmas Eve, about 50 volunteers set out against heavy rains, thick fog, and impenetrable jungle to search for any survivors of the crash. There were no trails in the rainforest, so every step of the desperate search would have to be hacked by machete.

> *There were no trails in the rainforest, so every step of the desperate search would have to be hacked by machete.*

On Christmas Day, the weather worsened, but the numbers of volunteers now reached 100, which enabled the searchers to divide into separate groups.

Later that day, the weather began to clear and volunteers Miguel Burac and Alfonso Burke spotted what appeared to be a piece of white metal higher on the mountain. After chopping the jungle growth for more than an hour, the three rescuers came upon the wreckage of the Cessna.

The bodies of the pilot and Michael Klein had been ejected from the plane at the time of impact. Under the front of the fuselage, they found the body of a girl.

And then they heard a faint sound. As they froze, listening carefully, they heard a girl calling for help.

It took the three men over 15 minutes to free Frankie Lewis from the pile of suitcases on top of her. The rescuers lifted Frankie carefully from the wreckage, acutely aware that she could have broken bones or internal injuries. When they could ascertain that there were no serious injuries, they wrapped her in a blanket and plastic bags in an attempt to keep her warm. Frankie was wearing only a T-shirt and shorts, and her lips were blue from cold.

Although the crash site was at 8,000 feet, Burac climbed higher up the mountain where his cell phone would work and called for help.

Additional rescuers could not reach them until daylight, so Burac and Burke, recognizing that Frankie was suffering from hypothermia and entering shock, continued to talk her through the night, giving her water and sweets to keep her alert.

More volunteers reached the site by morning. Frankie was carefully placed on a stretcher, and the rescue workers began what would be a five-hour descent that could only follow the path chopped out for them by the volunteers moving ahead of them.

Frankie was airlifted to a hospital in David, capital of Chiriqui province, where she was reunited with her mother, father, sister, and uncle, who had come down from the United States to be at her side. Although she was wearing a neck brace and had one arm bandaged when she met her family, the doctor said that Frankie only had some fractures and was suffering from hypothermia.

Truly, it was a miracle that a 12-year-old girl had survived an airplane crash and cheated death while trapped under a pile of luggage without food or water for 52 hours.

Danger at Sea

They Were Helplessly Adrift for Five Months and 2,500 Miles

In September 2002, the U.S. Navy rescued Californian Richard Van Pham, who was drifting off Costa Rica after he had been lost at sea for four months. Van Pham had survived quite well by collecting rainwater and eating turtles and fish that swam near his boat.

Even more extreme, in November 2001, two Samoan fishermen were rescued off the coast of Papua New Guinea where it was learned that they had survived for nearly five months helplessly adrift in the Pacific Ocean.

In June 2001, four fishermen—Lapahele Sopi, Telea Pa'a, To'o Loani, and Tofi Lauvi—had landed a huge catch of fish off Western Samoa. At first they were overjoyed with their success, then their 20-foot boat began to sink under the massive load. They cut away the fishing lines and even threw two outboard motors into the sea in a desperate effort to stay afloat.

The Samoan fishermen had been adrift at sea for five months.

Just as things were appearing to go better for them, strong currents began to pull their boat away from their usual fishing grounds near shore into the great open sea. For the next 132 days, the men were at the mercy of the ocean.

The fishermen waved to many passing ships, but they all ignored them. Even when they set off the flares that they had on board, the distant vessels did not come to investigate their signals.

As if to torment them, the currents kept them from drifting ashore on one of the many islands between Samoa and Papua New Guinea. They came very close to Fiji, but the relentless currents kept them away from help.

Once their food and water supplies had been exhausted, the four men caught birds and small fish and drank rainwater.

To'o Loani died one month after they had begun to drift out to sea. Tofi Lauvi succumbed to the rigors of their existence one month later.

In mid-November, Lai Luwaina, a villager on Normanby Island in the Milne Province of Papua New Guinea, spotted a small metal dinghy passing near the island. When he saw one of the occupants waving a blue cloth, he decided to investigate.

As Luwaina drew nearer to the dinghy in his canoe, he thought that one of the men on board was dead. When he climbed aboard, the man who was lying down, roused himself and both of the occupants asked him where they were. Later, it would be determined that the men had drifted more than 2,500 miles from home.

Telea Pa'a, 27, and Lapahele Sopi, 36, were taken to Alotua Hospital. After the survivors had been examined and treated for exposure, doctors said that they doubted if Pa'a would have been able to remain alive for very much longer. Sopi, however, was remarkably strong and in good condition considering the ordeal that he had just undergone. Perhaps it was thoughts of his wife and six children that kept him resolute that he would survive.

Sinking at Sea 4,000 Miles from Home, He Was Rescued by His Neighbor

John Fildes, 32, of the Hampshire Village of Warsash in Great Britain, was sailing his 40-foot trimaran *Dangerous When Wet* from St. Martin in the Caribbean to the United States in May 2007 when a sudden storm ripped off his mast and nearly sank him.

He had been adrift for two days, tossed by 20-foot waves. He had gone 48 hours without food and was beginning to sink when his frantic SOS was finally answered.

Ninety minutes later, the 116,000-ton super liner *Crown Prince* had pulled alongside the yacht. It was quite a delicate procedure because of the difference in size of the two vessels, but soon John Fildes was safely aboard the much larger ship.

Once on board, Fildes recognized Captain Alistair Clark, his neighbor from right around the corner in Hampshire. Captain Clark had heard the SOS from *Dangerous When Wet* and remembered that was the name of Fildes trimaran.

Both men marveled what a small world it is when your ship can be sinking in the Caribbean and you are rescued by your neighbor from 4,000 miles away. Perhaps it was more than a mere coincidence, more in the caliber of a miracle.

Previously, the men knew each other by sight and well enough to give a friendly wave when they met one another on the streets of Hampshire village. They were now likely to become very good friends.

Captain Clark dropped John Fildes off at San Juan, Puerto Rico, and bade farewell until they would have tea together back in their home neighborhood in England.

Drowning

Submerged in an Icy Lake, Clinically Dead for 90 Minutes

On the night of March 21, 1993, 32-year-old Ward Krenz was snowmobiling with two friends when they were caught in a sudden snowstorm. Deciding to speed across the ice of frozen Clear Lake, Iowa, to seek shelter, Krenz lost sight of his buddies

The snowmobiler couldn't see the large hole in the ice in front of him.

in the blinding snow. He was also unable to see the 200-yard hole in the ice that loomed before him.

In the desperate run across the frozen lake, Krenz had accelerated his snowmobile to top speed, so he traveled about 50 feet from the edge of the hole before the vehicle landed on the water and began to sink beneath him. He could see the headlight of the snowmobile disappearing into the depths of the lake.

Then he was in total darkness, and the cold water numbed his muscles so he couldn't swim. He had a fleeting thought that he didn't want to die, but his entire body felt numb, incapable of fighting what seemed to be the inevitable. He felt a sense of peace come over him, and he surrendered to the icy water of the lake.

Krenz's friends had gone as quickly as possible to get help, and members of the local Clear Lake volunteer fire department had responded. Krenz had probably been in the water for about 30 minutes when the rescuers arrived at the site of his descent into the lake. After nearly 45 minutes of probing the hole in the ice with searchlights, they spotted the top of Krenz's crash helmet bobbing in the water. The rescuers could see that his mouth, nose, and the rest of his face were under water. Later, it was determined that a pocket of air in his helmet had prevented him from sinking to the bottom of the lake.

By the time the rescuers pulled Krenz out of the lake, he had been in the frigid water for about 70 minutes and submerged for about 60 of those terrible minutes. He was rushed to St. Joseph Mercy Hospital, six miles away, where one of the emergency room physicians declared that his body temperature was 74 degrees. He was not breathing, had no heartbeat, and was declared clinically dead.

Although the doctors didn't think there was much of a chance of resuscitating Krenz, they hooked him up to a machine that was normally used during open-heart surgery to assume the functions of the heart and lungs. The apparatus took Krenz's blood, ran it through the machine, warmed it, and then sent it back to his body. Miraculously, even though Ward Krenz had been clinically dead for 90 minutes, the process restored internal warmth to his body until his heart was able to restart.

Krenz remained unconscious for three days, remained in the hospital for 13 days, and spent six weeks in a rehab center before making a full recovery. Initial fears that he might suffer brain damage because he had been without oxygen underwater for an hour were thankfully unfounded. Doctors explained that because Krenz had experienced such a rapid drop in body temperature, his metabolism had been turned off. His brain had not required oxygen because the cold had shut it down. *The Guinness Book of Records* lists the miracle of Ward Krenz as the longest time an adult has been submerged underwater and survived.

Nine-Year-Old Victim of Angelman's Syndrome Saved a Drowning Child

When nine-year-old Scotty Baston of Grapevine, Texas, received the 1996 White Helmet Award for heroism for his bravery in saving two-year-old Sean Maloney from drowning, all those in attendance at the award ceremony agreed with Scotty's mother, Joanne, that her son had accomplished a miracle. Scotty suffers from Angelman's syndrome, thus rendering him mentally retarded and unable to speak.

Although Scotty may not have realized that he saved a life, Joanne Baston told reporter Ruth Watts, he knew that he had done something good because everyone was making such a fuss over him. Physically nine years old, Scotty had about the same mental development as a three year old.

On that particular afternoon, neighborhood children had gathered to play in the Baston's swimming pool. When Danielle Maloney, Sean's mother, began to gather her kids, she removed the two-year-old's water wings preparatory to leaving. However, the moment that she turned her back to see to her other children, little Sean jumped unnoticed back into the pool. He immediately slipped below the surface of the water and was soon in great danger of drowning.

Unable to speak or call out for help from the adults whose attention was momentarily distracted from the pool, Scotty watched as the two-year-old boy struggled in the water.

Victims of Angelman's syndrome, a disease which affects one in 25,000 people, are very often affectionate and happy individuals, but, sadly, are handicapped by severe mental retardation, inability to speak, and unstable, jerky body movements. But as

Scotty's mother said, a miracle occurred. Somehow he sensed that little Sean was in trouble, and he reached down and lifted the boy out of the water.

Fire Chief Bill Powers, who dedicated the award for heroism to Scotty, said that Scotty had been alert enough to know that the two-year-old was in great danger and reacted as a true hero by removing Sean immediately from the swimming pool.

Joanne Baston was proud of her son and said that Scotty's actions demonstrated that even those children who are severely handicapped may still have wonderful gifts to share with others. People should never put limits on what such individuals might be able to do, she commented.

Although Scotty suffered from Angelman's syndrome, he knew what to do instinctively when he saw the little boy drowning.

Drowning Boy Saved by Visions of His Dead Cat and Dog

William Serdahley, professor of health sciences at Montana State University Department of Health and Human Development, spoke of the remarkable near-death experience of a seven-year-old boy who was brought back to life by the spirit of his dead dog.

It seems that the boy, who was named Pete, went fishing off a bridge one afternoon. According to the friend who had accompanied him, Pete lost his footing while casting his line and had fallen into the river. As he plunged beneath the surface, he had struck his head on a rock and was knocked unconscious.

By the time his friend had returned with help, Pete had lain submerged at the bottom of the murky river for five to ten minutes.

A policeman managed to find the boy's body, bring it to the surface, and pull it to a river bank.

But by this time, Pete had no pulse and his respiration had ceased.

By all appearances, the boy was dead.

What his rescuers could not know, however, was that the seven-year-old Pete was in the midst of an out-of-body, near-death experience.

Later, after he had been revived, Pete told Professor Serdahley that he had been floating in a special kind of place, a place where he had never been before. He floated into a tunnel, and he became somewhat frightened when he drifted deeper inside.

"Then I saw my old dog Andy and my old cat Abby come over to me in the tunnel," Pete said. "I was really happy to see them, because I hadn't seen them since they died a long time ago."

Andy and Abby were just as nice as he had remembered them, and Pete began to feel a lot better just knowing that they were with him. He no longer felt alone or frightened.

> *Andy, his beloved dog, drew closer to Pete and licked his hand.*

Andy, his beloved dog, drew closer to Pete and licked his hand. "I petted him," Pete said. "Then he put his head right by mine and began to lick my face."

And that was what had made Pete come back to his "regular body" and to wake up "in a hospital with people all around me."

Pete was examined carefully by a number of doctors and, thankfully, was found to have suffered no permanent damage, mental or physical, from his near-death experience at the bottom of the river.

Professor Serdahley expressed his opinion that "when Andy the spirit dog licked his face, it was a signal that Pete should return to his body. Andy was telling him it wasn't his time to die yet."

Well-known Author-Lecturer Remembers the Day He Drowned

John W. White, one of the founding members of the International Association for Near-Death Studies, calls the near-death experience a "crash course in spirituality and the human potential to expand consciousness."

White, an internationally known author, editor, and educator in the fields of consciousness research, parascience, and higher human development, has held positions as director of education for the Institute of Noetic Sciences, a research organization founded by *Apollo 14* astronaut Edgar Mitchell, and as president of Alpha Logics, a school for self-directed growth in body, mind, and spirit.

"My interest in spiritual experience and the nature of consciousness has been present from early childhood," White said, "but a near-death experience at age 14 certainly accelerated it."

It was during John White's fourteenth summer that he nearly died by drowning.

"The event was completely unnoticed by anyone," he recalled. "I'd gone swimming at Mixville Pond, about a mile from my home in Cheshire, Connecticut. The pond is my town's only public swimming area, although there was no lifeguard on duty in those days [c. 1953]. I rode my bike there one sunny afternoon and swam out to a platform that had a diving board."

Fourteen-year-old John had come to Mixville Pond by himself and had not met any friends there. The beach wasn't very crowded, and the platform was empty. A few people were sunning themselves on a nearby raft.

"Feeling the vitality of youth, I began to dive in a show-off manner. It was not that I was a great diver. I simply enjoyed the feeling of performing more than routine, simple dives as my body responded to my intention of swan dive, half-gainer, back flip, and so forth."

After a few of those warm-up dives, John decided to do what he had heard some of his buddies call a "sailor dive." Today, as an adult, John knows that there is no such thing, but somehow the prevailing adolescent wisdom at the time had declared that sailors were trained to dive headfirst with their arms next to their sides in front of them.

So he did exactly that.

"I sprang on the end of the board and sailed high in the air to enter the water head-first at a very steep angle of descent with greater than normal speed gained through attaining more than usual height. It was a really stupid thing to do."

John recalled plunging through the water toward the bottom, diving deeper than usual.

"So deep, in fact, that I struck my forehead on the sandy floor of the pond. The shock of the blow passed through my body at lightning speed, and I lost normal awareness.

"I was blacked out at the bottom, unconscious."

If he had been monitored by an EEG and an EKG, John knows that some vital signs would have showed, of course. His heart continued to beat, and his brain kicked in the drowning reflex, which clamps down the breathing mechanism so water can't be inhaled into the lungs. John knows that now, looking back on the experience.

> *"The shock of the blow passed through my body at lightning speed, and I lost normal awareness."*

"But at the time my understanding was quite different. I lay unconscious on the bottom of the pond for several minutes. I'm estimating that duration on the basis of two things: First, book knowledge of how long it takes before irreversible brain damage sets in from lack of oxygen; second, from contests I held with a friend during English class when we would sneakily challenge each other to hold our breath until the second hand of the clock crept around once, twice, and for me—because I usually won—a few seconds more. At that point I would have to give up and breathe—so I know that I could hold my breath for at least two minutes."

As his body rested on the bottom of the pond, John's awareness changed from blank nothingness to a sensation of wonderful, warm tranquility and security. He had no external perception, no sensory awareness.

"I was simply floating idly, feeling more peaceful than I had ever been.

"And while that languor, that serenity pervaded me, I had the fascinating experience of seeing my life pass before my eyes, as the saying goes."

John recalled that the "life review" was not sequential, but was more like "all at once." Yet, he said, "each scene was nevertheless discreet."

In reflecting upon this remarkable parade of images of his past, he commented: "I didn't watch it, strictly speaking. I lived it. I was in it. Yet I also knew that it had all happened earlier and that I was really reviewing it. There was a strange, simultaneous subjectivity and objectivity to it."

As he drifted at ease, feeling a vague sense of satisfaction, he slowly became aware of a pounding in his ears. Then he became aware of his chest heaving, trying to breathe.

"I developed a strong sense of danger and I started to panic. No light penetrated to the bottom of the murky pond. Everything was dark, so I was quite disoriented."

As John sank to the bottom of the pond, he felt a sense of tranquility.

Then John's hand brushed the sand, and he immediately regained a sense of direction.

"I kicked my arms and legs wildly to swim to the surface-yet amid that action I thought rather calmly, *I'm drowning.*

"There was an impossible pressure in my lungs. They swelled up, trying to take in air—but the airway-stoppage factor was still active."

He moved through the water for an "agonizing time" until at last his head broke the surface.

"I was surprised to find that I could see—but I still couldn't breathe, so powerful was that life-saving reflex.

"Neither could I cry for help. In fact, I was so traumatized that I could hardly control my arms and legs to tread water."

Somehow, John reflected, by the grace of God and a strong will to survive, he managed to remain above the water while his airway opened enough for him to begin breathing again.

The people sunning themselves on the raft had not noticed his plight, but after a few minutes John was able to swim slowly toward them.

"I hauled myself up the ladder with great difficulty and lay down to rest. After about ten minutes I felt well enough to swim to shore. Then I got on my bike and rode home."

John said that he never told anyone about the event until many years later when his writing brought him in touch with such NDE researchers as Kenneth Ring and Raymond Moody.

Today, as John looks back on his childhood near-death experience, he says that he is infinitely grateful for it.

Three Days before Her Due Date, a Pregnant Mother Jumps into an Ice-covered River to Save Her Children

Just three days before her due date, a very pregnant Christine Tanguay jumped into the ice-covered Yamaska River to save the lives of her two young children.

On March 24, 1996, Christine and her husband, Michel, were loading up their car after having eaten lunch at Michel's parents' home in Adamsville, Québec, when it occurred to her that she hadn't seen four-year-old Patrick or two-year-old Melanie for a while. Nine months pregnant and ready to deliver their third child, Christine prompted herself to go in search of the kids so they could go home.

Something told her to look down by the river. When she did, she felt as if she had been struck by lightning. There, in the middle of the ice-covered river, were the colorful jackets of her two children.

Christine screamed for Michel and began running as fast as she could for the shoreline. From what would she could see, Patrick and Melanie were both floating face down and quite obviously drowning in the freezing river water.

Thinking only of saving her children, Christine jumped into the icy Yamaska River. Within seconds, the freezing water had soaked through her coat and filled her boots and was making her "as heavy as a whale." She knew that if she got swept away in the current of the river or got trapped under the ice, she would drown without having a chance to rescue either Patrick or Melanie. At that particular moment, however, nothing meant more to her than achieving her goal of dragging her children to safety.

> *Something told her to look down by the river.... There, in the middle of the ice-covered river, were the colorful jackets of her two children.*

Somehow, she managed to reach Patrick and was alarmed to see that he wasn't breathing. Praying that he could be resuscitated, Christine pulled him over to the edge of the ice where Michel could reach him and pull him out of the river.

Then Christine turned around to swim out to Melanie, at least 25 feet away in the current of the river. Once again, praying as she swam, Christine managed to grab onto her daughter's coat. She turned Melanie face-up and was horrified to see that she appeared completely lifeless.

As Christine neared the shore, Michel and his brother Paul took Melanie from her arms, then began to pull her free of the ice and freezing water. Christine was so exhausted that she knew she would not have been able to climb out of the river on her own.

Michel and Paul gave the children CPR while Christine looked on, praying desperately for a miracle. She emitted a great sigh of relief and happiness when Patrick began coughing up water and breathing, but it took nearly 20 terror-filled minutes before Melanie took her first breath.

Later, at the hospital, a doctor told Christine and Michel that the fact that Melanie's body temperature had dropped to 78 degrees in the freezing river had lowered the oxygen demands on her body, thus helping to protect her from brain damage.

Three days later, right on schedule and none the worse for her frightening ordeal in the ice-covered Yamaska, Christine Tanguay gave birth to their new daughter, Veronique. In Christine's assessment of the past few days, she had been privileged to participate in three miracles.

Found Floating Lifeless without a Pulse, London Architect Makes Full Recovery

John Deeks, 35, an architectural technician from London, went for a swim while visiting his mother on the coast in Cape Town in South Africa in January 2008. The beach was not far from his mother's home, and Deeks looked forward to a refreshing dip in the ocean.

No one knows exactly how much time passed before a shark spotter sighted Deeks floating face downward. When members of the National Sea Rescue Institute, South Africa's lifeboat service, pulled him ashore, he was not breathing and he had no pulse. Estimates were made that Deeks may have been floating lifeless, without a pulse, for 40 to 60 minutes.

Once they had him on the beach, CPR was administered. According to medical experts, such immediate action saved Deeks's life. After two days on a hospital ventilator, he made a full recovery.

While no one on the beach noticed Deeks until he was seen floating face down, no one can say with authority how long the architect was "dead." A consensus was reached that he had been lifeless for at least 20 minutes.

A kind of medical rule of thumb has it that after four to five minutes deprived of oxygen, the brain is severely affected and may leave the surviving patient with some form of brain damage, such as slurred speech, muscular abnormalities, or other neurological problems. Yet John Deeks had none of these afflictions.

A consultant in emergency medicine pointed out that the water was quite cold that day and that temperature can make a difference. Hypothermia can affect the body greatly and slow its processes down considerably.

John Deeks remembered nothing of his return from the dead. He recalled that the sea had become very rough and the tide was high. He believed, upon reflection, that he must have got pulled over by a wave and caught in a current. Whatever happened, like most of those who witnessed his resurrection after being clinically dead for between 40 and 60 minutes, he believes it was a miracle that he survived.

The South African lifeboat service acted quickly to pull John Deeks's body onto the beach.

16-Year-Old Survives Miraculous Fall down Rouge River Gorge

Rudy Grahn, of Oakland, California, and his 16-year-old nephew, Vance Falls, who lives in North Carolina, had spent a wonderful summer of bonding, traveling up and down the West Coast. On August 3, 2008, they stopped at a scenic viewpoint of the Rogue River Gorge, and Rudy decided to rest a bit while Vance walked on ahead to take some pictures of the gorge.

Later, when Rudy got out of their vehicle to join his nephew, he heard people on the trail talking about the boy who had fallen into the water. A lot of people said they saw the teenager fall, but no one saw him come out.

Rudy felt his heart thumping his chest, and he prayed that the boy who fell into the gorge was not his nephew Vance. He ran the rest of the way to the gorge, then despaired when he saw Vance's red camera bag, but no Vance.

Sympathetic strangers gathered around Rudy to comfort him and to answer his questions about what had happened to Vance. According to observers, Vance had walked upstream beyond a fence constructed to prevent visitors from getting too close to the gorge. Some said that he was using a stick to balance himself in the rushing stream while he stretched forward to take a picture.

That was when the stick snapped and Vance fell in the water and was carried to the gorge, which drops 45 feet over a distance of about 500 feet.

> *And according to those gathered around him ... not even an experienced swimmer could survive the rough waters of the Rouge River Gorge.*

Behind him, Rudy heard people whispering that there had already been six drownings on the river that summer. Others sighed that no one could survive the tumult of the gorge and its jagged rocks.

Rudy knew he had to be strong and brave, but he was fast succumbing to the inner torment building up inside him. Vance couldn't even swim. And according to those gathered around him who were discussing the tragedy, not even an experienced swimmer could survive the rough waters of the Rouge River Gorge.

Some rescue workers had arrived and told Rudy to prepare for the worst. The river was pocked with lava tubes, and over the years, the bodies of a number of drowning victims had never been recovered.

Rudy reached for his cell phone. He knew he had to call members of the family and tell them what had happened to their beloved Vance. He felt truly crushed when he discovered that he could get no service in that location.

But it turned out to be a blessing that Rudy had not been able to contact family members and render them distraught, for a miracle was about to occur.

Remarkably, a hiker downstream came across the body of a teenaged boy on a ledge near the river. When he investigated further, he found the boy was just sleeping.

It was Vance Falls, alive and well, except for a nasty bump above his eye.

Later, after a few hours observation at the Rogue Valley Medical Center, Vance was released to Uncle Rudy. The teenager had survived the impossible with only a sore ankle, some bruises, and the big bump on his forehead.

Rudy Grahn said there was no rational reason for his nephew to be alive. To call his survival a miracle, he declared, just didn't go far enough.

Explosions and Fires

Angels Led Her through a Raging Inferno to Save an Elderly Couple

Thirty-year-old Anna Gallo, who lives in the Detroit area, has always been an extremely religious person. Each night at bedtime she joins hands with her children—Cathie, Susie, and Ben—to say their "good-night" prayers to Lord Jesus aloud together.

"And every night before I go to my own bed with my husband, I always pray that Jesus and the angels will protect our home from all evil and all harm—especially from fire," Anna said.

When she was just a girl of nine, Anna's aunt lost her beautiful home to a terrible fire that also left the woman horribly burned and scarred. Since that time, Anna has had an overwhelming fear of fire.

Then, one spring night in May 1994, Anna had just returned from the neighborhood supermarket when she began to smell smoke.

"Cathie, Susie, and I were putting away the groceries when I detected the acrid scent of smoke," she recalled. "At first I was afraid that it was our house that was on fire, and I prayed to Jesus to deliver us from harm."

She searched through their home, looking in every room for any sign of fire. When she couldn't find any source for the smoke in her own home, Anna stepped outside.

"I was horrified when I saw smoke and flames coming from the Pendells' home, just a few doors away," she said.

She knew that a family of four lived in the house with the wife's elderly parents, the Worsleys. She glanced around the front yard and saw that other neighbors were helping George Pendell and his two kids from the house. Some of them looked as though they were in bad shape from smoke inhalation. Anna knew that Linda Pendell worked nights, so at first it appeared as though everyone was present and accounted for.

Anna Gallo had an overwhelming fear of fire because, as a child, her home burned down and scarred her for life.

But then one of the Pendell Children started coughing violently and waving his arms wildly. "Grand ... pa, Grandma ... still upstairs!"

George Pendell had collapsed on the sidewalk, but he tried to get back to his feet. "Dear God," he cried, "my wife's parents are still in their upstairs bedroom."

The flames were spewing from every opening, and great black billows of smoke rose skyward. The house was now a raging inferno.

Anna heard someone near her say, "It's awful. Those old folks are trapped up there. Too late to save them now."

And then she heard another voice speaking directly to her: *Anna, you must save those people. You must enter the flames. It is up to you!*

Anna's knees felt weak and her heart pounded at her chest. How could she of all people walk into that blazing furnace? She had had a fear of fire since she was a child.

And then she thought of the Hebrew children thrown into the fiery furnace and how the Lord had kept them safe and untouched by the flames.

At the same time, she felt some kind of force drawing her toward the bright orange flames that curled around the rear of the house and snaked up to the second floor.

She remembered praying, "Lord, thy will be done!" And then she felt the force continuing to pull her, frightened and trembling, into the burning house.

"It must have been the hand of Jesus that moved me up a flight of stairs that was totally obscured by thick, black, suffocating smoke," Anna said. "Somehow I sensed that the fire had started in the kitchen, perhaps when grease caught fire and ignited the cupboards above the stove."

She was nearly to the top of the stairs when she gagged and choked on the thick smoke that rolled around her. She gasped for air, and her survival reflexes demanded that she turn back.

But the voice was insistent: *You must go on, Anna. The lives of two people depend on you.*

Once again she could feel the force moving her up the stairs. She began to cough as the smoke filled her lungs and stung her eyes.

Cover your face with your jacket! The voice told her.

Anna did as the voice advised her, and she finally reached the room where she could see the elderly man and woman lying on the bed.

"I thought they were already dead from smoke inhalation, because they lay so very still—but amazingly, they were only sleeping soundly!" Anna said.

She shook the couple awake and shouted, "Fire! Fire! We've got to get out of here— or we're all going to die!"

She helped them get to their feet and ushered them to the stairs. Within a few minutes, all three of them had stumbled outside to safety.

> *But the voice was insistent:* **You must go on, Anna. The lives of two people depend on you.**

By that time, the fire truck had arrived, along with its crew of professional firefighters. Anna was more than happy to relinquish the task of extinguishing the flames to their expertise. She had done all that the voice had asked her to do.

The neighbors were quick to declare that Anna had put her life on the line to save the elderly members of the Pendell family. An investigator from the fire department later called her a true hero.

Anna only shrugged and accepted her neighbors' thanks graciously. In her mind, she knew that the Lord Jesus to whom she prayed each night had chosen her to act on his behalf. It was her firm and unshakable belief that it had been Jesus' will that she help her elderly neighbors when they were threatened by flames of destruction and death.

"Jesus sent his angels to stay with me amidst the flames to keep me safe from harm," she said.

Guide Dog Leads Owner and 30 Residents to Safety

When Morris, her guide dog, awakened her at 11:30 P.M. on February 7, 1995, 41-year-old Sandy Seltzer knew that something was terribly wrong.

As she became more fully awake, Sandy could smell smoke and hear a lot of frightened and confused shouting.

Morris was nudging her out of bed, indicating as best he could that they had to get out of the place. The building was on fire.

Blind since her college days, Sandy knew that getting out of a burning apartment building from their room on the fifth floor would present a challenge to Morris, but she was confident that the big Labrador could handle it.

Holding tightly to his leash, Sandy followed Morris out to the fifth floor hallway and down the stairs. She could hear people shouting, some crying desperately, as they struggled against smoke, fire, and chaos to find their way to safety. There were eighty residents in the apartment house in Mineola, New York, and she prayed that everyone would escape the building unscathed.

When they reached the third floor, Sandy sensed that Morris was considering whether or not to further risk the stairs.

Morris backed up and began to walk along the third floor hallway. He had made a decision that Mineola Fire Chief William Mahoney would later say took intelligence and courage.

About a dozen third-floor residents had been carefully watching the guide dog as he pondered whether or not to continue down the stairs. Would they find their way to the street and safety—or would they walk directly into the flames and the suffocating smoke of a raging inferno?

When Morris finally backed away, the men and women decided that "his nose knew," that he had somehow sensed danger ahead, and they followed behind Sandy and her guide dog.

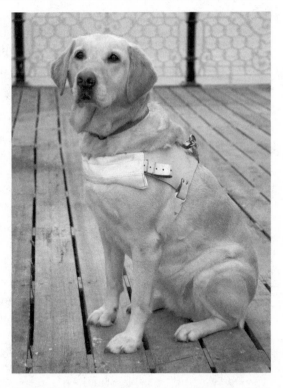

Guide dogs may lead the blind, but they are also loyal friends and, on more than one occasion, heroes.

When Morris sensed that the firefighters had poured enough water on the floors below to make the flames subside, Morris led Sandy and the other residents down through the darkness to the street outside the apartment house.

Fire investigator Dominick Mazza agreed with Chief Mahoney in declaring Morris a true hero. Mazza told reporters that those residents on the third floor might not have survived if it hadn't been for Morris.

Both Sandy and her courageous guide dog required treatment for smoke inhalation, and, in all, 14 tenants in the building suffered minor injuries. But there were no fatalities—thanks to the fast action of the Mineola firefighters and the bravery and steady nerves of a resourceful Labrador guide dog.

She Saved Her Family from a Fire She Saw in a Dream

In July 1991 Mrs. Gina Delatoso, 32, took a temporary factory job in a nearby city in order to help the family budget squeeze through the recession. During the summer she commuted, but in the winter when it was too cold and the roads were icy she stayed in an inexpensive motel near the plant rather than driving home.

At 3:00 A.M. on a January morning, Gina experienced a dreadful dream in which she saw herself surrounded by flames. The nightmare was so vivid that she awakened with the odor of burning cloth filling her nostrils.

Terrified by the thought that her motel room might be on fire, she got out of bed and checked the small room thoroughly. Although she found no fire, the feeling of danger persisted.

"All at once I knew that the fire must be in the house in which my husband, Jake, and our two sons, Frankie and Charlie, lay sleeping," Gina Delatoso said.

> *The nightmare was so vivid that she awakened with the odor of burning cloth filling her nostrils.*

She called their home, but no one answered. She continued to call, again and again.

At last she heard the click of the receiver being lifted—and nearly simultaneously with his "Hello" she heard her older son coughing.

"Are you all right, Frankie?" she shouted into the receiver.

"Mom! Mom! The house is full of smoke!"

Gina told her seven-year-old son not to panic. "Go wake up Daddy and Charlie. Find out where the smoke is coming from. Have Daddy put out the fire and call me back!"

After an excruciatingly long 30 minutes, Jake called her. The boys had put their mittens on an old electric heater when they came in from playing in the snow. Sometime during the night, the frayed electric cord had popped a spark onto a pile of newspapers and magazines. The papers had issued a great deal of smoke, and by the time they had located the fire, the flames were just beginning to nibble at nearby curtains.

Gina went back to bed, relieved that no real damage had been done to their ranch-style home.

"I know, however, that if I had not had that awful dream and awakened to smell that smoke in my mind—and if I had not called the house—my home would have burned to the ground along with my three loved ones," Gina said.

She Insisted Her Husband Was Still Alive in the Smoldering Ruins

Dr. Harry M. Archer was a respected surgeon and medical officer in New York City around the turn of the century. For a period of more than 30 years, this remarkable man was on the scene of every major fire in the city, rendering assistance both to fire victims and injured firemen. In 1912, he was awarded the Fire Department Medal in appreciation of his services to the city, and he later received the most coveted civic award of all, the James Gorden Bennett Medal.

Writer Frank B. Copley decided that Dr. Archer would make an excellent subject for a feature article, and the August 8, 1925, issue of *Collier's* magazine carried his testament to the many experiences and colorful reminiscences of the selfless medical man.

One of the most unusual experiences that Dr. Archer shared took place during a fire in 1920. He resisted trying to explain exactly what had occurred, but he commented that it "seemed to exhale an eerie suggestion of the supernatural."

Many firemen have lost their lives doing their jobs, but one firefighter given up for dead sent a miraculous message to his wife.

It was 7:30 P.M., a cold Sunday night in the city, and a fire had been reported in a rag shop on New York's Lower East Side. From an adjacent tenement, positioned on the fire escape, a group of firemen were aiming a fire hose onto the blazing five-story structure next door.

The fire escape was only a short distance from a third-floor window of the rag shop, so at about eleven, the lieutenant with the five men on the fire escape, plus members of Engine Company 32, were ordered to take their hose into the building through the window across from them.

This order proved to be a costly error. Within a half an hour after entering the doomed building, the firemen outside on the street heard a series of cracks and snaps followed by a tremendous roar. Within another few seconds, the interior of the building had collapsed, burying the hapless firefighters inside.

The lieutenant and two of his men were rescued almost at once, and they were brought to safety after having sustained only slight injuries.

A large contingent of firemen organized an extensive search through the smoldering rubble and ruins, but hours later, no trace of the three missing men could be found.

By 2:00 in the morning, it was decided that there could be little hope of finding the men alive and word was sent to their families, notifying them of the tragedy.

Dr. Harry Archer had been on the scene to treat the injuries of the survivors, and as was customary for him, he considered it his duty to remain on location until the last man had been recovered—alive or dead.

About an hour later, one of the firemen approached Dr. Archer with a request.

"It's Johnny Seufert's wife, doc. She's at the police line carrying on something dreadful and making a terrible fuss. Do you think you could help her out?"

Dr. Archer gave the fireman a quick nod of his head and went immediately in search of the distressed woman, whose husband could only be dead by this time.

"Dr. Archer!" she cried when she saw the famous physician. "You'll believe me, I know you will! You've got to make them listen to me. The others don't believe me, but I'm telling the truth."

He took the woman gently by the arm and walked with her a short distance away from the police line. "Please tell me how I may assist you, my dear lady."

"It's not me," she protested. "It's Johnny! Just before I got the telephone message telling me about the accident and that Johnny was lost, Johnny *himself* came to me."

Dr. Archer merely nodded in sympathy, uncertain exactly what the proper response might be to such a statement. Still, the woman did not seem hysterical or in shock.

"I'm telling you the truth," she insisted. "I saw him as plain as could be."

Before he could interject any kind of comment, she continued more resolutely than before.

"Johnny said, 'I'm a way down in the ruins of the fallen building. There is tons of stuff over me. They think I'm dead—but I'm not! Tell them not to let up until they find me. *Tell them I'm still alive. Tell them I'm not dead!*'"

Mrs. Seufert could not be swayed. "Doctor, I tell you Johnny is alive! I know he is. Don't let them stop. Tell them to keep digging and looking through the ruins. They can get my Johnny out. They *have* to get him out!"

And she resolved to cling tenaciously to her ground until they did find her husband.

At ten the following morning, the searching firemen did find another body. It was not Johnny Seufert.

At two that afternoon another body was discovered. Again, it was not Seufert.

Each time a body was brought outside the charred building, Dr. Archer tried to convince Mrs. Seufert to go home. She was in an extremely agitated state, and the doctor knew that if her husband's body ever was finally recovered, it would not be a pleasant sight.

But Mrs. Seufert steadfastly refused to move. After hours of fruitless searching, a crew of firemen came upon a long piece of pipe sticking up through the debris. Thirty-six hours had now passed since the building had collapsed, but one of the men thought that he had heard a tapping sound coming from the pipe.

They listened for a moment, then picked up a pattern to the tapping: three taps-pause; two taps-pause.

Three ... two. Three ... two. *Thirty two!* That was the number of Johnny Seufert's engine company.

The exhausted rescue team shed their weariness by responding to the need of a fellow firefighter—a fellow human.

The men listened once more as the signal was repeated. It was unmistakable.

Dr. Archer picked his way through the charred debris until he stood directly in front of the pipe. He placed his mouth over it and shouted:

"Seufert! Is that you?"

"Yes," came the barely audible reply.

"Are you all right?" Dr. Archer shouted again.

"You bet," came the answer. "I am now!"

It was later learned that Seufert had fallen into a hole of a few feet's depth just before the collapse of the burning building. It had been the pipe with its twisted end that had saved him, for it had bent over in the fall of the building; and as a consequence, no flaming debris had been able to suffocate the trapped man below. The pipe had kept Seufert supplied with air and had proved to be the physical agent that had saved his life.

But what of the nonphysical agent that had rescued Johnny Seufert? What of his image that had appeared to his wife and insisted that he was still alive, trapped beneath the rubble of the collapsed building?

It took two hours for the rescue team to free him. Finally rescued from the tons of debris, Seufert fell into the arms of his wife.

> **"Tell them I'm still alive. Tell them I'm not dead!"**

Miraculously, he had received few injuries, his largest discomfort having come from the cramping of his legs in the hole.

Dr. Archer gave him a quick physical examination, then asked about the incredible story that Mrs. Seufert had told. It had been her firm insistence that she had seen his living ghost and that this specter had insisted that the physical Johnny was still alive that was even more instrumental in saving his life than the fortuitous bending of a metal pipe.

How, Dr. Archer wanted to know, had he managed to leave his body and appear before his wife miles away from the scene of his physical entombment?

The only explanation that Johnny Seufert could offer was that he had just kept thinking about his wife—and about the seemingly impossible fact that for some reason he was still alive when by all logic he should have been dead.

Marine Sergeant "Iron Mike" Survives Direct Blast from Insurgents' Bomb

On September 24, 2005, the *Omaha World-Herald* printed a photograph taken by Jeff Bundy that soon became one of the most iconic of the Iraq War. Taken in the aftermath of a bomb blast, the picture depicted a Marine sergeant, pants blown away, legs bandaged, and standing on his own power.

The bravery of U.S. soldiers in Iraq is unquestioned, but sometimes it also takes a little luck to survive the battlefield against insurgents.

The photo had been taken on September 19, when Marine Gunnery Sergeant Michael Burghardt, 35, was summoned to disarm some improvised explosive devices (IEDs) near Ramadi, Iraq. Burghardt, a native of Huntington Beach, California, was on his third tour of duty in Iraq. Known as "Iron Mike," he had served with the Marine Corps for 18 years, 15 of them in bomb disposal. As an experienced member of an Explosive Ordnance Disposal Unit (EOD), Sgt. Burghardt was assigned to locate, identify, disarm, and dispose of the increasingly large number of home-made bombs that the insurgents had been placing along roadsides, in abandoned cars, and in vacated houses.

The man had become a legend after his second tour of duty in Iraq when he won the Bronze Star for having disabled 64 IEDs and destroying 1,548 pieces of ordnance.

Although Iron Mike had a reputation for being the best in the risky business of disarming IEDs, on September 19, 2005, it appeared that his remarkable career had ended. When he arrived on the scene, he learned that four soldiers had just been killed by a bomb. At the bottom of a five-foot-deep and eight-foot-wide crater, there appeared to be another IED.

He discarded his bulky bomb protection suit, telling unit members that it limited his vision. It was certain that insurgents were still in the area, but Iron Mike said he would rely on his standard issue helmet and flak jacket.

Unit members whispered their various words of caution and good luck as Sergeant Burghardt stepped carefully into the crater. He cut one of the wires on the IED, then he spotted a red wire that ran on the ground between his legs. It was at that moment that he realized the insurgents had lured Iron Mike into a trap.

The sergeant shouted for everyone to take cover. From some hiding place, carefully watching the scene, waiting for the right moment, an insurgent pressed a button on a mobile phone to detonate the bomb. The device exploded and blasted Iron Mike into the air along with dirt, shrapnel, and other debris.

During that strange phenomenon that occurs in such near-death experiences when time seems to be suspended, Sergeant Burghardt remembers feeling anger that the enemy finally got him. He fumed that they were able to do it.

His body landed back on the road leading to the crater, and he could not feel anything from the waist down. His father was a Vietnam veteran who was paralyzed from the waist down, and Mike had a somber mental image of the two sitting side-by-side in their wheelchairs. Then, as he lay there, he began to wiggle his toes, and he knew that he was not paralyzed.

Fellow members of the unit feared that Iron Mike had been killed instantly, but when they saw that he was alive, they ordered a stretcher and a helicopter for immediate evacuation.

But Sgt. Burghardt figured that the insurgents were definitely still watching the scene from some hiding place, so he refused the stretcher, got to his feet, and turned to a likely direction where the enemy was entrenched, and flipped them the bird.

Iron Mike wasn't going to let either his team members or the insurgents watch him being carried away on a stretcher.

After being blown into the air by an IED, Sergeant Burghardt's wounds were minor, primarily only burns to his legs and buttocks. He was off duty for less than a month, then, refusing a ticket home, he remained in Ramadi to continue to disarm the insurgents' increasingly ingenious bombs.

Falls from Great Heights

He Caught a Baby Who Had Fallen out a Seventh Floor Window

On September 11, 1991, Geraldo Silva was standing outside an apartment building in Rio de Janeiro, Brazil, waiting for a friend to join him, when something caused him to look up.

Plummeting headfirst toward him was a baby!

Instinctively, Silva knew that the child would surely die if it struck the sidewalk, so he stuck out his arms as if he were about to catch a football. The impact of catching the baby knocked them both to the sidewalk.

Dazed, Silva examined his surprise catch from the sky and believed the little girl was dead. Blood was pouring from her mouth.

He could see now that the baby was small, probably only 20 pounds or so, but when she landed in his arms, she had felt like a 100-pound sack of grain.

"Mama," the child cried in a weak voice.

Silva thanked God that the baby that had dropped down on him from somewhere up above was still alive. He called for help, and one of the shaken passersby that had gathered as witnesses to the remarkable event offered to drive them both to a hospital.

Meanwhile, seven floors above the scene, Najwa Safatli was washing dishes in their apartment when she heard the sound of glass breaking in the living room. Startled, she thought immediately of her 18-month-old daughter, Jasmin, who was seated in a high-chair in front of a window. Could little Jasmin have somehow managed to crawl out of the highchair and broken a vase or some other glass object?

When Najwa entered the living room, she was shocked to see that Jasmin was not in her highchair and that the window behind the chair was broken.

> *The young mother searched the living room, calling for her daughter. She could not yet allow herself to think the unthinkable.*

The young mother searched the living room, calling for her daughter. She could not yet allow herself to think the unthinkable. Jasmin could not have fallen out of the window. Perhaps a large bird or something had broken the window and frightened her baby. Jasmin must be somewhere in the apartment.

Najwa Safatli told journalist Christina Menzies that when she finally looked out the window, she was horrified to see that a crowd had gathered on the street below. At about the same time, a neighbor pounded on the apartment door and told Najwa that Jasmin had fallen out of the window and had been taken to a hospital.

Najwa was certain that Jasmin, their only child, was dead. She believed that it would be impossible for an 18-month-old child—or anyone else, for that matter—to fall out of a seventh-floor window and survive.

Frantic, she didn't wait for the elevator, but ran barefooted down the stairs to the parking garage in the apartment building. She rushed to the hospital, trying to calm herself to expect the worst. Once she learned the fate of Jasmin, she would call her husband, Ahmad, who was at work.

When the doctors at the hospital told the fearful mother that Jasmin was alive, Najwa said that she knew a miracle had occurred. Her baby had suffered only a broken leg and some bruises. Najwa thanked God and blessed Geraldo Silva for saving Jasmin's life.

Silva shrugged off all attempts to categorize him as a hero. In his opinion, a benevolent fate had managed to place him at precisely the very spot where he would be standing so that he might be able to catch little Jasmin as she hurtled through the air to the street below.

As the Safatli family recreated the accident, it appeared that Jasmin had stood up on the seat of her highchair and had lost her balance. Although she weighed only 22 pounds, she apparently struck the window with enough force to break it and fall through. According to a witness, Jasmin had bounced off an awning on the fifth floor, thus slowing her descent to some degree.

When his F-111's engines died, pilot Scott Kramer fell 12,000 feet without a working parachute—and survived.

But it was 45-year-old refrigeration technician Geraldo Silva who completed the miracle by being in exactly the right place at the right time to reach out his arms and catch Jasmin before she landed headfirst on the sidewalk.

Fighter Pilot's 12,000-Foot Fall Broken by a Child's Toy

In August 1992, fighter pilot Scott Kramer, 33, who was stationed at a U.S. Air Force Base on the outskirts of Bitburg, Germany, was putting his F-111 through its paces when the engine died. Kramer pushed the button for his ejection seat and was catapulted clear of the aircraft—but the parachute failed to open.

When he desperately attempted to open the backup chute, it, too, failed him.

Captain Scott Kramer was now falling toward the earth at 120 miles per hour. He thought of his family, which included three young children, and he shut his eyes and began to pray the Lord's Prayer.

Kramer's guardian angel was on the job that day, because the seemingly doomed pilot landed on the huge, inflatable castle that had been set up in the garden of bakery owner Manfred Luedendorff on the occasion of his daughter Ingrid's eleventh birthday.

Luedendorff later told journalists that the children had been celebrating Ingrid's birthday when the pilot came out of the sky and crashed into the inflatable castle. He had landed with such force that his impact sent many of the children flying off the castle and onto the lawn.

None of the children were injured, and Captain Kramer managed to fall 12,000 feet and receive only two fractured legs and a broken wrist.

Inflatable Diapers Saved a 22 Month Old from a Nine-Story Fall

In November 1992, 22-month-old Joshua Beatty fell nine stories out of an open window of a Southfield, Michigan, apartment and survived unharmed. In a strange kind of miracle, little Joshua's diaper snagged on a bush and cushioned his fall.

A maintenance worker, who witnessed the miraculous incident, said that it was as if God had held out his hands and caught the little boy.

Gina Beatty, Joshua's mother, said that she panicked when she entered his bedroom and saw that the screen had been pushed out of the window. When she could see her baby nowhere in sight, she remembers being shocked out of her wits.

When she first looked out the window in Joshua's room, she saw two girls on a balcony across the courtyard staring downward in horror. Then Gina heard awful shrieks from below. Forcing herself to look down to the concrete below, she felt her heart thumping as she saw Joshua's diaper on a bush.

And then she heard him screaming. He was still alive!

Rushing downstairs as quickly as possible, not knowing in what condition she would find her son, she was astonished to find him standing naked, surrounded by a small crowd of incredulous bystanders. As Joshua ran to her arms, Gina collapsed, shaking uncontrollably.

Miraculously, Joshua's diaper had snagged on a bush only a few feet a few from the concrete pavement. Then, somehow, the diaper held his weight long enough for him to hang suspended for moments before it snapped and allowed him to tumble harmlessly to the ground.

Sleepwalker Falls 17 Floors to Bounce off a Canopy

In September 1993, Paul, a 31-year-old construction worker from upstate New York, checked into a New Jersey hotel, intending to visit the nearby amusement park the next day to fulfill his ambition of making a bungee jump. Paul went to sleep, but he was so hyped to do a bungee jump that his subconscious took over. Dreaming that he was at the amusement park jump site, he tied a bed sheet around his ankle, walked to the balcony of his seventeenth floor hotel room, and jumped over the railing.

Even if the bed sheet had been tied to something solid in the room, it wouldn't have mattered a great deal. Paul would certainly have plunged to a certain death seventeen floors below.

Later, witnesses would describe Paul as a young man who definitely had a squad of guardian angels looking after him. Paul's plummeting body was seen to bounce off a lawn chair on a balcony four floors below his room, then bounce again off the hotel's canopy on the ground floor and land on the roof of a convertible that was parking in front of the building with its motor running. The impact of Paul's body knocked the car into gear and it ran across the street to crash into a bed store. He awoke beneath a pile of mattresses, wondering where he was.

Incredibly, Paul suffered only a few bumps and bruises as reminders of his real-life nightmare. The police filed no charges, but they strongly advised him to dream about something less adventurous than bungee jumping.

Sky diving can be a thrilling activity, but also a potentially deadly one.

A Muddy Pond Broke a Sky Diver's 4,000-Foot Fall

When experienced sky diver Klint Freemantle found that both his main chute and reserve chute had failed him while diving over Napier, New Zealand, at 4,000 feet, he thought initially that his life was going to end on that summer's day in 1993. Ironically, his girlfriend, Tracey, had pleaded with him not to jump that day, and he had promised that he might make it his last. It now seemed that he would keep that promise in a most unsatisfactory way.

Then, far below him, he saw a small pond. He knew it was a one-in-a-billion chance, but Klint did not see any other options open to him. He undid his harness so he wouldn't drown beneath the parachutes if he survived the fall and aimed himself toward the water as if he were a guided missile.

Klint's father, Terry, sister, Sarah, and Tracey ran in horror toward the pond where they expected to find his body. Instead, a man covered in mud rose to greet them. Klint Freemantle had fallen 4,000 feet without a parachute and suffered only a cut over his left eye.

He Stood Up and Brushed Himself Off after a 3,000-Foot Fall

On Easter Sunday 1994, Tom Molrooney gave his brother, Des, a joyride in a 25-year-old two-seater Jet Provost, once used as a trainer by Britain's Royal Air Force.

As they soared across the skies over Colchester, Essex, England, Tom decided to treat Des to some upside down rolls. On the second roll, Des's ejector seat broke free from its moorings and sent him through the cockpit canopy.

Des's helmet prevented him from being knocked unconscious by the impact, but he knew that he was in big trouble. He remained in the ejector seat for a few seconds before the safety belt snapped and he was free-falling at 120 miles per hour toward the ground 3,000 feet below.

Somehow, Des had remained calm. He reached for the parachute rip cord and pulled it. But the chute had been damaged when he fell through the cockpit canopy, and he was now twirling around helplessly in the straps beneath the fluttering chute.

Des remembered holding his breath for the remaining seconds of the fall, never giving up hope that he would somehow survive.

He landed with a loud thud in a grassy area near a supermarket. Numerous onlookers ran to the scene, fully expecting to see an unlucky parachutist's broken and battered body.

Remarkably, Des was able to stand up unassisted and dust himself off. He had fallen 3,000 feet and suffered only minor bruising and whiplash.

Football Wide Receiver Still Has the Touch, Catching Falling Baby

The experience and training that he had received as a wide receiver when he played high school football may have given park worker Don Hughes the steady hands and nerves that enabled him to catch 18-month-old Lydell Craig when the baby fell from a third-story window.

> Hughes looked up and saw a baby sitting on a third-story window ledge.

On June 6, 1994, 30-year-old Hughes and three fellow workers from the Baltimore Parks and Recreation Department were mowing around trees and shrubs when he noticed a crowd gathering outside of an apartment building across the street. There was a senior citizens' home nearby, and a lot of elderly men and women were shouting and pointing upward.

Hughes looked up and saw a baby sitting on a third-story window ledge.

In spite of the crowd milling around beneath him, the baby, little 18-month-old Lydell Craig, sat on the ledge, seemingly unaware of danger and blissfully taking in the new perspective. A woman, obviously the child's mother, was screaming at the baby, calling him by name, and telling him to please get back into the apartment.

Don Hughes had always been a religious person. And he felt that he had been used by God on a previous occasion in 1992 to rescue seven of his neighbors who had been trapped in a fire in a rooming house. When Hughes saw little Lydell Craig teetering on his perch three stories above the street, he heard God telling him to get over there fast.

He was walking across the street when the crowd screamed as if in one voice. The baby on the ledge was falling.

Hughes dashed forward and made the catch of his life. The momentum of his fall took Lydell Craig down within an inch or two of the concrete, but Hughes's powerful arms saw to it that the baby didn't touch it.

Lydell's mother, Shervonne, told journalist James McCandlish that Don Hughes had performed a miracle and that she would forever be grateful to him. She had left Lydell in the care of her uncle when she had gone shopping. Apparently when the uncle wasn't looking, the 18-month-old baby had crawled to the open window and had crawled out on the ledge to explore new territory. If a fast-acting Don Hughes hadn't heeded the orders he received from God to run across the street in time to catch little Lydell, the infant would likely have crashed to the concrete and died.

She Survived an 18-Story Fall down a Trash Chute

Twenty-one-year-old Laura Rodriguez was dumping trash in the very small utility room of her apartment building when the door closed behind her and jammed so that she could not open

In one television commercial, an actor jumps down a trash chute as if it were a fun slide, but for Laura Rodriguez it was no joy ride.

it. Unfortunately, Laura suffered from claustrophobia, so after she had banged on the door and screamed for someone to come and open the door, she began to panic. Again and again she cried for help, but when no one came, she began to lose control of her normal thought processes.

Although she was on the top floor of an 18-story apartment building, Laura reasoned that she could squeeze her body into the 14-by-16-inch trash chute and carefully work her way down to the utility room on the seventeenth floor.

As her husband, Mike, 29, later told the press on September 5, 1995, Laura was terrified. It was hot and dark in the chute, and Laura lost her grip.

Incredibly, Laura fell helplessly down the chute until she slammed into the trash dumpster on the ground floor, her legs shattering upon impact.

Laura managed to crawl out of the dumpster and scream for help. The superintendent heard her cries and immediately called rescue workers. Laura had lost a great deal of blood. Both legs were broken, and one shattered so badly it required steel pins and rods to hold it together.

Not only had Laura survived what was essentially an 18-floor fall, but if she had remained unconscious in the dumpster, she would have been compacted in the garbage container.

The Angels Saved Two-Year-Old Joey When He Fell 35 Feet

Doctors at the hospital in Mississauga, Ontario, pronounced two-year-old Joey Rodden to be the luckiest little boy that they had ever seen.

Early one morning in April 1996, Joey climbed onto a windowsill of the family's third-floor apartment while he was playing with his four-year-old brother, Robbie. For some peculiar reason, the game turned to one of throwing their toys out of a torn screen. As they were tossing toys out the window, Joey lost his balance and plunged 35-feet onto the pavement below.

> *They were astonished to find that Joey bore not a single scratch, bruise, or mark of any kind.*

Joey's five-year-old sister, Krystal, saw him fall out the window and ran into her parents' bedroom to tell them the awful news. Cherie and Gary Rodden rushed to the window and looked down in horror to see their son's limp little body lying on the pavement below. There had been no bush nor any snow to break his fall, and he lay still, face down.

Cherie admitted later that she was hysterically praying for a miracle when she and her brother Jon, who was staying with the Roddens, rushed down the stairs.

Jon got to Joey first, knelt beside him, and gently rolled him over on his back. Then his mother's heartfelt prayer for a miracle was granted. Joey opened his eyes, hugged his Uncle Jon, and got to his feet on his own power.

When the paramedics arrived and gave the boy a preliminary examination, they were astonished to find that Joey bore not a single scratch, bruise, or mark of any kind. To the contrary, rather than discovering a severely or fatally injured boy, the paramedics had to restrain Joey from wiggling free from their examination and running off to play with his brother.

Doctors insisted that the tot be taken to the hospital for two nights of observation, but the medical personnel were unable to find anything wrong with the extremely fortunate two-year-old Joey, who had fallen 35 feet without sustaining a single injury.

Truly, the Rodden family agreed, God had sent an angel to watch over their little Joey that morning. With grim humor, they joked that Joey was, indeed, a bouncing baby boy.

Sky Diver Survives 5,000-Foot Fall, Gets Five Broken Teeth

On a fine day in 1998, sky diver Bren Jones, 56, a veteran with 3,500 successful jumps to his record, went aloft to 5,000 feet above Harsforth, England, with four buddies. They bailed out, linked hands to form a star formation, intending to separate at 3,500 feet to allow their chutes to open.

At least that was the plan. A sudden gust of wind caused Jones's chute to become tangled with his fellow diver, Eddie Davies. Davies smashed into Jones, knocking him nearly unconscious.

They had been free-falling at about 125 miles per hour, the ground rapidly rising to meet them. Eddie managed to pull away from Bren and open his reserve chute.

Thankful that Davies was safe, Jones still faced his own awful situation. He was still wrapped in Davies' chute as well as his own, and the lines were coiled around him.

Desperately, he tried to tug his reserve chute from the entangled mess of chutes and lines, but he was unable to do so.

All 190 pounds of Bren Jones landed in plowed field, just a few feet from a concrete runway and his buddy Eddie Davies.

Doctors said it was a miracle that Jones survived the 5,000 feet fall with only five broken teeth and some painful bruises on his hips, back, and pelvis.

Father Quips Drinking Milk Helped His Two-Year-Old Son Survive Fall

Two-year-old Derek Anthony Darden of Bakersfield, California, fell out of a second-story window on May 19, 2002 and survived with only a few scratches.

Got milk? One father insisted strong bones saved his boy from suffering injuries after a fall.

The Darden family was still sleeping on Sunday morning when their neighbor rang the doorbell and informed them that their two-year-old son had fallen out of a window and onto the paved parking lot. It appeared that Derek, who shared a room with his seven-month-old brother, had pushed the crib against the window and had crawled up to check things out—and then ended up falling out.

After examining the two-year-old at a hospital, doctors released him to his parents, pronouncing Derek free from injury, except for a couple of scratches. The miracle baby's father quipped that he guessed drinking milk really did make a tot strong and healthy.

Two-Year-Old Didn't Even Cry after 50-Foot Fall to Concrete

Gordana Pavlicic thought that her two-year-old son, Vid, had died when he fell through the stair railing on the fifth floor of their apartment in Kragujevac, Serbia. One minute on that afternoon in October 2006 he was playing with his sister, the next he had slipped through the railing and had fallen 50 feet, landing on the basement concrete.

As Gordana knelt in dread and sorrow beside the still body of her young son, Vid suddenly sat up, looked about him in a confused manner, then got up and walked away. The mother was astonished that her little son did not even cry after surviving such a fall.

Later, at the hospital, doctors pronounced him completely uninjured.

Rushing to a Football Game, Mom Makes a Great Catch of Her Own

Mary Bussey and her son Brandon were in a hurry to get to the junior high school football game in Denver, Colorado, on October 3, 2006. The sound of crying caused them to look up and see a baby dangling by one tiny fist from the balcony of a third-story apartment.

Mrs. Bussey positioned herself just in time to catch the eight-month-old baby when she fell. She managed to get directly underneath the child so that she landed in her arms.

Police learned that the baby's 17-year-old mother had left the child in the care of her brothers, aged 13 and 10, while she had gone to work. The two boys hadn't noticed when their little niece had crawled onto the balcony.

Mary and her son were awestruck by the experience. If they had been a few seconds later, the baby would likely have fallen to her serious injury or death.

Sleepwalking Teenager Remains Asleep after Falling Four Stories

On August 28, 2007, a sleepwalking German teenager, who had just moved into an apartment with his sister in the eastern town of Demmin, fell four stories to the ground. Amazingly when the police arrived to answer a call for help, the 17-year-old was still sound asleep.

At the hospital, staff members attested to his claim that he had taken neither drugs nor alcohol. Although he had remained asleep after his fall, he did not escape a broken arm and leg.

Fourteen-Month-Old Baby Falls Three Stories to Land on a Roof Below

While his parents were celebrating a good, old-fashioned family celebration on Thanksgiving Day, 2007, fourteen-month-old Bradley Priebe had decided to check out the view from the window of his aunt's third-floor apartment in Brooklyn. He teetered for a moment—and then he fell.

Brandon Priebe, Bradley's father, said the boy landed three stories below on the roof of a music shop.

Anna, the toddler's mother, declared it a miracle that he didn't even suffer a single broken bone.

Christmas Miracle on East 66th: Window Washer Plummets 47 Stories and Lives

On January 4, 2008, Dr. Philip S. Barie, the chief of the division of critical care at New York-Presbyterian Hospital/Weill Cornell Medical Center in Manhattan, told reporters that if anyone believed in miracles, the case of Alcides Moreno, 37, would be an excellent example. On December 7, 2007, Moreno and his brother Edgar, clung to their three-foot-wide window washer's platform as it plunged 47 stories to the alleyway below. Unfortunately, Edgar had fallen under the platform and was killed by the 500-foot-fall, but firefighters found that a miracle had already begun, for Alcides was still conscious and sitting up in the debris at the Solow Tower at 265 East 66th Street, able to communicate with his rescuers.

Washing skyscraper windows is not a job for the timid who fear heights, and with good reason.

At a press conference, doctors predicted that Moreno's recovery would be complete in about a year. He would undergo surgery on his spine and other orthopedic surgeries—and then there would be the long months of rehabilitation. The medical experts were also confident that Moreno would walk again and that already in December the 10 fractures had all been repaired, with only one remaining.

The medical personnel were quite frank that Moreno's case was opening new vistas of research for them. Those who suffer falls above 10 stories seldom survive. A medical journal detailed the account of a patient who had survived a 19-story fall, but that was less than half the distance that Moreno had fallen. Those remarkable stories of people who manage to survive when their parachutes don't open, Dr. Barie said, constitute less than one percent of those who fall that distance and live.

Dog Chases Bird off Cliff, Survives 300-Foot Fall

In October 2004 James Frew of Orphington, Kent, United Kingdom, was walking with his family and their German Spitz, Max, along the cliffs near Charmouth, Dorset. All of a sudden, Max ran after a blackbird and chased it over the edge of a cliff.

Cats are famous for always landing on their feet, and some have also survived remarkable falls.

The little blackbird had wings and could easily outdistance Max and soar high above the sea.

Max did not have wings; therefore, when he no longer had solid earth beneath him, he plummeted 300 feet to the ground below.

Members of the Coast Guard helped retrieve Max and expressed their amazement that the dog was simply sitting calmly on the beach awaiting their arrival. He appeared completely unhurt in spite of the great distance that he had fallen.

A local dog expert explained that when a dog experiences a sudden, unexpected fall, such as Max's, they are unaware of the danger they're in and are completely relaxed.

Answers to an Age-Old Question: How Far Can a Cat Fall and Live?

And then there are those seemingly interminable discussions about how far a cat can fall and survive.

On a pleasant spring day in April 1993, Mogadon, an 18-month-old black and white cat, slipped from the window ledge that was 21 stories above the street near Leeds, Alabama, and plummeted to the sidewalk.

Claire Quickmire recalled that the descent to the sidewalk in the high-rise's elevator was the longest ride of her life. She fully expected to find her friend Mike's cat to be nothing more than a mangled mess of blood and fur. She was astonished to see the dazed and frightened Mogadon being comforted in the arms of a neighbor.

According to eyewitnesses, Mogadon had been seen streaking toward the cement when she struck a bush at the side of the high-rise and bounced onto the sidewalk. The befuddled cat picked itself up, walked off slightly dazed, but apparently not a great deal worse for wear than she was before she began the 21-story plunge to the sidewalk.

Just to be safe, Claire gathered Mogadon into her arms and rushed her to a veterinarian, who found no broken bones, but who located numerous cuts and bruises to testify to the cat's miracle survival. The supercat required 24 stitches, which seemed a very small price to pay for having survived an impossible fall.

A recent study published in *The Journal of the American Veterinary Medical Association* found that out of 132 cats that fell an average of 5.5 stories, 90 percent survived, including one that fell 45 stories.

Research has determined that a cat can reach a terminal velocity of about 60 miles per hour after free-falling about 130 feet in a few seconds. In actuality, the greater the distance a cat falls improves its chances for survival. In one study, of the 22 cats that scientists documented had fallen eight or more stories, only one had died.

According to an extensive study, a cat falling a great distance will have more time to relax and to position itself for minimum injury. Cats appear to accomplish this by arching their backs, twisting their torsos independently or their hind legs, and then bringing their hindquarters around. By thus spreading their limbs in a horizontal position, much like the position assumed by the so-called "flying squirrels," cats are able to distribute the points of impact fairly evenly throughout their entire body. By contrast, falling humans will reach a terminal velocity of 120 miles per hour after plummeting for a few seconds, thus greatly limiting the height from which they can survive a collision with earth or concrete.

Highway Incidents

Surviving a Near-Fatal Crash Became a Life-altering Experience

In August 1997, 28-year-old salesman Charles Groff of Vermont was returning home after two weeks of "dismal motel rooms and disinterested retailers" when he fell asleep at the wheel while driving on a lonely rural road.

"My '95 Taurus slammed into a concrete bridge abutment, then caromed down a ditch, rolling over twice before it flipped over on its top," Groff said.

Charles was unconscious for an undetermined length of time, and when he once again became aware of his surroundings, he realized that he was hanging upside down by his seat belt.

"The windshield was shattered, and I slowly became aware that the gritty substance in my mouth was bits of glass. My eyes were also trying to blink away tiny pieces of the windshield."

Charles was comforted to know that he wasn't dead, but he began to panic when it occurred to him that he didn't really know how much longer he might be alive.

"Although I could find the release button of the seat belt, for some reason it didn't work. I don't know if it was the weight of my body that prevented me from unbuckling the seat belt or what, but I seemed to be stuck there, dangling like a fish on the end of a line.

"And I was certain I could smell gasoline. I had an image of the car exploding and me burning to death."

He had a sobering thought of the world without him. "I knew that Wall Street and the U.S. Senate could get along without me, but I thought of my wife, Maryann, and my two kids, Keith and Kathy, our three-year-old twins. I wanted to be around to watch them grow up, to attend college, to get married."

"The headlights were smashed and dead, but the dash lights were still on. I caught a glimpse of my bloody face in the reflection of the windshield and cried out loud in anguish."

And then he heard the sound of footsteps in the gravel outside his crippled and overturned Taurus.

Flipping a car upside down is one of the most difficult and dangerous accidents for drivers to escape from.

"I heard this voice say that I had to get out of there fast. I answered that I had no argument there, but I couldn't get free. Immediately, this man was stretching his arms inside to help me. With one hand, he undid the release button on the seat belt. With the other, he helped me drop free without landing so hard that I would be injured."

Charles could not help noticing how strong the man was as he assisted him to move across the ceiling of the upside-down car and make his way out of the damaged vehicle.

"My rescuer turned out to be a rather slender, but well-built, man of medium height. He had long, shoulder-length hair and a beard. His voice was very soft and warm. For the life of me, I just can't remember how he was dressed. What I remember most about him was his soulful eyes."

The man's strong arms helped Charles out of the ditch and away from the crash site. "We must move away from the car," the stranger told him.

"I don't imagine that we had walked 30 feet when the car burst into flames. I shuddered and gasped when I thought how close I had come to being consumed by the fire that was now blazing from one end of my Taurus to the other."

Charles could feel that he was badly shaken and was cut and bleeding from numerous scratches, but he seemed all right. After all, he was walking away from the scene of the crash unassisted.

"There's a farmhouse with a good family not more than a hundred yards away," the stranger told him. "You'll be all right now."

And then as Charles turned to thank him and to ask his name, the man answered, "You've got a second chance now, Charles. Take full advantage of the opportunity. Change your ways and learn to appreciate all the wonders and miracles that God has given you."

And then Charles said that he was suddenly looking into "the brightest light that I have ever seen. It became so blinding that I fell to the asphalt of the road and covered my eyes.

"When I looked up again after a few moments, the light and my rescuer had disappeared."

Charles said that he has confided his experience with a few close friends. Some believe him. Some suggest that in his shaken and disoriented state, he was probably looking into the stranger's bright headlamps as he was driving away.

Charles remains convinced that it was truly an angel who came to deliver him from certain death that evening.

Baby Patrick Was Truly a Miracle from God

A newborn infant discovered by emergency workers when they came upon a grisly highway accident near Louisville, Kentucky, on December 19, 2000, was declared a miracle baby.

When 18-year-old Patricia "Trisha" Welch heard the sound of the crash from her grandfather's house nearby, she ran to the scene and found a truck driver kneeling over the body of a woman and a newborn baby, sobbing hysterically. Tragically, the woman had been thrown through the windshield of the truck and the baby had literally been torn from her womb. The newborn, blue and motionless, was still attached to its mother by the umbilical cord. Trisha placed a blanket over the infant, who lay on a snowy embankment.

> *The newborn infant, a little boy, was still alive, and Shepherd set to work to keep it that way.*

When paramedic Charles Shepherd arrived on the scene, he pulled back the blanket that covered the baby and grabbed the umbilical cord. Shepherd later said that he "praised the Lord" when his sudden movement on the cord caused the baby to start crying. The newborn infant, a little boy, was still alive, and Shepherd set to work to keep it that way. He cut the umbilical cord and began giving the baby oxygen. During the 15-minute drive in the ambulance to Kosair Children's Hospital, Shepherd said that he never stopped praying.

Although the mother, 31-year-old Olga Maria Nunes Bera-Cruz, was killed instantly in the collision, the baby's father, Furtado Boaventura of Miami, Florida, survived with minor injuries. Two days after the tragedy, Lisa Brosky, a spokeswoman for the children's hospital, said that the newborn boy's condition had been upgraded from fair to good and that the only physical evidence the infant bore as a result of the terrible ordeal was a scratch on his knee.

Boaventura named his son Patrick, in recognition of Patricia Welch, the teenager who had helped care for him until rescue workers arrived.

Jeff Landers, another rescue worker on the scene, found an open Bible near the crash site. He agreed with Charles Shepherd that, in view of all the hardships that little Patrick Boaventura had undergone, he truly was a miracle from God.

A Mysterious Hitchhiker with a Healing Touch

Wayne Fiske, 58, had been a cross-country trucker for over 30 years, driving for a number of major trucking firms.

"I'll always remember that cold December night in 1988," he wrote in his account of the remarkable experience. "My older brother, Eddie, 57, was riding with me on that job, more or less to keep me company, and also to hitch a ride to his daughter's home in Aberdeen, South Dakota."

Wayne said that it was good to have a chance to talk with Eddie and to catch up on events both major and minor in their lives.

Eddie was four years older. Although they had a sister born after Wayne, he would always be the kid in the family to Eddie. To his way of thinking, Wayne had probably had only two or three ideas in his whole life that he didn't think were stupid or off the wall.

In spite of an older brother's disdain for a younger brother's reasoning processes, Wayne said that the two men got along fairly well.

Their biggest conflict was over religion. While Wayne continued to raise his family in the Methodist traditions of their parents, Eddie thought church-going and Bible reading were bunk.

Wayne felt that Eddie's trouble was that he was just a kid when he had enlisted in the Marines during the Korean "police action," and he had brought his small town Nebraska innocence along with him into the tough outside world. The things he saw during service overseas had so shocked his unprepared sensibilities that he had returned home a virtual atheist.

On that special night, Wayne remembered stopping at a small roadside diner to tank up on coffee and cheeseburgers before they hit a long stretch of desolate highway.

"We got into another argument over our food when I gently—I thought—suggested that Eddie start watching his weight. He was at least forty pounds overweight, and I knew that he had started to drink hard liquor pretty steadily. Plus he smoked two to three packs of cigarettes a day. None of those things are good for the old ticker, and I reminded Eddie that Dad had died of a heart attack when he was about his age."

Shortly after they had returned to the truck and had traveled a few miles down the road, they spotted a hitchhiker at the side of the highway.

"Although company policy is strong against hitchhikers, I wanted to pick the guy up," Wayne said. "It was well below zero out there, and the hitcher barely had any clothes on—a light jacket, that was all. I figured he would freeze to death. And since there were two of us in the event that he should try any monkey business, I thought I should stop and pick him up."

Eddie raised no real objections. After all, he too was a passenger, and Wayne was the captain of the ship. But he stated firmly that the hitcher had better not mind his heavy smoking.

"The man looked to be about 35," Wayne recalled. "He was well-groomed, but his clothes seemed out-of-date, as if he had borrowed them from an older relative. Probably just a guy down on his luck needing a lift.

"The most noticeable thing about him was his eyes. You almost couldn't help staring at them. But you know, I can't remember what color they were. What was important, though, was that they were really kind and expressive eyes that made you feel friendly toward him right away."

But to Wayne's discomfort and annoyance, Eddie didn't seem to feel the friendliness and kindness emanating from the man, and he started picking on the hitchhiker as soon as he was seated in the cab.

Hitchhiking is not a safe practice, and it is not wise to pick up hitchhikers, either.

"Right away he asked him if he had been in the service, and when the hitcher said he hadn't, Eddie began to rail against peaceniks and beatniks and bums," Wayne said. "He made it sound like the guy must be all three and that to be all of those things was something like being a child molester, a dope addict, and a traitor rolled into one."

The hitcher, though, was unruffled, and very soft spoken in his answers. Wayne could see that the guy's quiet voice was only making Eddie all the more ticked off against life in general and the stranger in particular.

Eddie was shouting something about the alleged evils of welfare programs and food stamps when he suddenly clutched at his chest and emitted a terrible, gasping cry.

Wayne knew right away that he was having a heart attack, and he really started to panic. It was about 2:00 in the morning, and they were miles and miles away from any hospital. Wayne pulled over as quickly and as safely as he could, and he started to pray out loud to God to help Eddie.

"And that's when the hitcher does this incredible thing," Wayne said. "He reached out for Eddie's chest and put his index and middle finger against it. Right away Eddie stops moaning, and it is immediately obvious that he is feeling a whole lot better. I figured this stranger had to be some kind of martial artist who knew some kind of Kung Fu healing points in the body.

"But then the hitchhiker started to glow. I swear, there was a beautiful bluish-white light that seemed to emanate from his very being, all around his body. The entire cab of the truck was filled with that incredible light."

Eddie began to breathe easier, and Wayne could tell that his brother was truly feeling better.

"He had our complete attention at that point," Wayne said. "We knew that this was no common hitchhiker. This guy was from another world."

"He talked to us for a long time after that. How long, I don't know. It was as if we were somehow in-between ordinary time. He knew everything about Eddie and me and our families. It was incredible. Neither Eddie nor me said a word. We just listened."

"And then he disappeared. I mean, he was just gone. Like that. In the twinkling of an eye."

Wayne remains convinced that the mysterious hitchhiker was an angel or a saint or maybe even an alien.

"I hold mostly with his being an angel," Wayne said. "Eddie changed his attitude toward religion and nearly everything else that night. Really, the experience became a turning point in both our lives. Now we know for sure it is true what others have to accept on faith.

"We don't care what anyone else says or thinks about our experience that night," Wayne said, concluding his account. "We know that it really happened. Our families believed us. That's all that matters to us."

Man Confined to a Wheelchair Goes for a Wild Ride on the Grille of a Truck

Twenty-two-year-old Ben Carpenter, stricken with muscular dystrophy, was confined to wheelchair in 1999. Twice a week, Ben, a resident of Alamo Township in Kalamazoo, Michigan, took his motorized wheelchair for an outing. Around 4:00 P.M. on June 6, 2007, he had decided to go for a spin in nearby Paw Paw.

Ben didn't quite make the traffic light as he crossed Red Arrow Highway, and the driver of a semi didn't see him as he sped through the intersection. Incredibly, the truck collided with the wheelchair and the chair's handles became lodged in the semi's grille.

The loud hum of the diesel engine prevented the driver from hearing Ben's cries for help, and the truck roared down Red Arrow Highway going 50 miles per hour.

Ben was well aware that his wheelchair was going a great deal faster than it was made to go. At first his concern was that since the driver could not hear him, he might end up 60 or 70 miles from home before the truck made its first stop. After a few more minutes of riding in this precarious position, Ben became more concerned that his wheelchair would break into pieces and he would be run over.

Meanwhile, drivers approaching the truck were making 911 calls to the police. Some at first thought that they were witnessing some kind of crazy stunt that some reckless daredevil had rigged up on the truck's grille. Others saw the fear and pleading in Ben Carpenter's face and knew that some bizarre accident had occurred and the young man was in great difficulty.

When the reports first began coming in describing someone in a wheelchair stuck to the grille of a fast-moving semi, the police believed that they were receiving calls from an imaginative prankster. However, when the calls kept coming into Van Buren County Central Dispatch describing the same bizarre situation, they began to take the problem faced by some victim in a wheelchair seriously.

Just as the tires on Ben's chair began to smoke and leave dark streaks on the highway, the truck driver pulled over in front of the company that owned the vehicle.

When a state police car pulled up beside and told him that he had a man in a wheelchair stuck to his grille, the driver thought that he was being "punked"—the victim of a cruel television joke. Then he got out of the cab, walked around to the front of his truck, and met Ben Carpenter, who had, against his wishes, hitched a ride for five miles.

Ben was unharmed, and now that the wild ride had ended, he was not greatly unsettled by the event. All in all, he said, the road was quite smooth and there were not many bumps. He was, though, glad that it was over.

Drivers need to be especially vigilant about pedestrians using electric wheelchairs that might be hard to see in traffic.

Prayer Placed a Protective Shield around Her Vehicle

Delores Baca of Anaheim, California, told of the remarkable angelic visitation which occurred during a meeting of their church prayer group and explained how it miraculously helped to save the life of her daughter.

"Our priest had instituted a wonderful home enrichment plan in August of 1984," Mrs. Baca said. "Those of us who wished could gather in one another's homes in prayer groups and join with like-minded people who felt strength and unity in prayer.

"One night in November, when it was my turn to host and to conduct the prayer circle, I had a sudden frightening vision of my daughter Linda, who was away from home on an automobile trip. I had been very concerned about her safety, and I was at first fearful that my anxiety had forced a negative image of Linda into my mind. At the same time, I knew that I did not have to be embarrassed to ask my prayer partners to pray with me for my daughter's safety."

Mrs. Baca said that she next received a terrible picture of her daughter approaching a very dangerous stretch of highway. The vision seemed to acquire a life of its own, as if she were watching a motion picture beyond her control. She gasped aloud, hoping with all her being that she not seeing an image of true reality for she saw her daughter's car being struck by a large truck at a desolate intersection and being nearly demolished by the violent impact.

Delores Baca got quickly to her feet, and in a voice trembling with a mother's love and concern, asked each of the twelve women assembled in her living room that evening to begin to pray for her daughter Linda's safety.

> *The vision seemed to acquire a life of its own, as if she were watching a motion picture beyond her control.*

"It was at the very moment that I declared my heart-felt plea for succor that the miracle occurred," Mrs. Baca said. "As I spoke the last word of my request to pray for Linda, an overpowering spiritual influence seemed to envelop the entire room and everyone in it.

"Then before all of our eyes, a beautiful figure clothed in gold and white light walked through the very midst of our prayer circle and commanded: 'Pray!'

"Everyone understood that she was to pray for Linda as she traveled on the highway," Mrs. Baca said. "Each of us bowed our head in prayer, and we continued our supplications for about 30 minutes. At that time, we all heard a voice say: 'It is past!'"

Late the next afternoon, when her daughter returned from her automobile trip, she told her mother of the harrowing experience that she had undergone. According to Linda, she had been crossing an intersection in a desolate section of the highway when the brakes of a heavily loaded truck failed and sent it roaring unchecked straight for her car.

"It should have struck me broadside," Linda said, shaking her head in bewildered memory of the near-fatal experience. "I should have been history. But somehow my car gave a sudden surge of power and literally propelled me out of the truck's path. It almost felt as though my car were some kind of living thing that had the ability to jump out of harm's way."

When Mrs. Baca informed Linda of her vision and the combined prayer power of the group, she was very moved.

"That would have been at exactly the time that I was approaching the intersection," she verified.

And when Mrs. Baca told her daughter of the mother love that had summoned an angel to add additional energy to the prayers of the group of devout women, Linda crossed herself and set out at once for church to light candles and to offer prayers of thanksgiving.

"I can't explain why the heavenly being chose to answer my pleas and come to lend its energy to our prayer group that night," Delores Baca concluded, "but I shall be forever grateful that it did."

Trapped in a Blizzard, Their Car Dead, a Stranger Restores Their Power with an Angelic Touch

In December 1994, Catherine and John Bioletto of Los Angeles were driving to Lake Tahoe, Nevada, on a holiday vacation, when they spotted a bearded hitcher at the side of the road.

John and Catherine Bioletto were trapped in the snow. Should they trust a mysterious stranger to help them?

"Don't stop for him," warned 55-year-old Catherine. "He's probably some drug addict who'll try to rob us. Remember all the warnings about the hazards of picking up a hitchhiker. Just keep going!"

John, two months away from his sixtieth birthday, chuckled at his wife's concern. He read the papers and watched television news, too, but this guy didn't look like a junkie or a head case to him. "It's cold out there," he said. "Let's give the guy a break."

As they were slowing to a stop, John did work out a compromise with his wife's apprehensions. They would let the hitcher get in the front seat, and Catherine would climb into the back. If the man did try anything funny, she would spray him with the mace that she always carried in her purse.

"As the young man got into our car, I calmed my fears," Catherine told us in her account of the incident. "He had the most beautiful eyes, and there was a wonderful aura of peace around him. His quiet manner told you that he could be trusted."

They drove in silence, occasionally asking their passenger some questions about who he was and where he was headed. The hitcher said that he felt he had a mission to help people in trouble. He began to speak about how troubled so many men and women were in modern society and how so many had fallen away from God. When he began to quote a few passages from scripture, Catherine and John were giving each other furtive looks, wondering if they had picked up a religious nut.

Then, to their great concern, they were suddenly caught by a blizzard and were driving on a snow-packed mountain highway near Lake Tahoe.

At about the same time that Catherine and John were emerging from the stranger's mesmerizing talk of portents to come, John shouted that their automobile's electrical system had suddenly malfunctioned. The lights, wipers, heater, and windows no longer worked. Without the wipers and the defroster to keep it clear, the windshield soon became a white wall of snow and ice and it was impossible for John to see where he was driving.

> *"It could have been an angel of the Lord, I suppose."*

John managed to pull their car safely off the road and on to the shoulder without getting stuck in a snow drift.

"We're really in a jam," he said. "We have no headlights or taillights to warn approaching vehicles that we're stranded here. Someone could easily swerve on the slick highway and run into us before they see us. We have no heat to keep us from freezing to death, and it's too far to walk to the next town."

Catherine said that was when the stranger revealed his true presence. He stretched out his left arm and held his open palm just a few inches from the dashboard.

"A brilliant blue-white light like a bolt of electricity shot forth from the palm of his hand and struck the dashboard," Catherine said. "The light it made was blinding, and it filled the entire automobile. In that same instant, the hitchhiker disappeared right before our eyes. And in the next instant, the lights, wipers, heater, defroster, windows—everything—started working again all at once."

Catherine and John Bioletto were able to drive safely the remainder of the distance to Lake Tahoe.

"During the drive to our hotel, neither one of us spoke more than two words," Catherine said. "Since that time, though, we have discussed the marvelous experience over and over again. And we have shared it with many, many people."

And just what did they believe was the hitchhiker's true identity?

"It could have been an angel of the Lord, I suppose," Catherine said. "He told us that he was on Earth on a mission to help people. He certainly helped us. We could easily have been killed that day in that blizzard."

A Car Runs over Her Head, but She Lives with a Bump and Bruises

On July 3, 2008, 11-year-old Savannah Haworth had stayed late after school, rehearsing her role in Helmshore Primary School's presentation of the musical *Grease*. She was riding her bicycle home, being careful to avoid bumping into pedestrians, when she lost her balance and fell in front of a slow-moving vehicle. The driver was unable to stop the car in time to prevent hitting her, and the vehicle ran over Savannah's arm, shoulder, and head.

Fortunately for Savannah, her parents had been strict in enforcing the rule that she must always wear a helmet when riding her bicycle.

Taken to the Royal Blackburn Hospital in Helmshore, Lancashire, the girl was X-rayed and released after 24 hours. Although her helmet was crushed, Savannah escaped with only a swollen elbow, some cuts and bruises, and a bump on her head.

Miracles on the Train Tracks

My God! There's a Baby on the Tracks!

Larry DuBoise, assistant engineer on Amtrak's Southwest Chief, could not believe his eyes when the passenger train rounded a sharp curve on the outskirts of Isleta Pueblo, New Mexico, at 1:30 P.M. on May 16, 1992.

"My God!" he shouted to engineer John Vannoy. "There's a child on the tracks!"

As the Southwest Chief thundered toward the baby, the men watched helplessly as 18-month-old toddler Jeremy Abeita walked down the center of the tracks, his back to the train.

DuBoise yelled to Vannoy to slam on the emergency brakes, but both engineers knew that it would be impossible to stop the train in time to prevent hitting the child.

Many people—especially children—do not seem to be aware of the risks of walking along train tracks.

Vannoy blasted the horn, and the baby jumped and turned to see the train bearing down upon him.

"Baby! Baby! Get out of the way! Get off the tracks!" DuBoise shouted.

Confused and frightened, little Jeremy dropped to his hands and knees and began to crawl. DuBoise could see that the baby was trying to get off the tracks, but he knew that he could never make it before the train was upon him.

The 44-year-old engineer got out on the engine's front catwalk, then carefully moved down the metal stairs, wedging his legs in the bottom and second steps. He was now dangerously close to the shrieking front wheels of the locomotive and the cowcatcher—the metal frame on the engine's nose.

He grabbed a handrail, then lowered himself until his head was only about five inches above the steel tracks. His desperate plan was to attempt to catch hold of the boy and pull him out from under the crushing wheels of the train.

By the time the engine was about 50 feet from little Jeremy, it was still moving about 40 miles per hour. DuBoise said later that it felt that it was God's will that he should do his utmost to save the boy, but he felt his blood freeze when he heard Jeremy scream. The cowcatcher had brushed his body, and he fell under the metal frame toward the massive steel wheels.

DuBoise stretched out his arm in a desperate, blind attempt to grab the baby. He silently offered thanks to God when he felt his fingers clutch the infant's shoulder. With a great effort of will, he was able to pull Jeremy free and throw him onto the grassy ditch at the side of the tracks.

When engineer John Vannoy was at last able to stop the Southwest Chief, DuBoise saw the terrified mother sweeping her son up in her arms.

DuBoise remembered that he wanted to run to help her, but he stood next to the engine, rooted to the spot, as if paralyzed. He simply could not move after having accomplished his daring rescue of the baby.

A doctor and nurse who were passengers on the Southwest Chief gave Jeremy first aid before an ambulance arrived and he could be rushed to a hospital. The 18-month-old boy's lower left leg had been severed when he was struck by the engine, and he had also received abdominal and head injuries. But he survived.

Jeremy's mother, as well as the passengers, crew, and other witnesses of Larry DuBoise's remarkable, selfless heroism said that he had performed a miracle. DuBoise, however, gave all the credit to God. In his opinion, the Almighty had wanted him to intervene in what seemed like certain death for the boy, because He had something important for Jeremy to do in the future.

Later that year, Larry DuBoise was awarded the Carnegie Medal for heroism.

Ricardo Was One Lucky Guy

In February 1994, Police Lieutenant Moore of West Sacramento, California, pronounced 25-year-old Ricardo the luckiest man alive. At about 6:00 P.M. on February 3, Ricardo walked across some railroad tracks on his way to a bus stop. With his Walkman® radio playing at high volume in his ears, he didn't hear the freight train approaching on one track and the passenger train hurtling along on another.

Ricardo was struck first by the westbound passenger train. The impact tossed him into the air and into the path of the eastbound freight train. When Ricardo opened his eyes and looked up into the faces of two frightened-looking railroad employees, his first thought was that he must have been mugged. He started to get up, then one of the men told him to lie still, the paramedics were on the way.

For the first time, Ricardo noticed that he seemed to be covered with blood issuing from a head wound. When the asked the men what had happened to him, they told him that he had been hit by one train, then slammed by another.

After a brief stay in the hospital, Ricardo stated his firm belief that the good Lord had certainly been looking out for him. He had been struck by a fast-moving train and tossed like a rag doll into the path of another set of tracks where he was clobbered by another oncoming train. Other than having some stitches in the back of his head and the use of a temporary back brace, Ricardo was unharmed. West Sacramento Police Sergeant Hensley declared the whole incident of a man being struck in rapid succession by two trains and surviving with minor injuries to be "mind-boggling."

Dragged for Seven Miles, Then Struck Again by the Same Train

Marion, a 41-year-old clothing designer from Canada, was driving home late at night in her Mercury Capri along a road that she had traveled many times. As she approached a train crossing, she saw neither lights nor any kind of barrier, but suddenly a train was right in front of her. She slammed on her brakes and skidded into the side of the train.

The impact knocked her unconscious, and her automobile was wedged under the train as it moved down the tracks at 30 miles per hour. The crew was completely oblivious to the accident and had no idea that there was a woman in a car lodged under their train.

After about seven miles, Marion's mangled Mercury broke free and came to rest on the tracks. The train checked in at a nearby depot, then reversed direction, headed back along the route it had just traveled—and 30 minutes later hit Marion's car again. This time, however, the crew realized that they had struck something on the track and called for help.

Every year people die in car-train accidents, sometimes because there are no gates on the tracks, but other times because drivers swerve around gates in their haste.

The first rescuers on the scene did not believe anyone in the wreckage could have survived the double impact. To their astonishment, they found the driver unconscious, but alive. They used the Jaws of Life to free Marion from the twisted metal of the car, and then they rushed her to a hospital.

Although she had suffered a broken leg, a broken arm, and a generous assortment of bumps and bruises, Marion had survived what would have seemed an impossible one-two punch from a train. A Royal Canadian Mounted Police investigator explained that in this case the miracle lay in the fact that the first impact from the train had twisted parts of the car around Marion's seat, thereby literally providing a cocoon of protective metal that had saved her life.

Involved in a Train Crash, a Victim "Thought" Himself Home

William McFarland Campbell was a traveling insurance man with the Canadian Order of Chosen Friends for more than 30 years. In his position of Grand Organizer, he traveled from coast to coast from his home base of Hamilton, Ontario.

It was January 21, 1910. Train Number 17 arrived on time, and Campbell joined the other passengers for the half-block walk to the platform. With their suitcases in hand, the men and women swung aboard the train with no knowledge of what lay in store for them.

A rail lay broken at a point north of Toronto on the Soo Branch of the track where the Canadian Pacific Railway crosses the Spanish River at the eastern approach to an iron bridge. Before the engineer could even realize what was happening, the first-class car was off the tracks, plummeting down to the icy river below. With the first-class car came the dining car and the sleeping car, both pulled inexorably along. These cars pulled the second-class car with them—and then car after wooden car toppled over the embankment into the icy gorge below. As the cars tumbled over and over into the river, they left splintered wood and mangled bodies scattered over the wintry scene.

> She heard Will's unmistakable step on the front porch.

At 11:00 P.M., Mary Campbell turned up the gas lamp and rested her feet on the stool by her chair.

As she waited, she heard the sound of a taxi coming down the street. It turned on Grant Avenue and slowly passed the houses of their neighbors.

At last she heard it stop at their house, and the driver call out a "good night."

She heard Will's unmistakable step on the front porch.

Mary came forward, opened the door and welcomed her husband home.

But she frowned when she saw that Will's hat was pulled down low over his eyes, and his face was averted from hers.

"What's wrong, Will?" she wanted to know at once. "Did things not go well today?"

When he finally lifted his face, Mary could not halt a shriek of horror from escaping her mouth.

Her beloved husband's face was transparent. His eyes were two glowing coals.

Will was struggling to speak, but he could only manage a terrible gurgling sound.

Mary's frightened cries awakened the neighbors and brought them to her aid.

She was huddled on the floor when they found her, and it was evident that she was in an advanced state of shock.

When one of the neighbors answered the insistently ringing telephone, he learned of the terrible wreck of Number 17.

The following morning Mary Campbell managed to tell her story of Will's ghostly appearance to their family physician, Dr. John Bell.

Dr. Bell nodded in sympathy and said, "Sometimes when we have lived our lives together with someone, we become so attached to that person that we can recognize immediately when danger is at hand to threaten our loved one. Some believe that there is an aura, a body of energy, surrounding a person that is able to transmit thoughts or warnings—even at a distance."

After Dr. Bell had administered a sedative to Mary and saw that it was taking effect, he prepared to leave. Although he had provided the distraught woman with a "scientific" explanation for the apparition that she had claimed to have seen of her husband the night before, he did not really believe for one minute that Will Campbell had actually manifested before his wife.

As he was leaving the Campbell residence, however, he spotted Will's old hat on the rack in the hallway. He picked it up, feeling a sudden burden of sorrow. Will Campbell had been a fine man and a good friend.

"Poor Will," Dr. Bell reflected sadly. "He'll never wear this again."

As he turned the hat over in his hands, he saw the pink ticket in the hatband.

Once he had read the wording on the ticket, his face turned ashen gray. No matter how many times he read and reread the ticket, it still said: TRAIN NUMBER 17, FIRSTCLASS RETURN, SUDBURY, JANUARY 21, 1910.

How could a dead man ride home on a train that did not return? And how could he leave his hat behind in a house that would lie forever beyond his physical reach?

Dr. Bell's brain spun inside his skull, and he had to sit down on a sturdy chair to contemplate the mystery further.

Train Number 17 had been derailed before it had reached Sudbury. Was it possible for a ghost man to ride home on a ghost train?

No application of Dr. Bell's prized scientific procedure could adequately answer such an enigma, but Mary Campbell and all of their family and friends were overjoyed when William Campbell arrived home—in the flesh—on the wrecker the next day.

Will explained that he had been in the first-class car that had struck the bridge and had begun to burn. Somehow his body had been thrown clear during the impact of the collision, and he had been tossed out of the car into below-zero weather. He knew that he had been unconscious for several minutes, and when he returned to a kind of dazed state of semi-consciousness, he sat for several more minutes thinking of his wife and wondering if he would ever see her again.

Later, he roused himself, and set about rendering assistance to other injured passengers.

Electrified by Railroad Cables, Hit by a Train, His Mother's Prayers Pull Him Through

In November 1994, Lee, a Manchester (England) Metropolitan University student, had just celebrated his twenty-second birthday and was on his way home when he was chased by a gang of thugs who preyed on college students. To escape them, Lee jumped over a fence and landed on electrified railroad cables, then fell 20 feet onto the rail tracks where he was hit by a train.

Lee was not expected to live through the night. He had sustained an electrical shock of 25,000 volts which caused him to burst into flames. He had fallen onto the tracks below where a train had sliced the flesh off one shoulder, but, incredibly, had put out the flames with the rush of air from the wheels. His body was so mangled, blistered, and blackened that five people who saw him in the hospital fainted.

The electricity used to power a commuter train is enough to kill an unwary human being.

Although the medical staff at the emergency room informed his parents that they should expect their son to die before morning, his mother begged them not to give up hope. And she prayed for a miracle.

Lee was given more than 170 pints of blood, and his mother offered 20 percent of her total body skin for grafts so that he might live. Within 16 months of the horrible accident, Lee was exercising 14 hours a day at a rehabilitation center. Soon thereafter, he was playing soccer and anticipating his college finals, thereby providing a living testimonial to courage and positive thinking.

Struck by a Train while Saving His Two-Year-Old Brother, There Was Miracle Enough to Save Both Lives

Eight-year-old Corey Preston was horrified when he saw his two-year-old brother, Anthony, standing between the rails of the railroad track. Apparently, little Anthony had somehow slipped away from the baby sitter and had walked out on the tracks near their home in Ocean Springs, Mississippi. And now there was a freight train roaring down the tracks, moving rapidly toward Anthony, less than a minute away from running over him.

Corey, who had been enjoying a workout on his roller blades on that afternoon in May 1994, knew that it was up to him to get his little brother. Their grandmother Betty was at work, and their mother, Stephanie, who was in the Army, was in Washington, D.C., at the time.

As he sped toward the tracks on his skates, Corey yelled at Anthony to get off the rails.

But Anthony had suddenly become fully aware of the huge locomotive bearing down on him. Wide-eyed with fear, he froze.

Corey hobbled on his blades and got next to the tracks. He shouted at Anthony to take his hand so he could pull him off the rails.

The locomotive's whistle was shrieking an urgent alarm. The engineer had spotted the kids and was warning them to get off the tracks immediately. The freight train was hauling an extra number of boxcars, and it was far too big and long and moving too fast to be able to stop.

The freight train was hauling an extra number of boxcars, and it was far too big and long and moving too fast to be able to stop.

At the sound of the engine's piercing screech, Corey clambered awkwardly on the tracks, his roller blades making him teeter clumsily.

Since Anthony seemed unable to move out of harm's way, Corey shoved his little brother off the tracks. Better a skinned knee or elbow than to be run over by a freight train, Corey had reasoned.

But then Corey found himself in a nightmarish situation. The wheels of his skates had gotten caught between the crossties on the tracks.

Panic-stricken, the eight-year-old pulled at one skate and then the other. He could hear his brother crying out in fear.

The engineer slammed on the brakes of the massive locomotive, and Corey's world was overwhelmed with the sound of metal shrieking against metal and the sight of the huge engine bearing down on him.

At the last possible second, Corey managed to pull his skates free of the track, but it wasn't soon enough to prevent him from being slammed to the ground, unconscious and bleeding.

For a few moments, little Anthony stood beside the crumpled figure of his big brother, who was lying motionless in a pool of blood. And then it was the two-year-old's turn to be heroic. He ran all the way home and alerted nearby relatives, who called an ambulance.

The boys' grandmother happened to be at the hospital when the ambulance arrived, and she was shocked to see her minister and family members walk in with Anthony.

Doctors treated Corey for a smashed pelvis and hip socket and numerous cuts and bruises, and he was released five days later. Although he would have to use crutches until his injuries mended, the boy's courageous actions in saving his little brother could well have cost him his life. Some miracles have a price attached to them, and the tag on this one could have been a great deal higher.

"Calling Mom, 911, Anyone! I'm Trapped under a Train"

Nineteen-year-old Amber Scott was on her way driving back to Ball State University, Muncie, from her home in Anderson, Indiana, when she stopped for the red lights at a level railroad crossing. It was 7:00 A.M. on a very foggy early April morning in 1999.

As Amber looked in the rearview mirror of her 1989 Pontiac Grand Am, she could see the headlights of a truck fast-approaching the railroad crossing. The truck appeared to be going way too fast. Amber remembers thinking that she certainly hoped the driver would soon slow down or he could slam her right into the train.

Unfortunately, that is exactly what the truck did.

In the seconds before the truck crashed into her Grand Am, Amber gripped the wheel, closed her eyes, and prayed.

When she opened her eyes again, she was wedged under the thirty-third car of the train, being dragged along the tracks, making sparks fly in all directions as metal scraped against metal. The engineer driving the train was completely oblivious to the unwilling hitchhiker that he had acquired.

Amber knew that she couldn't just sit there being afraid, so she did what any American child has been taught to do—she reached for her cell phone and called her mother.

Patricia Scott was drying her hair at that very difficult moment in her daughter's life, so the answering machine picked up the call.

Amber called 911, but the dispatcher couldn't understand what she was saying over the loud screeching of her car being dragged along the train tracks.

Mrs. Scott finished drying her hair, noticed the blinking light on her answering machine, and clicked it on to hear an undecipherable noise—and then her daughter saying that she had been hit. Before Amber could say what hit her or where, the connection died.

It was a good thing that Amber had prayed before the collision and continued to pray, because after been dragged at right angles for nearly four miles and seven minutes, her Grand Am was knocked clear of the train by a highway sign beside the track.

Amber doesn't remember crawling out of her car, but when she came back to full consciousness, she found herself in the company of two old high school friends who had heard the screeching sound of metal against metal and had followed a trail of debris to the spot where the Grand Am had spun free. It was when Mike and James hugged her that Amber fully realized that she was covered with cuts, bruises, and had a very bad pain in her back.

A quick inspection of Amber's Pontiac told her friends that whoever was driving it should be dead. The roof was caved-in, the hood was crumpled, and the back of the Grand Am was smashed up against the rear seat.

Patricia Scott, assessing the damage done to her daughter and the vehicle, pronounced a miracle, surely an act of divine intervention.

Few people can survive the deadly power of an avalanche.

In addition to the power of prayer, Amber's friends pointed out that the T-shirt that she was wearing with the declaration "Too Tough to Die" inscribed across the chest may have helped to keep her from being killed by the train.

Law enforcement officers soon tracked down the truck driver whose carelessness on a foggy morning had nearly cost Amber Scott her life. The 25-year-old, who was traveling nearly 60 miles per hour when he had struck Amber's Grand Am and shoved it onto the tracks, was charged with driving without insurance.

Buried Alive

Buried by an Avalanche, She Had Time Only to Pray

The drive to her country home outside of Allegany, Oregon, had begun pleasantly enough for Diane Wallis, 31, on that late afternoon of March 5, 1991. As she came around a curve near the home where her two children and husband, Bob, would be waiting for her, she had to slam on the brakes to avoid running into a pile of earth and rocks that had fallen onto the pavement from the high bank alongside the road. As she began backing up so that she could go around the roadblock, she saw a massive avalanche of rocks, trees, and dirt cascading directly toward her.

Instinctively Diane moved toward the passenger seat as rocks and trees crushed the roof of her automobile as if it were made of paper. She had only time to utter a prayer for God's mercy before she was pounded by debris breaking through the smashed roof and pinning her face down on the seat.

Diane was able to move only her left arm. Her right, slashed by shattered glass, was wedged between the two front seats. Although at the time she was unable to visualize the full scale of her predicament—her car was completely buried under several feet of rocks, trees, dirt, and debris—Diane Wallis did comprehend that her car had been swept off the road by an avalanche on a route that was seldom traveled by any but those who lived in that remote area.

After several minutes, she found it difficult to breathe. She tried desperately not to become hysterical, not to envision that she was trapped in her own tomb.

She realized that as strange as it might seem, the engine of her car was still running, and the fumes from the exhaust could soon be robbing her of vital oxygen. Her left hand managed to find the keys and shut off the ignition. And that was when it occurred to her that her hand could also reach the horn on the steering wheel.

Although he thought at first that it was his watch beeping, Jim Kellum, the Wallis' neighbor, had come to investigate the avalanche. Diane's guardian angel must have directed Jim to stand on the right spot at the right time, for after a couple more blasts of the horn, muffled though they were, he was able to distinguish that there was someone in an automobile somewhere under the heap of rocks, dirt, and trees.

Bob Wallis, who was becoming concerned that Diane had not yet returned home from work, joined Kellum and other neighbors at the spot where the faint sound of an automobile horn was working itself way up through the rubble. An instant consensus was reached that everyone needed to run home and get whatever power equipment they had available. That had to be Diane entombed by the avalanche.

In two and a half hours, the men had Diane freed and on her way to the hospital to be examined. Again, her guardian angel was at her side. Diane Wallis suffered only cuts and the mild effects of exposure and was sent home to be with her family.

✳

A Patch of Yellow Miracle

On April 1, 1991, rescue worker Hubert Haddukiewicz was astonished when he found an unharmed month-old baby girl amid the rubble of a five-story apartment house that had been blown to bits by a gas explosion.

Later, Haddukiewicz declared that little Laure Claes had to have been protected by the wings of angels to have survived a fall of 50 feet with the walls of the building crumbling all around her.

Imagine the horror of 23-year-old mother Cathy Claes of Salbris, France: She had just given her month-old daughter her 9:00 A.M. feeding and had placed her in her crib when a powerful explosion knocked her off her feet. As Cathy watched in terror and disbelief, the walls of their fifth-floor apartment crashed down around her—and the room in which little Laure lay in her crib broke away and crumbled to the ground along with the four floors beneath it. Only a narrow section of their apartment remained, and Cathy was left clinging precariously to a small portion of the floor to avoid falling to certain injury or death.

After what seemed an eternity of fear and anguish, firemen with ladders rescued Cathy and lowered her to safety. She had sustained a broken nose and a multitude of cuts from the blast, but she had no concern for her own injuries. She felt only the awful pain of believing that her beloved Laure had surely been killed in the explosion.

Cathy was placed on a stretcher and was being carried to an ambulance when she happened to see a man running toward them carrying her baby.

"She's alive!" Hubert Haddukiewicz shouted. "This little baby is alive!"

Cathy got off the stretcher and ran to claim her month-old baby girl. "She is my Laure!" she exclaimed, taking her child from the rescue worker. "Thank God, she is alive! Bless you for finding her!"

Later, Haddukiewicz, a computer technician, told how he had left his nearby home as soon as he had heard the thunderous explosion. He ran to the scene to see if he might be able to help anyone who may have been injured by the blast.

> *As Cathy watched in terror and disbelief, the walls of their fifth floor apartment crashed down around her.*

No emergency crews had yet arrived when Haddukiewicz arrived. He had stood near the piles of rubble, trying to see through the clouds of dust, hoping to detect some sign of life.

Then a patch of bright yellow caught his attention. It appeared to be an infant's blanket or dress.

Haddukiewicz made his way through the clouds of dust and crawled over bathtubs, tables, beds, chairs, and the debris from crumbled walls and floors. He found the baby on top of a pile of rubble with her little head nestled in the center of a plaster wall partition. Just above the spot where the baby lay was an overhanging portion of floor that appeared ready to fall at any moment.

The rescuer wasted no time. He grabbed the baby from the crevice in the wall partition where she lay and got out of there as quickly as possible.

Just as he cleared the pile of rubble with little Laure in his arms, the overhanging section of floor crashed down on the place where she had been.

Haddukiewicz said that the look of joy on Cathy Claes' face when he handed her little daughter would remain with him always. He declared that it was all the reward that he would ever need for his unselfish act of heroism.

The doctors who saw to Cathy Claes' injuries also examined Laure and pronounced her completely unscathed. To the immeasurable relief of Cathy and her husband, Herve, lucky Laure hadn't even suffered a scratch.

Trapped in a Coal Mine for Six Days without Food or Water

On August 18, 2007, brothers Meng Xianchen and Meng Xianyou were trapped in a coal mine collapse in Beijing's Fangshan District. After two days, all rescue

Coal miners in China risk their lives every day to eke out a living.

efforts were discontinued, and the Meng brothers' relatives mourned and burned "ghost money" at the entrance of the mine to ensure their spirits peaceful departure from Earth.

After six days trapped in the mine, the brothers crawled out of a hole and emerged to a disbelieving, but joyful, family.

The brothers discovered that if they broke coal into small pieces they could eat it. Xianchen said that he found the little chunks bitter, but not at all unpleasant. In the mine, they had found two discarded water bottles, and they took small sips of their own urine as their only liquid intake.

After only a few days in the hospital, the Meng brothers were released in remarkably good shape after their ordeal of six days trapped underground.

Both Xianchen and Xianyou said they would find some other work than to return to mining.

He Survived Five Hours under Tons of Dirt through Meditation

Wang Jianxin, 52, had his back to the wall of the 15-foot trench that he was digging at a construction site in Ningbo city, eastern China. Suddenly, without warning, the wall collapsed and Wang found himself buried alive.

Immediately, his coworkers began digging furiously with their shovels to free him. Some men ran to get firefighters to help with the excavation.

A doctor at the scene said that Wang did not have a chance of surviving. If the dirt around him were somewhat loose, the doctor estimated, the longest that the construction could survive would be five minutes.

Urged on by the doctor's prediction, Wang's fellow workers were still only able to free him after five hours had passed.

When the men pulled him free of the trench, they were all astonished to find him alive and quite well. The doctor unhesitatingly pronounced Wang's survival as a miracle.

How had Wang managed to stretch five minutes of air into five hours of life?

Meditation was his answer. Wang Jianxin was quite aware that the air in the small pocket around him would not last very long, so he made himself relax and focused on his breathing by meditation. Since it was so very quiet under all that dirt, Wang said that he found it quite easy to achieve inner calm.

AMAZING ANIMALS

Animal Attacks

Courageous Friend Saved Him Being Eaten by Four Lions

In July 1992, African game preserve guide Ronald Neluheni, 24, and conservation advisor Tuba van de Walt, 46, were supervising the construction of a fence inside South Africa's Nwanedi National Park, a 245,000-acre game preserve, when one of the laborers indicated that there was a lioness creeping from the bush toward Neluheni.

Ronald turned to face not one, but four crouching lionesses less than five yards away.

The workers screamed and climbed the fence.

Ronald decided to try to make a run for the Toyota Landcruiser 30 yards away. He had barely taken a few steps when a lioness slammed into his 118-pound body and brought him down.

The guide felt terrible pain as the beast's claws and fangs tore into his flesh. Ronald couldn't scream, not even when a second lioness sank her teeth into his thigh. A third hungry lioness clamped her jaws around his arm, and he could see the fourth one coming to join in the meal of his body.

By this time, Tuba had made it to the truck. He could think of no other way to get four savage lionesses off his friend than to ram them with the four-wheel drive. Careful not to hit Ronald, Tuba positioned the Landcruiser over his friend's body to protect it from the lions.

Tuba was astonished when the four man-eaters quickly recovered from being struck by the truck and came charging back to begin crawling under the truck to continue their meal. They had tasted blood, and they would not be denied their prey.

Lions attack in groups, and when a game preserve guide found himself the intended prey of four lionesses, he was lucky to escape with his life.

Ronald would always have the horrible memory of the huge ravenous creatures pulling him out from under the Landcruiser and dragging him over stones and into the bushes. He actually recalled the four of them beginning to feast on his body.

Tuba followed the four lionesses into the bush and charged them again, once more positioning the truck carefully over his friend's mangled and bloody body.

Although the Landcruiser had momentarily scattered them, the four hungry lions regrouped and prepared to charge the vehicle and reclaim their prey.

As the man-eaters approached, Tuba courageously left the safety of the truck with a box of tools in his hands. One by one as the lionesses approached, he would pelt the beasts with a heavy wrench or a hammer.

At first, snarling angrily and charging the truck with vicious determination, the lionesses began to lose their enthusiasm with each direct hit on their heads or bodies from the heavy metal tools that Tuba threw with an accuracy inspired by desperation. At last the four retreated into the bush, roaring their rage at being denied their dinner.

Wrench in his hand at the ready, Tuba saw that he had finally beaten the man-eaters away from the badly injured Ronald. Tuba grabbed Ronald by the legs, placed him in the cab, and began a frantic 50-mile drive to the nearest hospital.

Although Ronald had been severely bitten in the thigh, arm, chest, and throat and had been clawed deeply on several parts of his body, he recovered and returned to work in the park. He has said that he owed his life to a brave friend with an ability to pitch heavy metal tools with unfailing accuracy.

Cat Attacks and Drives Away Bear Threatening the Family

During their summer vacation in 1993, John and Cassandra Kraven headed for a cottage in the Adirondack Mountains in upstate New York with their two-year-old daughter, Jane—and their cat, Socks, named after President Clinton's feline. Actually, they had not wanted to bring the cat along, fearing that it would be too much bother, but a friend who was supposed to kitty-sit for them was called out of town at the last minute.

The first few days at the cottage had truly been relaxing, but their tranquility was nearly irreparably shattered when a black bear suddenly stormed into their yard. Before John or Cassandra could respond to the situation from within the freeze frame of shock that had enveloped them, the huge animal had grabbed their daughter and was shaking her in his snout as if she were a rag doll.

At that moment of ultimate horror, Socks leaped onto the bear's head, fastened his back claws into its flesh, and scratched at the brute's eyes until it dropped the baby in order to better direct its wrath at the attack cat.

Socks, beholding victory with Jane now released from the behemoth's jaws, jumped to the ground and deftly avoided the clumsy giant's swiping paws. Then, with the bear in hot pursuit, Socks ran into the forest.

John and Cassandra ran to their child, who, though crying in terror, seemed unharmed. Miraculously, the bear's teeth had snatched at the girl's playsuit and had not punctured her flesh. If it hadn't been for Socks' dramatic intervention, however, they were horrified to think of what might have happened.

After about two hours, Socks returned to the cabin, completely unharmed. The Kravens theorized that their courageous kitty led the bear on a merry chase deep into the forest, far away from their cabin, in order to ensure the return of peace and quiet for the remainder of their vacation.

John and Cassandra know that they owe their daughter's life to the bravery of a little cat that they didn't even want to bring with them on vacation.

Desperate Mother Fights to Protect Her Children
from an Angered Mama Bear

In the spring of 1993, Irene Govis, 32; her daughter Nevin, five; son Zachary, seven; neighbor's daughter, Natasha Winch, six; and the Govis' dog, Petie Bear, were hik-

One of the worst things you can do while out in the wilderness is come between a protective bear mother and her cubs.

ing to observe a beaver pond in the thickly wooded area outside North Bay, Ontario. They were all excited to have the opportunity to watch the beavers busy at work in their native habitat.

Zachary's enthusiasm got the better of him and he rushed ahead of the others on his bike, just missing a black bear and her cubs as they were emerging on the trail after snacking on some berry bushes.

Ever since she was a child, Irene had been warned never to mess with a Mama bear's ultra-protective instinct toward her cubs. She yelled at Zachary to freeze in his tracks. No more sudden movements that might be interpreted as threatening to this Big Mama's babies.

As Irene turned to reach for Nevin, the bear attacked her from behind, knocking her down, biting and clawing at her flesh. Irene felt terrible pain as the angry bear ripped mercilessly at her thighs and backside.

But far surpassing the pain that she was enduring was the horror that Irene felt when the bear dropped her and lunged for her five-year-old daughter. Irene screamed in anguish and fear when the massive jaws of the enraged creature closed around Nevin's neck, its fangs puncturing her jugular.

That was when Petie Bear charged the bear, snapping and growling at the monster that was mauling and biting the members of its human family. Although the dog was no match for the black bear, Petie Bear managed to distract the enraged beast long enough for Irene to throw herself protectively on top of her badly injured daughter.

Irene prayed that Nevin would not bleed to death from the slashing wounds in her throat before she could get her to the hospital.

And then the bear was once again ripping and biting at Irene's back and the helpless mother wondered for a terrible moment if any of them would survive long enough to get to those who would be able to provide major medical care for their wounds.

At last the perturbed mother bear felt it had exacted enough punishment to compensate for the perceived threat to her cubs, and she summoned her babies to her side and the three of them crashed off into the bushes from whence they had come.

Although her own wounds were severe and bleeding profusely, Irene, a registered nurse, ripped off her shirt and wrapped it around her daughter's neck to stem the bleeding. Then, calling upon all the bodily reserves that she could muster, she cradled Nevin in her arms and ran with Zachary and Natasha to the nearest home, where the startled owner called an ambulance.

Dr. Paul Preston, who treated the mother and daughter at North Bay Civic Hospital, said that little Nevin had come within a "millimeter" of death, while Irene had suffered 24 puncture wounds.

The powerful force of a mother's love had enabled Irene Govis to fight off a savage bear attack to save her children and to use her own body as a shield against its vicious claws and fangs as it tried to kill her little girl.

Remaining "Cool" Is Key to Surviving a Bear Attack

In June 2000, Second Lieutenant Jason Sansom of the Canadian Air Force and his wife, Jamie, were hiking in Glacier National Park when they suddenly noticed that two bears were about 15 yards ahead of them on the same trail. The Sansoms dropped back a bit, but one of the bears seemed curious about them and began to stalk them.

The couple decided to hide behind some trees and hope that the bear would leave them alone. Jason was behind a large V-shaped tree, and he reported later that he and the bear went around and around the tree for several minutes as it tried to claw him.

Eventually, the bear got hold of one of his legs, but only managed to rip Sansom's jeans.

Jamie, hiding behind a nearby tree, managed to throw something at the bear, and it was taken by surprise and appeared to back off. Taking advantage of the bear's sudden confusion, Jason made a dash for a more protected spot.

Now began a new game of hide and seek, as the bear stalked Jason around the larger tree for another 10 minutes.

Then it charged him.

Jason said that he immediately dropped to the ground and went into the fetal position. He tucked his fingers under him and gave up only the outer part of his arms.

The brute began walking around Sansom, curiously smelling him, licking him. And then it began biting Jason, just little nibbles at first, then methodically biting harder and harder.

From her vantage point, Jamie could see the bear toying with her husband, lying curled in the fetal position on the ground. Since she had no weapon of any kind, she wisely understood that the best thing she could do to help her husband was to run for help.

Fortunately, the bear paid no attention to Jamie, but its bites were becoming harder and deeper. Jason knew that he could not lie still and take the pain any longer. He managed to get his car keys out of his pocket, spread them out on his fingers as if they were some kind of knife or brass knuckles, and he struck the bear in the snout.

The sudden painful blow took the bear by surprise, and he backed up around 10 or 15 yards to review the situation.

> *Sansom had done exactly the right thing in keeping a calm and cool head.*

Sansom got up and ran to get behind some more trees. The bear followed, but at a distance. It still seemed to maintain a curiosity about Jason, but it would wax and wane. The bear would walk toward him, and then scratch some bark off a tree.

At last, the bear grew tired of the diversion to its routine day in the woods and began to walk back down the trail. When Jason estimated that it was about 40 yards away, he left the safety of the trees and ran back along the trail.

Later, park officials said that Sansom had done exactly the right thing in keeping a calm and cool head. Jason Sansom said that he had just tried to do his best to be resourceful so that he and Jamie would be able to survive. Sansom received over a dozen bite wounds on his arms and bruises on his chest, but the couple knew that the encounter could certainly have ended much worse.

Alaskan Biologist Sets Record for Surviving Two Bear Attacks

On March 21, 2005, Scott MacInnes, 51, a biologist who lived in Alaska, set a record for which one cannot imagine any contenders who would harbor the slightest envy. On that date, he became the first resident of that state who had survived two bear attacks.

The earlier attack occurred in 1967 while MacInnes was hiking on a popular trail in the Chugach National Forest. The biologist received wounds on his legs and an arm, but he was able to be on his feet in a few days.

The second mauling took place during his early morning jog when he encountered a brown bear and her cubs near his home in Soldotna in the Kenai Peninsula. An Alaska Department of Fish and Game spokesman summarized the incident by pointing out that there was the presence of a dog, food source, and a freshly killed moose near the trail. Such factors would certainly contribute to the likelihood of a bear attack.

In this instance, MacInnes received wounds on his head, neck, and abdomen, but was expected to make a full recovery.

Usually, wolves are shy animals that avoid human contact, but encounters, though rare, can be perilous.

Mano-a-Mano with a Wolf on New Year's Eve

Attacks by wolves against humans are rare, but they do occur, especially if the animal has become rabid.

On New Year's Eve 2005, Fred Desjarlais, 55, who worked for Cameco Corporation, which has a facility in Key Lake, about 400 miles north of Saskatoon, Saskatchewan, decided to jog the three miles back to camp instead of taking the shuttle bus. It was 7:00 P.M., relatively early in the evening, and he was wearing thick winter clothing, so what could be the harm in an after dark jog?

Fred had not run far when he heard something running behind him. He looked behind him and saw a large wolf come up out of the ditch. The wolf began to circle Fred, and the lone runner hoped that the big guy hadn't brought the pack with him.

The wolf was alone, but when Fred shouted at the animal, hoping to frighten it away, the beast lunged for Fred's face with its jaws wide open.

Fred side-stepped the wolf and shouted again, trying to end the confrontation.

The wolf reared up on it hind legs and looked down on Fred, who was amazed at how large the creature's head was and how wide its jaws could open.

When the wolf lunged again, it bit Fred on the shoulder, and the two combatants fell to the ground, wrestling with one another in the snow. Because Fred was wearing a heavy coat and several layers of clothing on his upper body, none of the wolf's bites penetrated to his skin, but then his attacker managed to deliver two very painful bites to Fred's pelvic area that did rip through an area where he wore lighter clothing.

Angered and in a great deal of pain, Fred managed to get on the wolf's back and pin him down in a headlock. He had no idea how long he could maintain his hold, but fortunately some fellow employees in a shuttle bus spotted the desperate struggle and came to his aid.

The wolf ran away, but it was tracked the next day, shot, and tested for rabies.

Fred was taken to a medical facility at the camp where he received stitches for his wounds in the pelvic area. The bites on his upper body did not penetrate his coat or the several layers of clothing he wore, but the vicious attacker's teeth left a good number of bruises. Later, he was taken by air ambulance to a hospital in Saskatoon for additional treatment.

Battling Rattlesnakes Will Not Be Added to the Competition Categories for Mrs. America

On August 30, 2007, the Mrs. America contestants who had gathered in Tucson, Arizona, for the national pageant were competing in horseshoes and team pinning at the Tanque Verde Ranch.

As Mrs. Tennessee, Christina Ryan, was coming down a flight of stairs on her way to a rehearsal, she recognized a deadly brown recluse spider on the ground and instinctively backed away from it. Unfortunately with her complete focus on the spider, Mrs. Ryan didn't hear or see the rattlesnake directly behind her.

After Mrs. Ryan was bitten by the snake, her screams alerted Mrs. Iowa, Taryn Schuyler, who is a trained nurse. She pulled the fang out of Christina leg and helped calm her—and the other ladies, as well, who were now very much on the watch for rattlesnakes.

It became a united effort as Mrs. Iowa began preliminary treatment of the bite, Mrs. Wisconsin called 911, and Mrs. Mississippi helped calm Mrs. Tennessee.

Christina Ryan was taken to the hospital and spent several hours in intensive care, receiving injections of antivenin. She swore that she would still complete in the pageant, even if she had to hobble across the stage.

Birthday Boy Remains Calm When Mountain Lion Crashes Party

The family was celebrating Paul John Schalow's tenth birthday with an outing in Arizona's Tonto National Forest. Paul, known as "PJ," loves riding ATVs, and the

10 adults, plus PJ and his cousin Brittany, 9, spent the whole morning of March 8, 2008, exploring the picturesque area.

Around 2:00 P.M., the family stopped to have lunch on a sandy beach next to a river. That was when an uninvited guest arrived.

A female mountain lion sauntered into their camp and began to focus her attention on the Birthday Boy.

The more experienced adults in the group suspected that the lioness had to be rabid to approach the party in such a casual manner. Mountain lions are by nature primarily nocturnal and very shy of humans.

PJ and Brittany heard everyone telling them to freeze, to remain completely motionless.

Demonstrating remarkable courage and self-control, PJ became a living statue—even when the lioness scratched his back with its claws.

Next the mountain lion put its paw on PJ's shoulder and opened its mouth, attempting to fit its jaws around the boy's head. To the terrified family members watching the scene, it was very apparent that the lion had plans to carry PJ off as its evening dinner.

Fortunately, PJ's uncle had brought along a handgun, and he slowly worked his way to his vehicle to get it. PJ's grandfather, Newton Smith, told him to shoot the animal while it had backed slightly away from PJ and was trying to decide if it could fit the boy's head in its mouth.

One well-placed shot ended the incredibly tense situation, and Grandpa Smith gutted the mountain lion in order to have its carcass examined by wildlife officials. After tissue tests had been conducted, the family was informed that the mountain lion had an advanced stage of rabies.

Newton Smith remained convinced that if the children had screamed and ran, rather than standing stock still, the mountain lion would have gone into attack mode and clawed and bitten not only PJ and Brittany but quite possibly several other members of the family as well.

The somber news from the doctors who had conducted the tests on the female lion was that all those who had been exposed to the erratic behaving interloper to the birthday party would have to begin a series of six rabies shots to be administered over a period of several weeks.

Florida Teenager Said God Was with Him in Struggle with Huge Bull Alligator

Kasey Edwards, 18, is a Florida man who had grown up around alligators. He remembers as a kid when he and his friends went swimming, the alligators stayed on the bank or went after some fish and left humans alone. But times have changed, he commented, and the environment for the gators has become more competitive as humans

Alligators have powerful jaw muscles and can bite down with over a ton of pressure, enough to easily snap and crush bones and rip off limbs.

squeeze in on their territory. That is why he doesn't blame the nearly 12-foot-long monster that took most of his left arm off on June 22, 2008.

Edwards and some male and female friends had spent the day partying at Vero Beach on Saturday, June 21. He strongly denied that anyone was intoxicated when they left the beach around 6:00 P.M. and decided to hang out along a canal that fed into Lake Okeechobee, the large freshwater lake between Miami and Orlando.

It was about 2:00 A.M. when Edwards decided to jump in the canal for a swim. A number of his friends tried to talk him out of it, because they had spotted alligators in the area. Kasey dismissed their concerns by reminding him that he had been swimming with alligators ever since he was a little boy. They had never bothered him.

Edwards dove into the canal and swam across to a row of buoys on the opposite bank. It was then that he heard his friends yelling and screaming, but he thought they were just cheering him on or telling him to swim back.

The next thing Kasey knew was that something had clamped down hard on his left arm, and he was looking into the terrible jaws of an 11.5-foot, 600-pound bull gator. Kasey's right hand clutched the rope of a buoy, and he knew that he must not let loose or the gator would next try to pull him under in a "death roll," the creature's technique of dragging its prey underwater to drown it.

Edwards said later that he knew that God was with him and would save his life. Although the huge gator pulled him under five times, Edwards maintained his desperate hold on the buoy rope and he was always able to surface to keep from drowning. He knew with all his being that God was helping him keep his head above water.

Kasey heard a harsh cracking sound, and the alligator released him long enough to swallow his left arm.

The realization that he was missing a good portion of his left arm hadn't quite settled in on Kasey's consciousness, and he began to swim as fast as he could to reach his friends.

He had not been able to get too far before the big bull gator had come back to complete his main course. The massive brute bunted Edwards in the stomach, knocking the wind out of him, intending to sink him beneath the waters of the canal.

Kasey Edwards had had enough. He plunged his fingers into one of the gator's eyes and gouged with all his might.

Again, he said, God was on his side, and that painful eyeball gouging was enough to discourage further attacks from the bull gator.

Edwards paddled back to shore, and two of his friends pulled him out of the canal and wrapped a shirt around what remained of Kasey's left arm and apply pressure to slow the bleeding until a medevac helicopter arrived to transport Edwards to Holmes Regional Medical Center.

Although the monster alligator that had attacked Kasey was hunted down and killed, his arm, found in the animal's stomach during a necropsy, was in no condition to be reattached. However, after a surgery to clean up the six-inch stump remaining of his left arm, doctors are confident that Kasey Edwards will be an excellent candidate for a prosthetic limb.

Sharks

Dolphins and Angels Saved Her from a Shark Attack

It has been 40 years now, but Sherry Steiger's "shark toes" still occasionally shed the entire nail, and they remain more sensitive to pain than any of her other toes. But she doesn't complain. She was able to keep her foot, her leg, her entire body—thanks to the timely intervention of dolphins who protected her from a shark attack.

In 1968, under the sponsorship of a Lutheran church in Austin, Texas, Sherry assisted in planning and organizing a spiritual retreat for 40 teenagers to be held just off the coast of South Padre Island in the Gulf of Mexico. They had traveled together some distance in a caravan of cars and vans, and when the caravan arrived. The weather was hot, sunny, and sultry—perfect for enjoying the beach and the ocean.

The head pastor and several adult chaperones were more familiar with this part of the country than Sherry was. In fact, it was the first time that she had ever seen an ocean.

Sherry recalled the events of that awful day of the shark attack:

"The next day, during free time, I made a beeline straight for the beach. There was a perfect blue sky and the water was gorgeous. After goofing around with some of the kids in the water, I parted company from the crowd and set out for a good swim.

"I had been a lifeguard at a well-known summer resort, and I had always been a strong swimmer, so I eagerly swam out beyond the breaking waves. Lost in the beauty of the moment, I rolled over to my back and just floated, noticing every wisp of cloud that accented the sky and the seagulls overhead in their endless frolic. Feeling the caress of the warm sun on my body, I drifted off—literally. It was as though I had fallen into a meditative trance—and when I returned to my senses, I realized the current had carried me so far out to sea that the shoreline was barely discernible.

> "Big fish *was all that came to mind as I tried to make out what it was that was hitting me with such force.*"

"Although I realized that I had a long swim ahead of me, I was not concerned, for I knew I had the endurance to accomplish the distance without undue effort. I firmly told myself not to panic, to start swimming in the direction that most of the waves were heading. If I ended up on another part of the beach, I would simply walk back to my group. Getting to shore was the main objective.

"I swam steadily back to shore, occasionally treading water to make sure of my bearings. Soon, thankfully, I was able to see the shore. But I knew that I was still fighting against a strong current that seemed just as determined to keep me out to sea as I was to reach the beach.

"I was treading water to get my bearings again when something huge slammed against my legs.

"Again something hit me with such force that I was swept off balance.

"Another jolt and I was screaming for help.

"My training as a lifeguard had taught me not to panic, but it was all that I could do to stay above water.

"Whatever it was, it kept on whapping me, and I went under the waves several times. I kept attempting to swim toward shore, but I was being battered back to sea with every attempt.

"*Big fish* was all that came to mind as I tried to make out what it was that was hitting me with such force. Or perhaps big *fishes*, for there seemed to be two kinds of skin hitting against me—one very rough, the other smooth.

"At last I was near enough to shore so that someone heard my screams for help. I went under, came up, and saw a friend about 10 feet away from me, coming to rescue me. Almost the instant I spotted him, a look of absolute terror came over his face.

"I was going under for the third time. I couldn't get air.

"I couldn't swim. I just kept being hit. Then I passed out.

"The next thing I knew I was in some wonderful stranger's strong arms, being lifted out of the water. As I came to, I saw that I was covered with blood from head to toe.

"I was brought immediately to the first aid ranger station, where I interrupted a long line of people awaiting treatment. The ranger took one look at me in the arms of my rescuer and cleared the emergency table. I thought the man who was already on the table looked in worse condition than I—he had a sword from a stingray piercing his entire thigh.

"The ranger looked me over carefully, wiping away the blood and examining the scraped areas. When his attention centered on my feet, he yelled to the other rangers in the first aid station, 'Shark! Clear the beaches. Put out the shark alert signs. And get to the loudspeakers. Now!'

"Then he turned to me and said, 'My dear, you are one lucky woman to be alive.'

"I had been scraped from head to toe by the sandpaper-like skin of a shark, he explained. 'And look at those shark teeth in your toes. Do you want them when I get them out?'

"I declined the offer of the trophy. Later, I was transported to a hospital for shots and further examination. Then I was released and solemnly informed once again how fortunate I was.

"When I arrived back at the camp where my teenage charges had pitched their tents, my reception was less than enthusiastic. Of course everyone was thankful that I was safe, but, at the same time, they were disappointed by the news that the rangers had declared the beach off limits for several days because of my shark attack.

"The rangers theorized that the monster had been taking its time, casually bumping up against me, nibbling at me, preparatory to making its final strike. However, before that fatal lunge could be made, something else in the water—something of which I was dimly aware—had caused the shark to change its mind.

"It took more than six months before I could wear a shoe on the foot where the ranger had pulled out the shark's teeth.

"Later, as I was recounting the incident to some friends, I said that I had been aware of a couple of large marine bodies other than the shark in the water with me. One of the group who was listening to my account was a noted authority on dolphins. He stated emphatically that it was most likely dolphins that had saved me from the shark.

"'Sherry, I believe your guardian angel was a dolphin,' he said. 'My research indicates that dolphins are among the few creatures that will take on a shark.'

"He went on to say that since sharks' teeth had been taken from my toes, the likelihood of the blood from the scrapes on my body and the bites on my feet drawing other sharks to the area was overwhelming. He continued to tell of a few examples in his work with dolphins in which a dolphin or a group of dolphins had moved in on a shark to ward off an attack.

"I sensed instantly that he was correct. A dolphin had saved my life. I had always been thankful to God for the unnamed person who pulled me out of the water. But for me to have survived to that point, I believe that he had already sent an angel to protect me in the water.

"Now I consider it likely that both of my rescuers, both in human and dolphin form, were my guardian angels that saved my life.

Being Eaten Alive, Dolphins Appeared to Drive away the Great White

In July 1996, Martin Richardson, a 29-year-old adventurer from Colchester, England, left the dive boat when he spotted three bottlenose dolphins in the Red Sea off Egypt's Sinai Peninsula. He thought it would be wonderful to join them and play with them in the water, but they disappeared when he entered the sea.

He was floating on his back and relaxing in the warm waters when a Great White shark suddenly emerged from the sea and clamped its monstrous jaws around his shoulder.

That very first bite punctured a lung and tore away part of a rib and some muscle.

Richardson tried to swim for the dive boat and he shouted for help, but his friends were over a hundred yards away.

Within a few seconds, the monster struck at his left side, once again tearing away flesh with its massive jaws.

Richardson did not wish his final resting place to be in the belly of the ugly brute. He punched down on the shark's head and nose as hard as he could, and once again the sea beast released him.

Reeling from shock, Richardson did his best to swim away from all the blood in the water that had poured from his terrible wounds, but the vicious predator tore into him a third time.

Somehow, even though the third strike had ripped away even more flesh and exposed Richardson's spine, the Englishman, fighting desperately for his survival, managed to punch the shark away once again.

But seconds later, the hideous, beady-eyed monster was on him again, chewing flesh from his chest.

It was at that awful moment, Richardson said, that he prayed to God for a miracle. He shouted to the heavens that he had never before asked for very much, but now his life was in his hands.

Richardson knew the next strike from the Great White would finish him off. The pain was beyond anything that he could imagine, and he was so weak that he could barely stay afloat.

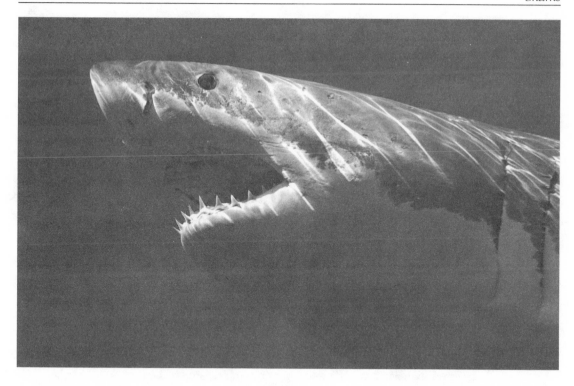

The 1975 movie *Jaws* exaggerated the capabilities of a Great White Shark, but the real-life predator is nothing to sneeze at.

And then God answered his plea for a miracle by sending the three bottlenose dolphins that had first attracted Richardson into the warm waters of the Red Sea.

The dolphins formed a protective ring around him and beat the water with their tails and fins in order to frighten the shark away from its prey. And they continued their defensive tactic until Richardson's friends in the diving boat were able to pull alongside him in an inflatable boat.

The Recanati Center for Maritime Studies at the University of Haifa in Israel stated that such a defensive measure by dolphins is common when they are protecting their young from predators.

Associated Press reports said that doctors at the hospital in el-Tur, Egypt, placed 200 stitches in Richardson's left shoulder, stomach, and back. Attending physicians told him that he had lost 11 pounds of flesh to the Great White and that he could anticipate a hospital stay of at least a week. Miraculously, the doctors informed him that their prognosis suggested that he would experience a full recovery.

Later, when they measured the teeth marks on his body, it was estimated that the beast had a jaw span of nearly two feet and was probably about 14 feet long.

Richardson told the media that he had always loved dolphins—and now he owed his life to them.

Dolphins Provided Safety while Shark Attack Victim Made It to Shore

On August 28, 2007, Todd Endris experienced a miracle very similar to that of Martin Richardson. Todd, 24, was the owner of Monterey Aquarium Services, and he had decided to take a day off to enjoy surfing with some friends at Marina State Park off Monterey, California. He recalled that he had no warning when a shark, estimated at 12 to 15 feet, hit him.

Endris was sitting on his surfboard when the attack occurred, so the monster was unable to get his razor-toothed jaws around both the surfer and his surfboard. On its second pass, though, those terrible jaws clamped down on both Endris and his board, peeling the skin off his back.

On the third pass, the shark attempted to swallow Endris's right leg, which, the surfer stated, was actually a good thing, because he was able to kick it in the head and snout until it released him.

It was at that time that some dolphins, which the surfers had previously noticed playing in the surf, appeared to form a protective circle around Todd. While the dolphins kept the brute at bay, Endris was able to get back on his board and catch a wave that took him to shore.

After Endris made it to the beach, a number of lifeguards took one look at the surfer's mangled body and told his friends to prepare for the likelihood that he would not survive the vicious attack.

Fortunately, one of Todd's friends, Brian Simpson, was an X-ray technician in a hospital trauma center and focused on his training when he saw the blood pumping out of Endris' leg, which had been bitten to the bone. Simpson used his surf leash as a tourniquet and slowed the blood loss.

A medevac helicopter flew Todd to a hospital where a surgeon determined that the victim of the shark attack had probably lost half of his blood. Surgery, doctors commented later, was like putting together a jigsaw puzzle.

Six weeks later, Todd Endris was back surfing at Marina State Park.

Sea Lions Risked Their Own Lives to Save Two Humans

The DeGraffenreid brothers had certainly not planned on their small fishing boat sinking on that late spring afternoon in 1990, and they only had water-ski vests to keep them afloat in the turbulent, shark-infested waters of Channel Islands National Park off the Southern California coast. Daryl told Gary that he would swim for an island several miles away in an effort to bring help.

As he swam, Daryl noticed that he had attracted the attention of a baby sea lion. After a few moments, the little guy came so close to him that the two made direct eye contact.

Daryl suddenly had the seemingly crazy thought that rather than simply swimming beside him, the sea lion could go for help. When the creature continued to stare at him, Daryl suddenly found himself shouting, "Go get some help!"

He may have felt momentarily ridiculous for telling his troubles to a baby sea lion, but he had to wonder if it was only his imagination when the little fellow turned and quickly swam away—just as if it had truly understood that the human struggling in the water needed some big-time assistance.

Daryl lifted his head above the waterline for a moment and saw that he really did need help. Sharks had begun to circle him.

And one of them was monstrous. He estimated that it was more than 20 feet long.

Daryl was getting weaker by the second. The swells kept coming at him, and he was going under each time. He was beginning to lose consciousness. And the sharks were circling closer and closer.

Then, miraculously, 15 to 20 sea lions suddenly appeared to form a wall of protection around him.

Knowing that sea lions themselves were a favorite meal for sharks, Daryl marveled at the bravery of these creatures that had created a living barrier between him and the toothy sea marauders.

Sea lions often fall prey to sharks, and so when a group of sea lions rescued the DeGraffenreid brothers from shark-infested waters, the feat was doubly heroic.

Somehow, the combined forces of such a large number of sea lions managed to drive the sharks away. But in spite of the bravery of his marine benefactors, Daryl found himself steadily sinking beneath the waves as his ski vest became increasingly waterlogged.

But as Daryl said later, God must have had something very special in mind for the DeGraffenreid brothers, for just then a Coast Guard boat with Gary on board arrived to pull him out of the sea.

In reviewing the remarkable case of the band of sea lions that gathered to save Daryl DeGraffenreid from a shark attack, park ranger Don Morris said that while it was common for curious sea lions to swim up to humans in the water, he had never before heard of an instance wherein the sea-dwelling mammals had banded together to assist one of their landlocked cousins.

You Need Not Fear a Shark in Hawaii If It Is Your "Aumakua"

Traditionally, the words *shark* and *safety* don't go together, but in Hawaiian Thelma Spencer's case, it was literally a shark that *saved* a family.

In 1991, while Brad and Sherry Steiger were lecturing in Hawaii, Thelma told them that when she was very young, her parents would sit and, as they used to say, "talk story" or, in other words, sit around the campfire and share different personal experiences from when they were younger. Of all the many wonderful stories Thelma's mom and dad shared with her, it is easy to understand how this particular adventure made a life-long impression on her.

"Mother told us that our family *aumakua*, or guardian spirit, was the 'mano,' or shark, and that when we were in the water, should we ever get into trouble, the shark would protect us," Thelma recounted.

"Needless to say, 'aumakua' or not, I was not going to make it a point to get real close to any sharks!"

Thelma said that the "aumakua" was a serious matter, and to prove that what her family had told her about the shark being their aumakua was true, she described her mom's firsthand experience.

A long time before Oahu, Hawaii, became commercialized, when Thelma's mom was just a little girl, she had gone fishing with her cousins and uncle. The fishing was usually better at night, so they all went out in the family canoe for the big catch.

They went out as far from the shore as they could and still be able to see the flicker of light from the lantern left burning on the porch for a marker. Mom's Aunt Tutu, who stayed behind, was sitting there on the porch, with the lantern, rocking in her chair and waiting for their safe return.

Mom said that she and her cousins were really having a great time catching fish and playing around. They must have been playing around with a little too much fervor, because the canoe started to rock.

No matter how much Uncle chastised them and warned them about the danger, they kept on, and the boat got to rocking real bad. No one was listening to Uncle or paying attention to his warning, so over the canoe went! When the canoe flipped, everyone went into the water.

The night was extremely dark, with no visible moon, so it was difficult to see. Not only that, but the water wasn't very warm, either.

The first thing was to make sure everyone was there. All were accounted for, so Uncle told them to try to stay together and start swimming toward shore. Well, it's a good thing they could all swim, but not a good thing that they now realized they could not see the shore.

In their folly, they hadn't been aware that the canoe had drifted out farther than the eye could keep sight of the lantern. It was so dark that they couldn't tell which direction to swim to head for shore. They were completely disoriented.

Suddenly, one of them yelled out that something had just brushed past her and that whatever it was, was very, very big! Everyone else started to thrash around the water in fear to try and keep away from whatever "it" was. Then one by one, each of them started yelling too because they each felt something swim past them.

Whatever was brushing against them appeared to be swimming around them in a circle. It continued to circle and circle. By now, everyone was really in a panic, as they knew they were far enough out in the ocean that there could be sharks—big sharks.

Uncle tried to regain control and calm everyone down. He told them all to come together and hold hands, forming a circle in the water. Remaining quiet and staying there in a circle must have been quite a challenge when the temptation would be to take off, but they listened and did as Uncle said.

In the stillness, Uncle said he was able to see a fin circling and circling them. Instead of becoming more fearful, Uncle had the sense that something else was happening. He could tell for sure that it was a shark. But each time it would swim around them, it seemed to brush up against them and then do the circle around them again.

> *Uncle told all the nieces and nephews to follow him and the shark. What other choice did they have?*

The shark continued this behavior, when Uncle finally said, "I think the shark knows we don't know which direction is the shore and he's trying to tell us that he will show us the way if we follow him."

Uncle told all the nieces and nephews to follow him and the shark. What other choice did they have?

Finally, they braved it and started to follow the shark, staying as close together as they could in a tight group. They were not being attacked; that became evident. So they swam and swam, following the shark. The shark would swim awhile, then encircle them again to be sure they were all there, and then swim some more, leading the way.

Following this pattern, soon they were able to see that the shark was leading them right—they could see the shore and the flickering light of the lantern on the porch! Then they really bore full speed ahead.

By the time they all reached shore, Aunt Tutu was standing there waiting for them. By now, she knew trouble was brewing and she had been praying for their safety.

Once everyone was safely on land, the shark made one final circle, as if to say goodbye, and off he swam. That was when Aunt Tutu told them all that the shark was the family aumakua—and you can bet, they believed her!

Animal Rescuers

A Dolphin Lifeguard Off Land's End

In the early 1970s, Bob Holborn, a plumber turned deep sea diver, trained "Beaky," a Cornish dolphin, to become an accomplished lifeguard. According to writer Dennis Bardens, the amiable sea mammal was responsible for the saving of many lives in the waters off Land's End.

Holborn tells of the time when a sailor fell off the side of a boat and Beaky held him up in the water for several hours until help finally arrived.

On another occasion, one of Holborn's friends was diving off Land's End when a sudden thick fog separated him from his boat. Beaky saved his life by actually guiding the man to the steps of his diving boat.

Man's best friend ... and angel in a dog's body?
Some people may think so.

On April 20, 1976, an accomplished diver named Keith Monery found himself in a desperate situation off Penzance, Cornwall. He had shed his life jacket after it had become filled with water and he had discarded his 15-pound weight belt, but he was still having great difficulty reaching the surface.

The sea had become rough, and Monery was rapidly nearing exhaustion. Although a friend had spotted the diver's distress signal—a clenched fist waved frantically to and fro—and had entered the water to attempt a rescue, another "friend" was much quicker.

Beaky streaked past the human rescuer, then got underneath the exhausted Monery and kept pushing him upward until he reached the surface and could be rescued.

Saved by His Dog and Two Angels in Doggy Disguise

Little Ernest Mann, a frail two-year-old who barely weighed 18 pounds, wandered away from his family's cabin in the rugged hills west of Albuquerque, New Mexico. After a frantic two-hour search of the area immediately surrounding their summer cabin, James and Angeles Mann were forced to conclude that their tiny son had gone for an unauthorized walk with Ivy, their spotted white dog. They had no choice other than to call Sheriff Ed Craig of Cibola County, who quickly organized a search party of deputies, state police, and volunteers.

Mann, a high school mathematics teacher, and his wife struggled not to allow their emotions to disintegrate into panic. Although the temperature had nearly reached 70 degrees on that June day in 1989, by 8:00 P.M. it had dropped to the mid-50s. Soon it would be in the 40s. Before dawn it would lower into the 30s.

And frail, little Ernest was wearing only a thin cotton shirt and pants when he strayed away from the cabin and into the woods.

After a few hours of searching, the Manns felt their hearts sink when they learned that trained bloodhounds were unable to pick up the scent of either Ernest or Ivy. They tried not to think of the awful possibilities that their son and their faithful dog had been set upon by a mountain lion, a black bear, or coyotes. What if the two of them lay injured, bleeding, freezing to death? James and Angeles Mann spent a night of terror, trying their best to keep their hopes as high as possible.

By morning the search party had grown to more than 100 officers and volunteers. There were searchers on foot, on horseback, and overhead in an air force helicopter. But there appeared to be no trace of the boy or his dog.

Then, about 10:00 A.M., a most peculiar thing occurred to a searcher who was walking through a forest clearing. A black dog approached him and gently placed its jaws over his wrist. The searcher was wise enough to understand that the strange dog wanted him to come with him.

The searcher signaled to others in his group, and they followed the black dog directly to the spot where tiny Ernest Mann lay sleeping between Ivy and another stray dog. When the black dog was certain that the searchers had seen the lost boy, it, too, snuggled up next to the others.

Ernest sat up, frightened, dirty, confused, but very happy to see the party of searchers surrounding them. Sheriff Craig said that the two-year-old cried out, "Doggies! Doggies! Warm, warm!" as he hugged the three dogs. The little boy was literally smothered in their fur.

Sheriff Craig went on to state that the three dogs had arranged themselves in a tight circle around Ernest, keeping him snug and warm throughout the long, freezing night. The sheriff said that there was no other way that the tiny two-year-old could have survived.

Interestingly, as Sheriff Craig carried Ernest to the patrol car, the two stray dogs ran off, as if they understood that they were no longer needed now that the little human was safe.

James and Angeles Mann, together with Sheriff Craig and the unselfish, tireless searchers, agreed that Ernest owed his life to the faithful family dog and the two stray mutts that Ivy had somehow managed to enlist to help keep her little master warm until human help arrived.

Sheriff Craig commented that never in all his years in law enforcement, including many searches for people lost in the wilderness, had he ever witnessed anything like those three dogs huddling around little Ernest to make certain that he survived the freezing cold.

Battling Burt, Attack Parrot Supreme

Seventeen-year-old Tawnya Sutherland of Kearns, Utah, came home on the afternoon of February 6, 1994, to find herself confronted by every young woman's worst nightmare. She was home alone, and she had just discovered a burly stranger in the kitchen.

The blonde high school junior screamed at the intruder to get out of her family's house, but the big brute simply glared at her, making it clear that he had other plans.

Tawnya quickly sized up the situation and concluded that at five-feet-six, 125 pounds, she offered little threat to the stranger who was a six-footer weighing well over 200 pounds.

As he began to move toward her, Tawnya was dimly aware of the sound of Burt, her Amazon parrot, whistling for her, just as he always did whenever he heard her come home.

However, this fateful afternoon, she had much more serious matters on her mind than attending to her bird. She figured that she would soon be fighting for her very survival.

In desperation, Tawnya threw a glass at the intruder, but he easily sidestepped the missile.

As he closed in on her, she managed to kick him in the groin, but he only grunted and seemed annoyed, rather than hurt.

The brute reached out to grab her shirt, and he punched her hard in the ribs.

> *Burt had been her constant feathered buddy for five years, and Tawnya knew that he was jealous and protective of her.*

Later, Tawnya said that at this point she felt that something too horrible to imagine was about to happen to her.

And then, incredibly, that was when little one-pound Burt became suddenly transformed into a vicious attack parrot. Squawking a fierce battle cry, he flew into the kitchen, landed on the thug's shoulder, and began biting at his neck.

Burt had been her constant feathered buddy for five years, and Tawnya knew that he was jealous and protective of her, but what could he do against a creep 200 times his size? She feared for her brave little parrot, because it seemed as though the intruder would be able to crush him with one solid blow from his heavy hands.

But Burt had launched a kamikaze attack, and it was obvious that nothing would be able to make him let loose of the lout who threatened his beloved owner.

Regardless of how the intruder twisted and turned, the enraged parrot could not be shaken loose of his clawhold on his shoulder. And those claws and beak were drawing blood.

The teenager marveled as she witnessed yet another remarkable transformation. The big, brutish thug had become a whining crybaby right before her eyes.

When he finally managed to break away from the world of pain inflicted by the parrot's unyielding beak and claws, he burst out the back door, cursing his bad luck as he ran away.

Satisfied that the intruder had been vanquished, Burt flew to Tawnya, as if to see for himself that she had not been harmed. The grateful teenager could see by his heaving chest that her brave Burt was exhausted from the awful struggle, and she began to quiet him and reassure him that he had heroically saved the day.

Later, Deputy Jim Potter of the Salt Lake County sheriff's office stated that never, in his twenty years of police work, had he ever heard of a bird that went to the aid of its owner. Brave little Burt had saved Tawnya from great possible harm.

Blitzen the Bird Dog Kept a Cougar at Bay

On a late winter's morning in 1994, Heidi Kahlke of West Jordan, Utah, was horrified to witness a cougar jump over her fence and land just inches away from the spot where her neighbor's daughter, eight-year-old Becky Biggs, was playing in the Kahlkes' yard.

From time to time, especially during the winter months, hungry mountain lions ventured down from the mountains to scavenge food from small towns and villages. Unfortunately, on occasion, the cougars will pounce on a small dog or a cat—or even attack a human. The big cat had apparently spotted little Becky playing in the yard and added her to its select menu.

But before the cougar could lift a paw to harm Becky, Blitzen, her constant canine companion, a 10-year-old Hungarian bird dog, put a stop to any intentions the lion might have had of dining on his beloved mistress. Leaping in rage at the unwelcome invader from the mountains, Blitzen startled the hungry cougar and sent it sprawling under the Kahlkes' pickup.

Here it was that the brave Blitzen kept the cougar cornered for two hours until police and wildlife officials arrived and knocked the big cat out with a tranquilizer dart. The cougar was carted back to the mountains where it belonged, and Blitzen gained a new neighborhood title: Hero Hound Dog.

Police Dog Saved His Human Partner from an Icy Death

Thunder, a German shepherd police dog, was inducted into the Wisconsin Pet Hall of Fame in 1996 for the heroic act of pulling Sheriff's Deputy Stanley Wontor out of an icy river.

Deputy Wontor and Thunder, his faithful K-9 partner of seven years, had been pursuing a burglary suspect across a 20-foot-wide stretch of frozen river when the lawman crashed through the ice four feet from the snow-covered bank.

Wontor could feel the river's current pulling him under the ice-covered surface. He was certain that it would be the end of him.

He realized that his only lifeline to survival was Thunder's leash. He had wrapped the leash around his wrist when they ran in pursuit of the burglary suspect, and he still gripped it in his hand.

Fortunately, the dog was powerful enough to stand his ground at the edge of the hole in the ice, and he had planted his paws solidly against the sudden pressure on his collar, thereby providing an anchor for Wontor against the current.

> *Wontor could feel the river's current pulling him under the ice-covered surface. He was certain that it would be the end of him.*

The Deputy knew very well that Thunder could not withstand the pull on his leash and collar for too much longer. If the two of them did not act soon, it would soon be too late for both of them.

"Pull, buddy! Pull!" he yelled.

The command may have been a new one, but Thunder seemed clearly to understand that his partner did not belong in the freezing cold water of the ice-covered river.

The big German shepherd dug his powerful paws deep into the snow and began to inch backward up the bank, slowly dragging Deputy Wontor toward the edge of the hole in the ice.

Summoning hidden reserves of strength, Wontor managed to climb out of what had seemed for several terrible minutes to have been destined to become his icy coffin.

While it is certain that the 55-year-old law enforcement officer, the father of three grown children, thought about his family and gave thanks for his rescue, he also remembered being "mad as a hornet."

Although he was soaked to the skin and freezing, he told Thunder that the burglary suspect was not going to get away from them. Especially after he had nearly lost his life in pursuit of the man.

Amazingly, 10 minutes later, Deputy Wontor and Thunder had the suspect under arrest. Later, the man led police officers to a cache of over $40,000 in stolen snowmobile parts, and he was subsequently convicted for burglarizing a Marinette, Wisconsin, sports center.

Reflecting upon his narrow escape from the icy river, Deputy Wontor said that as long as he lived, he would know that he owed his life to Thunder, his faithful partner and wonder dog.

Priscilla the Pig Saved a Boy from Drowning

Pigs suffer from countless inaccurate, centuries-old stereotypes that portray them as dirty, stupid, lazy animals. On the contrary, they are only as dirty as their environment dictates, clean enough to be considered ideal house pets by some contented pig owners. And when it comes to a survey of the IQ of barnyard animals, the pig will quite likely be found near the very highest mark for native intelligence.

In 1995, Priscilla, a three-month-old pig, became the first animal inducted into the Texas Veterinary Medical Association's Pet Hall of Fame when she saved an 11-year-old boy from drowning.

Priscilla had been swimming with her owner in a Houston lake when they heard the frightened cries of Anthony Melton, who had panicked and begun to drown. The little pig responded at once and began to paddle toward the screaming boy.

Once she was next to him, Priscilla nudged Anthony with her snout, grunting and signaling for him to grab on to her harness.

Perhaps it was the extraordinary circumstances of a paddling pig bobbing next to him that banished the boy's panic and allowed him to focus on the animal's obvious pantomimed communication. He reached out to grab hold of the pig's harness, and Priscilla towed him straight to the safety of the shore.

Pot-bellied pigs are highly intelligent and, many say, make good pets. That's especially true of Honeymoon the pig, who saved her owners from a house fire.

Pot-bellied Pig Saves Family
from Fire while Watchdogs Slept

Pam and Fred Abma of Ramsey, New Jersey, bought Honeymoon, a pot-bellied pig, on their wedding trip as a gift to each other. As it turned out, Honeymoon was definitely a gift that kept on giving.

On February 2, 1998, about 8:00 A.M., a fire broke out in the laundry room of the Ramsey home. Fred and Pam were still sleeping, but Honeymoon, now a robust 18-month-old, 100-pound porker, kept scratching at their bedroom door until they were awakened.

When the couple went to investigate Honeymoon's persistent bother at their door, they discovered smoke filling the house.

Fortunately the local fire department quickly extinguished the flames, but the Abmas were pretty disgusted with their two watchdogs, who slept through the entire potentially tragic event.

There was no question in Pam Abma's mind that it was Honeymoon who had saved everyone's bacon. "She was the only one who smelled the smoke. Our dogs were clueless," she told reporters.

Fred said that he had heard that pigs were very intelligent. Some of them, he commented wryly, were obviously much smarter than dogs. "And it was lucky for us."

Cows Rally to Save a Kindly Farmer from a Raging Bull

In August 1996, a number of newspapers in Great Britain carried the remarkable story of how a farmer's fair treatment of his cattle came full circle when the bovine ladies worked together to save him from death at the hooves of an enraged bull.

Fifty-four-year-old Donald Mottram had driven his four-wheel bike into a field on his farm in Meidrim, near Carmarthen, Wales, to give a calf an injection.

Before he devoted himself totally to the task, Mottram checked the location of a three-year-old French Charolais bull that he had on loan for breeding his cattle, a mixture of Welsh Blacks and Aberdeen Angus, and saw that the 3,300-pound brute was at least 300 yards away. Satisfied that the bull was quiet and uninterested in his presence, Mottram directed his attention to the injured calf that he hoped would one day become a member of the breeding herd of 90 cattle that he kept on his 78-acre farm.

He was shepherding the calf when he suddenly felt a "horrendous thump" on his back. Mottram and his vehicle were tossed 30 feet away.

He landed on his back, and as he lay there in a daze, he found himself looking up into the snorting, enraged face of the bull.

The powerful young bull began tramping on the farmer, stomping on his chest and shoulders. Mottram tried to turn away, but the huge animal kicked him into unconsciousness.

Later, he estimated that he had been unconscious for 90 minutes, and when he came to, he saw that he was surrounded by a large group of his cattle. And it was immediately apparent that Daisy, his 14-year-old "bell cow," had assumed charge of the other ladies and they had formed a protective circle around him.

Daisy had always been one of Mottram's special favorites. Whenever he wanted the herd back in the barns, all he had to do was to call Daisy, and she would lead the other cattle back home. And now she had saved his life by summoning the other cows to join in standing with her against the bull.

As he lay injured and dazed within the circle of cattle, Mottram could hear the bull snorting, stamping the ground, and bellowing his rage. From time to time, he would charge into the circle of cattle, but Daisy would see to it that the wall of bovine flesh held firm.

With Daisy keeping the circle of cattle intact and shielding him every inch of the way, Mottram was able to crawl 200 yards to the gate and get to the house where he could call for help.

He was in the hospital for six days with a dislocated jaw, broken ribs, damaged lungs, and bruised shoulders. In addition, there was a hoofprint on his chest that took five months to heal.

When he was asked for his explanation of why he thought Daisy and the others had intervened and taken up his cause against the bull, he replied that he had always treated the animals reasonably, and they looked after him in return. Mottram said that he had always believed that you reap what you sow.

When Fire Broke Out, Ivan Dragged the Baby to Safety and Awakened His Deaf Owner

If Ivan hadn't come to their rescue that day in April 1997, Tanya Brumleve of Redmond, Washington, is certain that both she and her daughter would have burned to death. Ivan, a Siberian husky/Labrador mix, dragged the three-year-old Alexandra from her bed, then awakened his deaf mistress as she lay unconscious from smoke inhalation.

The Brumleves had rescued Ivan from a death-sentence at the pound and trained him to be Tanya's "ears," because she was legally deaf. On that terrible day when their apartment became transformed into a blazing inferno, he more than repaid the debt.

Twenty-four-year-old Tanya had just put Alexandra into bed upstairs for a nap. Her husband, Michael, a housekeeping manager at a major Seattle hotel, was at work. Tanya had sat down on the couch to relax, Ivan at her side as always.

Ivan always alerted her when the phone rang and when there was someone at the door. He went everywhere with her—even into the shower.

> *Tanya was certain that both she and Alexandra would have died from smoke inhalation if it weren't for Ivan.*

Tanya apparently dozed off, and the next thing she knew, Ivan was jumping on her chest and barking. His seemingly violent actions came as a total shock to Tanya, for Ivan had been trained not to display any aggressive behavior toward her.

Once she had been jolted awake by the big dog, Tanya realized that the room was thick with smoke. Ivan had already pulled Alexandra down the stairs and was tugging her toward the front door. He was barking anxiously at Tanya, demanding that she get up, open the door, and leave the place immediately.

Later, Tanya and Alexandra were treated for smoke inhalation, but they otherwise escaped unhurt. It appeared that Alexandra had been playing with matches that she had found and had accidentally set her room on fire. Her bed, toys, and books were all destroyed. Tanya had fallen asleep on the downstairs couch and had subsequently been overcome by the smoke.

Calling the big Siberian/Labrador a guardian angel in a dog's coat, Tanya was certain that both she and Alexandra would have died from smoke inhalation if it weren't for Ivan.

A Redmond Fire Department spokesman agreed that Ivan was a true hero, and Michael Brumleve added that Ivan had saved the lives of his wife and child, a debt that he would never forget.

Faithful Trixie Nursed Her Owner, Victim of a Stroke, for Nine Sweltering Hot Days

In 1998, 75-year-old Jack Fyfe awakened to find the left side of his body completely dead of all sensation. He felt as though a boulder had crashed through the roof of his home in Sydney, Australia, and crushed him to his bed.

After he managed to collect his thoughts, he realized that he must have had a stroke while he was sleeping. With a great effort of will he attempted to roll out of bed, hoping that he might be able to drag himself to the telephone and call his daughter for help. But he was completely unable to move.

That was when the horror of his predicament truly struck him full force. A widower, he lived alone with Trixie, his six-year-old Australian Kelpie-Border collie mix. His daughter was going to pick him up to attend a social event, but that was nine days away. A virtual recluse such as he would be unlikely to be missed in those nine days.

Jack did his best to fight back the panic that had begun to flood every corner of his mind. Only Trixie, whining at his bedside, heard his agonized pleas for assistance.

It was very hot in the house. Jack knew it had to be over 90 degrees. He was very likely to die a slow, torturous death of thirst long before anyone missed him.

After a few hours, he pitifully cried out for water as he drifted in and out of consciousness. Trixie heard his hoarse cries and understood that her master very desperately needed something to drink. She suddenly left the bedroom and went into the kitchen. Jack could hear her lapping water from her bowl.

Perhaps Trixie's method of transport wasn't the most sanitary of methods—but who would worry about such petty concerns when he was dying of thirst? Trixie jumped up on Jack's bed and released a snoutful of water into his mouth.

Jack had often repeated the word "water" as he filled Trixie's bowl, but for her to interpret his feeble gasping of the word as a request for her to fetch water and deliver it mouth-to-mouth seemed a miracle.

For days, each time Jack would call out for water, Trixie heeded his cry. When her water dish ran dry, the resourceful dog got a towel and dipped it in the toilet bowl.

Jack had no qualms about where the life-preserving water was obtained. He thankfully sucked on the soaked towel as if he were a helpless baby.

For nine days, Trixie kept him alive until Jack Fyfe at last heard his daughter at the front door. From time to time, his telephone had rung, and he assumed that it was she calling to discuss plans for the social event that they were to attend. He had prayed that she would soon become concerned because he never answered the telephone. And now she was there—and she had brought paramedics along with her. He was saved.

Jack's daughter and his attending physician were astonished to learn how faithful Trixie had kept her master alive those nine awful days.

Boy's 35-Foot Fall Was Cushioned by His Dog

Eleven-year-old Alfredo Iannone of Salerno, Italy, knew very well that he and his friend should not be climbing around on the roof of a building under construction. That neglected bit of knowledge probably acquired a whole new dimension of truth when he walked too near the edge and tripped.

As he plummeted through space, Alfredo remembered screaming and thinking that he would surely die.

If not death, then surely terrible injury would have been his fate from having fallen 35 feet if it had not been for Stella, his big, German shepherd mix, who made a self-less dash to position herself directly under her master's falling body.

Later, Alfredo recalled that it had been like failing onto a mattress. In front of startled eyewitnesses, the boy bounced off the back of the stalwart Stella and onto the ground. Except for a few bruises, he was completely unharmed. Stella, too, was none the worse for wear for having served as living safety net for her careless master.

Alfredo's friend said that Stella had been barking at them from below, as if she had been warning them to be careful and scolding them for being so foolhardy. Stella had run like a bullet to position herself under Alfredo.

A physician at the Salerno Public Hospital was yet another voice of praise who declared Stella a hero. In his opinion, Alfredo would have been killed if the big dog had not raced under him to cushion his fall.

Stray Dog Earns a Home after Catching Falling Four-Year-Old

Four-year-old Livia Ungureanu had no doubt been scolded many times for throwing food to a stray dog that hung around their house in Baile Olanesti in central Romania. She had grown fond of the mutt and had given it the name of Nusa.

On May 26, 2004, Livia was leaning over the balcony on the third floor of their home, cheerily ignoring her grandmother's admonition not to feed the dog, when she leaned too far and fell.

Her grandmother, Jeni Ungureanu, 77, who had looked away after warning Livia not to throw any more food to the stray animal, ran to the balcony and saw her grand-daughter lying on the ground. Immediately, she thought the worst. Her beloved, strong-willed Livia was either dead or severely injured.

Then she saw the dog struggling to get out from under Livia. The four-year-old had fallen on the dog, and it had cushioned her fall. With renewed hope, Jeni ran out to the street to gather her granddaughter into her anxious arms.

Doctors at the local hospital pronounced Livia extremely fortunate to have suffered only minor injuries. On the same day, a village veterinarian gave Nusa a clean bill of health.

Jeni Ungureanu clearly recognized a miracle when she saw it. And she also agreed to permit Livia to keep Nusa as a pet.

Tiny Pekingese Saves Owner from Bear Attack

Petre Preda, a Romanian shepherd, was checking his flock pastured in the mountainous region of Magurii Casinului in Vrancea county when a bear charged out of the bushes.

Preda ran as fast as he could, but then he stumbled and broke his right leg. He thought that now only God could help him, and he began a prayer that he was certain would be his last.

Pekingese are small in stature, but big in heart. One man's pet proved to have the bravery to match a bear's!

That was when Preda heard the sharp barking of his little Pekingese pup. For the 12-pound fierce warrior to attack a huge bear was suicide.

Preda's wife had given the Pekingese to him as a birthday gift, adding that the puppy would take care of him in the mountains. Preda had laughed at the image of such a tiny dog protecting a grown man, and he had named the Pekingese "Bear" as a kind of joke, just as a man who owned a St. Bernard might name him "Mouse."

Amazingly, Bear's angry barking distracted the brute. The bear made a vicious swipe with his paw at the Pekingese that would surely have torn him to pieces if it had connected with his little body. Bear ran between the bear's legs to nip it on its stomach.

That aggressive action on the part of the Pekingese appeared to make up the bear's mind which of the two victims it would attack first. It dropped once again to all fours and began to chase Bear.

Preda screamed in terror as he saw the little puppy running as fast as its legs could carry him. Bear ran into the woods with the large, shaggy giant close on his heels. The shepherd feared that he had seen the last of his brave, little Pekingese.

Petre Preda was only half-conscious when a fellow shepherd discovered him lying a few feet from the flock of sheep that had begun to gather around their fallen master. After his friend had fashioned a crude splint for his broken leg, Preda told him of the bravery of little Bear, who had given his life to draw the bear away from him. In spite of his pain, Preda insisted on going into the woods in search of his courageous Pekingese's body.

Preda had just begun limping toward the forest, leaning on his friend's shoulder for support, when Bear came running out, completely unscathed, barking triumphantly. The little Pekingese had managed to outrun his much larger adversary and had managed to evade the bear in the woods.

Preda had thought that he was doomed when the bear suddenly charged him from the bushes. He would always be grateful that his little Pekingese had other ideas how the encounter would end.

Dog Rescues Newborn Baby by Sheltering It with Her Puppies

Late at night on August 20, 2008, a rural resident who lived outside of La Plata, Argentina, was certain that he heard a baby crying in a field behind his house. Since it was a very chilly 37 degrees that night, the man decided to investigate.

There, in the field, he found what appeared to be a newborn baby huddled next to a female dog and her six puppies. Startled by his unexpected discovery, the man ran back into his house and called the police.

Later, Dr. Egido Melia, director of the Melchor Romero Hospital in La Plata, said that the 8-pound, 13-ounce baby had only superficial scratches and bruises and was in good condition. It was apparent that the dog had carried the baby from a nearby area where its mother had abandoned it and brought it to be with her puppies. If the dog had not done so, Dr. Melia said, the baby would surely have died.

Police, who declared the dog an angel and a hero, eventually located the baby's mother, who was immediately hospitalized and given psychological treatment. The young woman appeared to remember little of the incident.

Giant Turtle Kept Her Afloat for 48 Hours until She Was Rescued

On June 2, 1974, Mrs. Cassandra Villanueva, 52, was aboard the *Aloha* when it caught fire and sank 600 hundred miles south of Manila, in the Philippines. Unable to make it to a lifeboat, the woman grabbed a life jacket and was tossed to the mercy of the ocean.

Forty-eight hours later, Mrs. Villanueva was spotted by the *Kalantia*, a Philippine naval vessel. The sailors who made the initial sighting stated that the woman appeared to be clinging to an oil drum.

However, as the vessel drew nearer to the fortunate survivor and someone threw her a life preserver, the sailors involved in the rescue said that the oil drum suddenly sank from view. It was only when the team was hauling Mrs. Villanueva up to the deck of the *Kalantia* that they saw that she had been clutching the shell of a giant sea turtle.

According to reports in several international wire services, one of her rescuers stated that the giant turtle was first sighted beneath Mrs. Villanueva, propping her up. It even circled the area twice before disappearing into the depths of the sea, as if to reassure itself that its former passenger was in good hands.

> *The giant sea turtle appeared beneath her and lifted her out of the sea.*

Mrs. Villanueva told reporters that after the *Aloha* sank, she had been floating in the water for more than 12 hours when the giant sea turtle appeared beneath her and lifted her out of the sea. She said that its head was as large as that of a big dog.

Later, a very small turtle climbed on her back as she rode on the giant turtle's shell. As though the little turtle had appointed itself her assistant guardian angel against the dangers of the sea, it bit Mrs. Villanueva every time she felt drowsy. It was as if it wished to prevent her from submerging her head beneath the waves and drowning.

His Prayers for Help Were Answered by an 11-Foot Stingray

On January 15, 1990, 18-year-old Lotty Stevens and a friend left to go fishing from Port Vila, Vanuatu, an island in the South Pacific. Although both of the two young men were experienced fishermen, they were caught off guard by a sudden storm that capsized their boat.

Helplessly, Lotty and his friend were tossed about by waves as they desperately sought to stay above the water. Fortunately for Lotty, it was his habit always to wear a life jacket when fishing in the ocean.

Later, when the sea was calmer and the height of the waves had subsided, he looked around the wreckage of their boat for his friend. After calling his name for several minutes, Lotty was forced to conclude that his companion had drowned during the storm.

For three days, Lotty clung to the overturned boat, bobbing lazily up and down as the wreckage drifted aimlessly. Then, with only his life jacket for support, he decided to swim in the direction in which he felt Port Vila lay.

For two days, the teenager alternated swimming as hard as he could, then floating to rest, praying all the while for a miracle. If only some fishing boats would come upon him and rescue him.

He tried hard to fight against despair. He knew that even a large ship could pass relatively close by and not be able to see his head bobbing in the vast ocean.

Toward the end of the fifth day after the raging storm had sent him into the sea, Lotty Stevens got his miracle. He had been floating with his eyes closed when he felt something big lift him from the water. There beneath him was a giant stingray, at least 11 feet long—including its six-foot poisonous tail. And the massive sea beast was taking him for a ride.

At first Lotty was frightened. Stingrays were not known for performing benevolent acts.

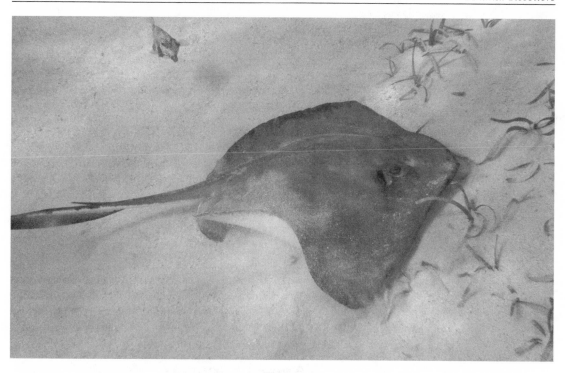

Stingrays can attack people with their barbed tails, but usually they remain aloof. One teenager, though, befriended a stingray that saved him from three sharks.

But soon, he later told journalists, he began to realize that the giant sea creature was his friend. He would pat it as if it were a dog—a big slimy dog with a hard and strong body.

One afternoon, after several days as a grateful hitchhiker, Lotty suddenly found himself dumped in the water as the stingray dove and disappeared. Lotty shook his head to clear the sea from his eyes—then wished that he hadn't. An enormous shark was heading straight for him.

Dear Lord, he screamed in his mind, why did his friend leave him now? Was the stingray afraid of the killer beast coming toward him?

Then the teenager saw a second shark—and a third. Suddenly Lotty's angel of the sea reappeared, swimming in a fast circle around him. Amazingly, the three sharks turned fin and swam away. Apparently they feared the stingray's long poisonous tail more than they felt the desire to feed on a human.

Lotty gave his thanks to God and the stingray that had once again saved his life. The great sea creature came alongside Lotty and nudged him, so he climbed back aboard its strong back.

Until the joyous morning when he at last sighted land, the teenager survived for eight more days by catching fish from atop his seaborne savior. The stingray also spotted the beach, for it headed for the shallow water and slid Lotty off near the shoreline.

Lotty remembered staggering like a drunken man, then collapsing on the sandy beach. The next morning he was awakened by a fisherman.

It took the teenager several moments to realize that he was not dreaming and that he was actually once again on solid land. As he slowly came to appreciate the fact that he was no longer in danger of drowning or of being eaten by sharks, he also realized with a sudden pang of regret that he hadn't had a chance to thank his remarkable friend from the ocean for saving his life.

> *It took the teenager several moments to realize that he was not dreaming and that he was actually once again on solid land.*

The fisherman helped Lotty to a doctor, and later, a hospital on the main island pronounced the teenager in good shape except for some dehydration and a few sores from salt water and chafing against his life jacket.

When he telephoned his family, their grief turned to joy beyond understanding, for they had already had a funeral service for him. It had been 21 days since Lotty and his friend had disappeared in the ocean storm.

Lotty does not argue with those who would seek to denigrate the facts of his remarkable rescue. He is living proof that somehow he survived 21 boatless days adrift in the ocean. In the opinion of Lotty Stevens and his family, that most certainly qualifies as a miracle.

Animal Survivors

Cat Survives 46 Days Trapped in Coffee Table Drawer

On December 8, 1989, Rhea Mayfield of Brownwood, Texas, asked her daughter to help her move the coffee table from their apartment to the building's storage room to make space for the Christmas tree. When they returned to the apartment, they noticed that Kelly, their tabby, was missing. After several minutes of calling for her, they concluded that Kelly must have wandered out of the apartment while they were lugging the table to the storage room.

Rhea called the police and placed ads in local newspapers. Every day she would allot some time to searching the neighborhood for her missing cat.

It was not until January 22, 1990, 46 days later, that the manager of the apartment building happened to hear the weak cries of a cat while he was in the storage room. It took him a few moments to locate the source of the pathetic cries, but he opened the compartment of the coffee table to discover a very emaciated cat, barely recognizable as Rhea Mayfield's robust and slightly plump Kelly.

Kelly barely had the strength to purr against her owner's cheek, so Rhea took her directly to a veterinarian. Here it was determined that the cat that had previously weighed in at 17 pounds, now tipped the scales at less than five.

A professor of veterinary medicine reviewing the case remarked that a dog would not last a week without water, and the longest that he had ever heard of a cat surviving without liquids was 30 days—never 46! He theorized that the temperatures in the storage room, sometimes dropping several degrees below freezing, might have helped to save Kelly's life by slowing down her body functions.

50 Days without Food and Water
Sealed in Metal Container

In 1990 when the employees of the freight company in Kent, England, were sealing the metal container that was to protect the Mercedes-Benz during its sea voyage to Australia, they had no idea that they were also enclosing a stray black cat inside the box. The unwilling feline stowaway—who came to be called "Mercedes"—survived an astonishing 50 days without food or water, locked securely in its metal sea-going tomb. In an unparalleled feat of endurance, Mercedes traveled 17,000 miles in her metallic crypt; and when the ship arrived in Port Adelaide, Australia, nearly two months later, customs officials were stunned when the skin-and-bone cat stumbled out of the container.

Dr. John Holmden, a veterinarian and chief animal quarantine officer in south Australia, theorized that Mercedes must have had a full stomach before she became trapped in the container. By licking drops of condensation and by spending nearly all of her time resting, she managed to stay alive.

"Wally" Endured 45 Days
Trapped behind Bathroom Wall

After several days in her new home, Winnie Wagner of Orange Park, Florida, decided that either a cat was somehow trapped inside the wall near her bathtub or she had lost her mind.

Finally, in late February 1994, she had the marble paneling removed from around her tub, and a small cat blinked at them from inside the wall.

"Wally," as he was appropriately christened, was carefully removed from the bed that he had made of insulation, and Winnie took him to Briarcliff Animal Clinic in nearby Jacksonville.

Dr. Susan Ridinger weighed Wally in at only three and a half pounds, but stated that although dehydrated and weak, he was in amazingly good shape, considering what he had been through.

The veterinarian theorized that Wally had lived off condensation from pipes under the tub in Winnie's bathroom, but doubted that the cat could have survived for much longer.

No one could venture any more than a guess as to how Wally had found himself trapped in the walls of the home, but educated estimates concluded that he had somehow managed to endure 45 days sealed up in solitary confinement.

Curious cats frequently manage to get themselves in pretty tight situations, getting trapped behind walls and inside holes, where they find themselves in need of a helping human hand.

Tabby Stayed Alive for Six Weeks
in a Deserted Woodchuck Hole

In autumn 1997, Vivian Browning of Damascus, Maryland, hired some workmen to fill in a hole that had been left under her back porch by a pesky wood chuck. What the 73-year-old woman didn't know was that her beloved Tabby had been exploring the burrow when the men began dumping dirt into it.

That night when Tabby didn't come home, Vivian was very upset. Tabby was so very precious to her. And although sometimes Tabby would stay out a bit late, she would never fail to come home.

After several nights of searching and calling for her dear cat, the heartbroken woman decided that she must accept the reality that Tabby had been taken from her by some accident.

One afternoon, six weeks later, Vivian was pushing the snow off her wooden deck when she thought she heard Tabby meowing from somewhere near her. Within minutes, Vivian had a crew in her backyard, ripping the boards apart with chainsaws and wrecking bars.

Tabby was lifted out by one of the workmen, who tenderly handed her to Vivian. Her dear cat was nothing but fur and bones. While Vivian cradled Tabby in her arms, one of the men rushed Vivian and Tabby to a veterinarian.

The veterinarian went on to theorize that the only way that Tabby could have survived six weeks trapped under the deck was if she had managed to find a little water to drink and a few moles to eat.

Danish Sheepdog Found Alive after 68 Days in a Dry Well

Flossy, a sheepdog from Gilleleje, Denmark, was found alive after 68 days trapped down a dry well. When the dog was discovered on August 12, 2003, it was lifted out by fire rescue workers.

Flossy's owners, Birgitte Pontoppidan and Hans Ibsen, had searched for days after their sheepdog had gone missing, but they had long since given up hope that she would ever return.

A local veterinarian theorized that Flossy had only been able to survive by licking condensation off the well walls. She had had no food at all for over two months.

Shadow Survived Five Weeks in a Pit in Death Valley

On April 18, 2004, the Schwartz family of Trona, California, were hiking near the ghost town of Panamint City on the western edge of Death Valley National Park when their dog Shadow fell into a pit. The chasm was so deep that they could not see Shadow, but they could hear her whimpering so they knew that she was still alive and had survived the fall.

The pit was four-feet wide, but the Schwartzes could not determine its depth. They secured an aluminum ladder from a nearby ranger station and attempted to rescue their 10-year-old cocker spaniel-beagle friend from the hole. They planned to lower the ladder to the bottom of the pit and then descend to retrieve Shadow. When they accidentally dropped the ladder and it fell out of reach, they realized that the pit was much deeper than they had estimated.

Seventeen-year-old Stephen continued to call to Shadow, but finally the dog ceased responding. After a family counsel, Stephen's father, brother, and two cousins decided that Shadow had died. The pit had to be 30 or more feet in depth. Poor old Shadow had probably received fatal injuries from and the fall and had just managed to hang on for several minutes more. The Schwartzes fashioned a wooden cross to mark Shadow's final resting place, said a prayer in memory of their faithful friend, and sadly returned home.

On May 16, five weeks after the Schwartz family believed that they had lost Shadow to an abyss in the desert, brothers Darren and Scott Mertz were trying to discover the source of a spring near Panamint City. They were daring one another to climb down inside the hole when they were startled to hear barking coming from its darkened depths.

Horrified that there seemed to be a dog down in the pit, the brothers resolved not to leave until they had rescued it. Darren, 34, used an old hose from a nearby water storage tank to lower Scott, 36, down to the ladder that the Schwartzes had lost in their attempt to rescue Shadow. Scott descended farther until he reached a very frightened and skinny dog. Although she was obviously malnourished and starved, Darren and Scott had no idea that Shadow had been at the bottom of the pit for 35 days.

> *Darren and Scott had no idea that Shadow had been at the bottom of the pit for 35 days.*

When they returned to Scott's home in Temecula and had given the dog some food and water, the brothers called the number on her tags and told the Schwartz family that they had retrieved their dog from a pit in the desert.

An astonished Stephen could hardly believe that Shadow was still alive after the family had left her for dead five weeks before. He admitted that he had prayed for such a miracle and had asked that he would once again see Shadow alive.

Sealed in a Container, Cat Lives after 30-Day Trip from China to Tampa

In mid-April 2004, a cat jumped out of a container of parrot cages when the shipment arrived at Goldberg's warehouse in Tampa, Florida. The container had been sealed a month before when it had left a factory in China.

The metal container had arrived by boat in Los Angeles in early April and had been transferred to Tampa by rail. The cat had chewed up a number of cardboard boxes that held the bird cages, but no trace of water or food could be found that would explain how the cat had managed to survive locked in a metal container for a month. Veterinarians who examined the cat and treated her for dehydration said that she would soon be ready for adoption.

Bubbles Endures Eight Weeks Trapped under Garden Deck

Amazingly, according to the June 25, 2004, *Daily Record* of London, Bubbles the cat survived eight weeks trapped under a garden deck. Emma Dearie, Bubbles' seven-year-old owner, had continued a desperate search for her kitty for two months and had even walked to farms as far away as two miles to inquire about her beloved pet.

The Dearies' neighbors, John and Anne McMillan, had no idea that they were sealing poor Bubbles in a makeshift kind of tomb when they put in their garden deck. When they at last heard a faint mewing issuing from under the deck, they called a carpenter to pry up a portion of the decking. There was a very thin and very desperate Bubbles, very glad that someone finally had paid some attention to her cries.

Workmen Accidentally Wall Cat under Bathtub for Seven Weeks

On August 26, 2008, Bonny, a four-year-old cat, was found after having been walled in beneath a bathtub for seven weeks. Her owner, Monika Hoppert, a 60-year-old widow from Stradthagen, Germany, declared that Bonny had to have a guardian angel to have survived without nourishment for such an incredible period of time.

On June 19, workmen replaced pipes in several apartments and had removed the cladding around the bathtubs in Mrs. Hoppert's and other residents' flats. Bonny had apparently exercised feline curiosity and crawled underneath the open area before the tiles were sealed up again.

Seven weeks later, Mrs. Hoppert's neighbor insisted that she could hear a cat meowing under her bathtub. Upon investigating, Monika Hoppert recognized the distinctive sound of her missing Bonny's voice. The cat's weight had dropped from 13 pounds to four, but she was being nursed back to health with kitten food.

LOST AND ALONE

A heavy storm, which marooned Mrs. Arthur Horton, of Chicago, in Clinton, Iowa, must be credited with helping her find her father, W. J. Murphy, from whom she had been separated for 29 years.

While waiting out the storm in Clinton, Mrs. Horton happened to mention her long lost father to a restaurant owner. The man tipped her off to a Mrs. Murphy, who turned out to be a cousin, and through her she was able to trace her father.

* * *

While browsing through an army surplus store in Centralia, Illinois, an ex-G.I. found his old tunic on a counter. The faded serial number identified it as the one he had returned to supply on his discharge. The manager returned the tunic with his compliments.

* * *

Mrs. Magdalene Vanover was chatting idly with a grocer in Corbin, Kentucky, while he filled her order. The grocer remarked that her German accent reminded him of his days as a soldier in World War II.

He pulled out an album of pictures that he had snapped while he was on leave in Germany.

One photograph was a close-up of Mrs. Vanover as a young girl.

* * *

How would you classify the above true stories? Would you say that they are examples of fate, serendipity, luck, or coincidence? Or would you go so far as to say that they were all small miracles?

Numerous polls and surveys have demonstrated that over 80% of American adults believe in miracles—extraordinary events that seem to make strange dents and openings in ordinary reality, things that cannot easily be explained by the rigid laws of physical science or the flexible rules of chance.

Wedding and engagement rings are small and easily lost, yet sometimes they manage to make it back to their owners years later.

Reunited

An Engagement Ring Reclaimed from the Sea after 89 Years

During a routine dive around the wreck of the HMS *Opal* off the coast of the Orkney Islands in 2007, diver Peter Brady found an engagement ring with the inscription, "To Stanley from Flo, 6 March 1916."

The HMS *Opal*, together with the HMS *Narborough*, ran aground during a snowstorm on January 12, 1918, with a combined loss of life of 188 seamen. Peter and his diving partner, Bob Hamilton, both of Liverpool, had explored the site numerous times but had never found any item of value. They both agreed that they should try their best to return the ring to the family.

An examination of the casualty list revealed that there was a Stanley Cubiss who perished in the disaster. Checking the 1901 census, they discovered a Cubiss family in Yorkshire. Pursuing the lead, they learned that Stanley and Florence had wed in June 1917, but some years after her husband's death aboard the *Opal*, Florence Cubiss had remarried. A search of the telephone books produced a listing for a J. M. Cubiss in York.

Bob Hamilton only managed to get a few words out explaining that they were divers who often visited certain underwater sites when Cubiss, Stanley's nephew, a retired brigadier, interrupted his caller to utter, "The *Opal*."

Marveling over the fact that such a personal item of his uncle's had been found after 89 years, Brigadier Cubiss requested that the divers present the ring to a naval museum in Orkney so that people might always remember the tragic events of that night in 1918. Hamilton and Brady agreed, and mused that the million-in-one chance of finding the ring had seemed quite eerie—almost like a miracle of some sort.

A Memento of Love to Her Airman Husband Found after 50 Years

In 1992, Eleanor Thomas flew from her home in the United States to the village of Fontan, France, to participate in a ceremony unveiling a monument honoring the 11 crewmen of the *Dallas Lady*, who had been shot out of the sky on September 12, 1944. For decades the people of the region had left the wreckage intact in reverence to the U.S. airmen who had given their lives in the liberation of France. Then in the early 1990s, war veterans and grateful French citizens decided to build a monument in the center of the debris.

As Eleanor Thomas stood among the honorees, the family members of the valiant crew of the *Dallas Lady*, a villager approached her and silently handed her a medallion that he had found while gathering mushrooms. The metal was still shiny and the engraving was clearly legible: "I love you, Eleanor."

To her joy and amazement, she clutched once again the medallion that her husband had been wearing when he had been shot down nearly half a century ago.

He Found His Fiancée's Jewelry in the Belly of a Fish

On December 28, 2007, Kristy Brittain, 25, was kneeboarding behind a boat off Slopen Main on the Tasman Peninsula, east of Hobart, Australia, when suddenly rough conditions tossed her into the sea. Although she was not injured, she felt peeved that she had lost a nose stud that she had acquired only a week before Christmas.

Three days later, on January 1, Darren Triffett, her fiancée, found the stud as he was filleting a flathead that he had caught in roughly the same area where Kristy had taken her spill off the kneeboard.

While one can easily conceive of a sparkling metal object appealing to the eclectic appetite of a flathead, try to figure the odds of Triffett catching the one fish in the sea that had swallowed his fiancée's nose stud.

Lost 1968 Class Ring Was Found in a Stranger's Jewelry Box in 2007

In 1968, Tony Brown was a junior in Lexington, Alabama, high school who had a summer job at a car wash. One day, his hands covered with soapy water, his class ring slipped off his finger. Brown and his coworkers searched everywhere for the ring, pulling off the cover of the drain, sifting through mud and water. Back in 1968, class rings meant a great deal to the wearer, and Tony was deeply upset that he had lost his.

In January 2007, Rick Ritter, a 1972 graduate of Lexington High, was looking through a jewelry box that had belonged to his recently deceased aunt. Ritter was puzzled to find a 1969 Lexington High class ring among his late aunt's personal effects.

Another member of the Ritter family explained that their aunt had found the ring under the seat of her 1968 Buick many months after she had sent the automobile to the car wash. She had no idea whose ring it was, so she just put it in her jewelry box and forgot about it.

Ritter noted the initials TMB inside the ring, so he went to his old high school yearbooks and found two or three individuals to whom the ring might have belonged.

When he called Brown, Tony responded that, yes, he had lost his class ring down a drain when he worked at a car wash in the summer of 1968.

With great delight, Ritter informed Tony Brown that he would once again have his class ring after 38 years. It hadn't slipped off his finger when he was washing the outside of his aunt's Buick, but when he was wiping down the backseat.

Class Ring Lost on Beach Found in Belly of Shark

Just before the 1969 Mount Dora High School prom in Enterprise, Florida, Norman Lewis gave his class ring to Janice, his girlfriend. The next day, following their high school's after-prom custom, they went to New Smyrna Beach. Janice put Norman's ring on a bracelet just before they went for a swim, and to their dismay the prized token of young love slipped off in the water.

How could a ring lost three decades earlier turn up in the stomach of a shark?

Although they searched for the ring for hours, Norman and Janice finally gave up on finding the ring. They did not, however, give up on each other. The couple had been dating since they were 14, and four years after graduation they were married.

In July 1999, a young boy caught a four-foot shark in the surf at New Smyrna Beach. When he cut the shark open, he found a Mount Dora High School class ring. The boy and his father contacted officials at the high school, and it was determined that it was Norman Lewis's class ring that Janice had lost 30 years ago.

Lewis was astonished. How could a ring lost three decades earlier turn up in the stomach of a shark that a young boy had just caught? Had a fish swallowed it in 1969 and then been swallowed by a larger fish and had the incredible cycle of fish swallowing fish continued until 1999?

Lewis was pleased to have his class ring returned to him, but he said that he had not really missed the ring since he had Janice all those years. She was definitely the better choice of the two.

A Ring Thrown Away Because of a Lovers' Quarrel Is Found by a Grandson 67 Years Later

Leighton Boyes, 33, had heard the story many times. Just months before his grandmother Violet Booth, 88, was to marry his grandfather Samuel in 1941, the two had a lovers' quarrel, and she threw her diamond engagement ring into a field in Gilmorton, where they were out walking.

Samuel Booth, who was remembered by everyone who knew him as a very nice man, searched many hours for the ring after the couple made up. When it appeared lost to them forever, Samuel simply bought a new ring and he and Violet went on to become happily married.

Grandfather Samuel had died in 1993, and lately Grandmother Violet, who lived in Thurmaston, Leicestershire, had been thinking a great deal about that diamond that she had tossed away in a tiff. Boyes, who lived in Mowmacre Hill, Leicester, decided to have a go at the field in Gilmorton with a metal detector to see if he might reclaim the ring that had been so angrily discarded 67 years ago.

The farmer who owned the field granted his permission, but cautioned that the land had been ploughed many times since 1941. He also added that occasionally metal detector enthusiasts had asked to search the field for ancient relics.

Astonishingly, it took Boyes only two hours to find the ring, which seems in itself a small miracle. It was buried about four inches beneath the soil and was not damaged in any way. Boyes just wiped the dirt away, and that was it. Since it was gold, it hadn't tarnished a bit.

His grandmother was moved to tears when Boyes presented her with the ring that she had thrown away so many years before. Grandmother Violet found that the ring fit her little finger, but she decided to keep it safe in a box. She, her son Andrew, and other members of the family, only wished that Grandfather Samuel had lived to see the return of the once-rejected ring.

Two Look-a-Like Firefighters in New Jersey Discover They Were Twins Separated at Birth

Firefighter Jimmy Tedesco of Tintin Falls, New Jersey, was surprised when he visited the firehouse in Paramus, about 65 miles away, and met a fellow who seemed to be a carbon-copy of his buddy, Jerry Levey. Jerry was a bachelor and a volunteer fire captain who installed fire sprinklers.

When Jimmy told Jerry that he had met his double in Paramus—a man with the same bald head, sideburns, broad shoulders, big nose and the same style of eye glasses—Jerry scoffed. As far as he knew, he was an only son.

Jimmy continued his detective work and found out that Mark Newman in Paramus had the same birth date as his friend Jerry. With a little subterfuge, Jimmy managed to get Newman to drive to the Tintin Falls firehouse. When Mark Newman and Jerry Levey met, they exclaimed that it was as if they were looking in a mirror.

When they all went out for a beer, the other firemen laughed at the way Mark and Jerry held their bottles in an identical manner, made similar remarks at the same time, and used the same gestures when they spoke.

In their getting-to-know-you discussion, they learned that when they were younger they had both worked at a supermarket, then a gas station, before they decided to study forestry. Later they both were employed by a lawn-service company before they had found that they were attracted to firefighting. They favored the same style of clothes, wearing belts with extra-large buckles, aviator glasses, and long, jangling key chains. In addition, they had both had hernia operations when they were boys.

Mark Newman and Jerry Levey pursued their identical images, likes, and dislikes, and discovered that they had been twins born in New York who were separated at birth.

Best Friends in College Discover
Years Later that They Are Sisters

When Fiona Cooper and Wendy Croft met in college in the late 1980s, they took an instant liking to each other. In fact, they were rather taken aback when they had the same bleached blonde hair, liked the same music, bought the same kind of clothes, raided each other's wardrobes, and even had the same preferences in men.

Throughout their years in college, fellow students were always asking the two if they were sisters. Although Fiona and Wendy knew that they were both adopted, neither ever thought that they might really be siblings. Upon graduation, they both got married and found themselves both settling down in York, where they remained best friends.

> *Throughout their years in college, fellow students were always asking the two if they were sisters.*

It wasn't until the summer of 1994 that Wendy, then 26, became determined to locate her natural mother. When she found the woman living 60 miles away, Wendy learned that her mother had another daughter a year later, whom she christened Lorraine and placed in an orphanage. In one of their numerous discussions over the years, Fiona had told Wendy that she had originally been named Lorraine, but her adoptive parents had rechristened her Fiona. When Wendy asked Lorraine's birth date, the woman named Fiona's birthday.

Wendy was so excited with the revelations that she immediately picked up the telephone and informed Fiona that not only did they act like sisters, they really were sisters. When Fiona realized that Wendy was not joking, she confessed that being raised as an only child, she had often prayed at night for a sister—and now there was proof that her best friend was that longed-for sister.

Two Co-Workers Learn through
Health Records that They Are Sisters

Jeannette Pyden, 44, and Darlene Meadows, 38, who worked at the Kmart in Port Huron, Michigan, always took their lunches together and sometimes met after work to have a few laughs, because they had good times together.

In November 1994, Jeannette's daughter, Amy, happened to be looking up biological information for her two sons' health records when she stumbled across some interesting data. She called her mother at work and told her that the lady that she loved having lunch with and going on breaks together was actually her sister.

Although the two women had hit it off from their first meeting, there was no great mystery why they hadn't recognized each other. Jeannette was one of five brothers and

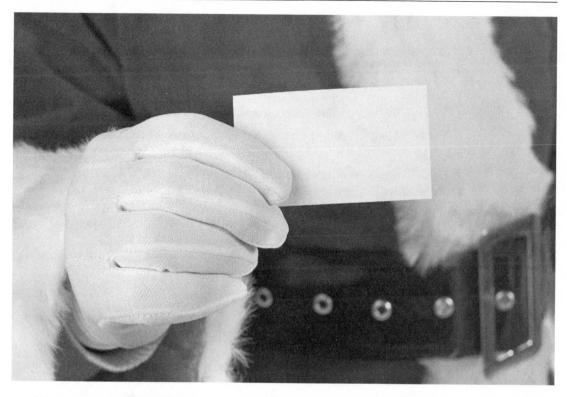

Santa may be prompt with deliveries, but sometimes the U.S. Postal Service is not quite as prompt.

sisters who were taken from their poverty-stricken parents and placed with foster families. By the time Darlene was born, Jeannette had been fortunate to be adopted.

Interestingly, many years later, Darlene had made a deathbed promise to her mother to one day find her siblings. But who was to know that destiny was to bring one of them to the same Kmart where she worked?

After sharing tears of joy and reunion, the two women sought to fulfill Darlene's vow by combining forces to locate their other brothers and sisters.

A Christmas Card Arrives 93 Years Late

During the Holiday season in 1914, a group of ladies from Alma, Nebraska, selected a colorful Christmas card depicting a young girl and a jolly Santa Claus to send their cousin Ethel Martin of Oberlin, Kansas. It was postmarked December 23, 1914. It arrived in perfect condition on December 17, 2007—93 years late.

Ethel Martin was now deceased, so the card ended up with Bernice Martin, her sister-in-law. Postal employees could not guess where the card had been for nearly a century, but someone found it and saw that it got delivered.

A Student's Postcard Assuring His Parents All Was Well Arrives 40 Years Too Late to Comfort Them

In 1966, Zygmunt Kubiczak, a Polish student, sent a postcard to his parents on the other side of Poland to let them know that everything was going well for him.

On October 17, 2006, the postcard finally arrived. Kubiczak's parents were no longer alive, but thoughtful neighbors sent it on to him when it finally arrived.

Kubiczak mused that since he had sent that postcard Poland had thrown off the Communist system; he had gotten married; brought up two children; sailed around the world in a boat; and survived a serious heart operation. And somehow the postcard he had written as a student to reassure his parents that all was well with him in college was having its own mysterious journey and taking a very roundabout route to be delivered.

Separated for Seven Years after an Off-Duty Nurse Saved His Life, the Young Man Returns to Save Hers

In July 1999, 11-year-old Kevin Stephan was acting as batboy for his brother Rob's baseball team at a field across from Erie Community College's North campus in Buffalo, New York. Kevin was entering the practice cage between innings to pick up some bats when a batter whose back was turned to Kevin struck him in the back with a powerful backswing.

Kevin remembers the blow, then taking a few steps toward the dugout. Then he woke up with someone kneeling over him.

Penny Brown, a registered nurse, was in the stands when she saw Kevin get hit. She could see clearly that he was beginning to have a seizure and was entering cardiac arrest. Immediately, she came rushing from the stands, smacked him hard on the chest, and then began CPR. Within a few moments, Kevin began breathing again.

After several hours in the hospital, Kevin was cleared and released to his parents, Lorraine and Gregory Stephan. Later, the Stephans both broke down, tearfully comprehending the enormity of their son's injury and the fact that they had nearly lost their child. Penny Brown had saved Kevin's life.

On January 27, 2006, 17-year-old Kevin Stephan had no school because it was Regents week, so he had begun his dishwashing shift at a local restaurant early that day. Since he was back in the kitchen, Kevin was unaware that his mother had entered the restaurant around 2:00 P.M.

Shortly after she was seated, Lorraine Stephen recognized Penny Brown, the nurse who had saved her son's life, seated with her family eating lunch. A few minutes later, when Lorraine glanced toward the Browns, she was startled to see Penny clutching at her throat, struggling to get air, and obviously choking.

Lorraine Stephen ran toward the kitchen, shouting for Kevin to come out at once. The manager of the restaurant, aware that Kevin was a volunteer firefighter, also called for his assistance.

Kevin moved behind Mrs. Brown, applied the Heimlich maneuver and after two thrusts, the food was dislodged.

After Mrs. Brown was out of danger, Kevin's mother told him that this was the woman who had saved his life seven years ago.

Kevin said that he had always wanted to find some way to adequately thank the off-duty nurse who had saved his life.

Then he walked back to the kitchen to resume his dishwashing duties.

Now a senior at Lancaster High School, Kevin sought no publicity for his part in saving the nurse's life. Once, when pressed by journalists to make some kind of statement in regard to the incredible coincidence, Kevin firmly stated his belief that it was no coincidence. Although he admitted that there was no way to explain the unusual happening, he expressed his opinion that on occasion the Lord set things up to occur in a certain way, but nothing is a coincidence.

Penny Brown, currently an intensive care nurse at Buffalo General Hospital, said that such an incident was almost impossible to believe, but she was most appreciative that it had occurred.

Kevin's mother perhaps summed it up best when she declared that somehow the life of her son and the life of Penny Brown had been touched by the hand of God.

And who can truly divine if Penny Brown had saved Kevin's life so that seven years later he might save hers?

Surviving on Their Own

Pinned beneath a Tree for 11 Hours, He Was Forced to Cut Off His Own Leg

Sixty-six-year-old Al Hill was well-known for clearing trees on terrain too rough and dense for professional loggers. On June 6, 2007, Hill had been working alone outside his remote home near the tiny village of Iowa Hill, about 60 miles from Sacramento, California.

Accidents happen to even the most experienced. Hill was unable to get out of the way of a tree that he had just chopped down and it fell on his leg and held him fast.

Grimacing through the pain, Hill was able to reach his mobile phone, but he was unable to get a signal that far in the wilderness.

He began calling for help, but no one heard him.

Al Hill was pinned under the tree for 11 hours when he decided to take matters into his own hands. With a pocketknife as his only tool and his courage his only anesthesia, Hill cut off his own leg.

Stuck beneath a tree he had just cut down, Al Hill was miles from help when he took desperate action.

At last one of Hill's neighbors, Eric Bockey heard his cries for help and found him lying near the tree that had held him captive for so long. Bockey ran for two miles before he was able to get a signal strong enough to call the Iowa Hill fire service. Bockey said later that as he ran for help he knew that God had to be with them that day.

Iowa Hill, a community of 200, has no electricity and few services, but another neighbor was alerted to the emergency and arrived on the scene with his pickup truck. Bockey and the driver loaded Al onto the truck bed and drove him to an emergency landing site where a helicopter flew him to a hospital.

In spite of his painful ordeal, the tough Al Hill never succumbed to shock. Once at the hospital, he received much more professional amputation surgery.

Luana Dowling, head of the Iowa Hill volunteer fire brigade, commented on what a remarkable individual Al Hill was. Al and her brother, Randy Campbell, often worked together in the toughest of terrains. Campbell agreed that Hill loved cutting the big trees, but added that fluke accidents could happen to even the most professional of loggers.

Hand Caught in a Corn Picker, Flames Beginning to Engulf Him, He Cuts Off Own Arm with a Pocketknife

Sampson Parker of Kershaw County, South Carolina, was harvesting corn on September 11, 2007, when some stalks jammed the rollers on his rusted old picker. As so many farmers have done to their lasting regret, Parker didn't shut the machine off, thinking he could reach in and quickly grab the troublesome stalks from the rollers without wasting any time. The rollers first caught his glove, then his hand.

For more than an hour, Parker called for help, but he was working in an isolated cornfield, far from anyone who could free him from the clutching rollers. Desperately, he tried to pull his hand free, but the relentless rollers only dragged more of his hand, his forearm, his elbow into the machine.

Parker had been able to grab an iron bar and jam it into the chain-and-sprocket that drove the rollers that pulled his arm into the corn picker. The sprockets, grinding against the bar, cast off sparks that set the dust, corn husks, and ground litter on fire. Parker knew that in a very few minutes, the whole corn picker was going to burst into flames and burn him to death.

The farmer managed to open a pocketknife and began to saw at the arm held fast in the rollers. The fear of the fire probably kept him from passing out from the pain of cutting off his arm.

When Parker got to the bone, he dropped to the ground, using the force of his own weight to snap the bone. He had barely touched the field when a tire exploded on the picker and the force of the blow out tossed him about five feet and free of the flames.

Somehow, Parker found the strength to run from the burning corn picker and get into his pickup. He drove out to the highway, parked on the roadside, and tried to flag down a passing vehicle to get help.

When no one would stop to help him, Parker drove to the middle of the road, hoping to force a car or truck to stop.

Vehicle after vehicle drove onto the shoulder to get past him.

When, at last, someone did stop to investigate, it happened to be Doug Spinks, a first-responder, trained to deal with emergencies. Spinks was visibly shocked as he quickly appraised Parker's condition. He stopped the bleeding from his amputated arm, but he later admitted to inner doubts that his efforts could save the man.

While they awaited a rescue helicopter, Parker told Spinks that he would not give up. He had a wife and three children who loved him, and he would live.

Because of the injuries that he had suffered from the flames that had begun to engulf him as he was cutting off his arm, Parker had to spend three weeks in a burn center before being released from the hospital. While he was recovering, about 25 of his neighbors had joined together to finish harvesting his corn.

By November 26, 2007, Parker had been fitted for a prosthetic arm and was back on his job supervising an $80 million highway construction project. Grateful for the support tendered him by his friends and neighbors, Sampson Parker accepts full responsibility for his fate. He admitted that he had stuck his hand where he shouldn't have.

Paramedic Trapped under ATV for Four Days
Forced to Eat Rotten Meat and Fight Off Coyotes

Ken Hildebrand is a paramedic who teaches classes on first aid and how to work with heavy equipment at Keyano College in Fort Murray, Alberta. On January 8, 2008, he was riding his ATV in Crossnest Pass to check on some property that he owns there and to see if he could help ranchers with the problem they were having with wolves attacking their cattle.

On his way, Hildebrand was collecting animal traps that contained dead and rotting animals. He was about 80 miles southwest of Calgary when his ATV struck a rock. Before he could jump free of the vehicle, it rolled and pinned him underneath, face down on the frozen ground.

Perhaps one of the factors that made Ken such a sympathetic caregiver was his having been a victim of polio, which left him with a weak leg. Now, as fate would have it, his overturned ATV was resting on his strong leg, preventing him from getting up.

Vehicles like ATVs allow us to explore remote wilderness areas, but we should never do so by ourselves.

He was able to reach the axe that he had in the vehicle. Hoping to be able to use its handle to pry himself free, he was unable to get enough leverage to get the ATV off his good leg.

It wasn't long that first evening before coyotes began to ring Hildebrand, attracted by the stench of rotting meat from the dead animals in the traps. As a paramedic, he knew that he must guard against hypothermia from rapid loss of body heat, so he had used a number of beaver carcasses as improvised coats, blankets, and windbreakers. He was able to keep the hungry coyotes in retreat by blowing on a whistle he had with him whenever they appeared ready to charge. Thankfully, the shrill sound managed to drive them back from their intended meal.

Ken had no food or water with him, and, unfortunately, he had landed on a patch of dirt near the rocks that had no snow covering. He began to suck on mouthfuls of dirt to try to get some moisture from the frozen soil.

By the second night, he was so hungry that he tried eating some of the rotting beaver—but it only made him sick.

He knew he was becoming dehydrated, but all he had for moisture was the dew that collected on some surveyor's tape that he had carried with him.

As the fourth day of his imprisonment dawned, Ken Hildebrand had begun to accept the grim reality that he might not be found before the cold, dehydration, mal-nourishment, or animals finished him.

Later that day, after nearly 96 hours trapped under his ATV, he saw a friendlier ani-mal approaching him and checking out the scene. A few minutes later, a hiker joined his dog in discovering Hildebrand's very difficult circumstances.

As rescue workers were arriving on the scene, the hiker said that something had told him to hike that particular terrain that morning. Although he had never before had any desire to visit that area, he just had a strange feeling to hike there that day.

Ken Hildebrand spent a night in the Crow Pass Hospital, then was transferred to Lethbridge where he underwent several operations to treat severe frostbite and injuries to his legs.

Friends of Hildebrand's said that it was typical of the man that despite suffering hypothermia, frostbite, dehydration, and other injuries, his primary concern was that he would not be able to make his next paramedic shift.

Pet Survival in the Wilderness

Bobbie, the Famous Collie of Oregon

One of the most famous of all the accounts of a dog finding its way back to the home of their owners after conquering seemingly insurmountable odds in the wilderness is that of Bobbie the collie, who made his way alone from Indiana to Ore-gon. Although Bobbie had only his canine instincts to guide him, he managed to find his human family after walking 3,000 miles through forests and farmlands, mountains and plains, scorching heat and freezing cold.

In August 1923, Mr. and Mrs. Frank Brazier, owners of a restaurant in Silverton, Oregon, began the long journey to Indiana to visit relatives. Bobbie rode on top of the luggage in the back seat of the open touring car.

When the Braziers stopped to visit relatives in Wolcott, Indiana, before continuing farther east to Bluffton, their final goal, Frank and Bobbie drove the car to a garage for a carburetor adjustment. As the big collie leaped from the back seat, he accidentally bumped against a formidable bull terrier.

Frank had no real concern for Bobbie. But what Frank didn't know was that the cranky bull terrier commanded a whole pack that ganged up on Bobbie. Bobbie beat it out of town with the pack of growling, snapping dogs at his heels.

When the work on the Braziers' automobile was completed, Frank drove up and down the town's streets and the nearby country roads, sounding the horn to summon his beloved collie. But Bobbie had disappeared.

The next day, the Braziers placed an ad in the local paper, offering a reward for the return of their dog, but no one seemed to have seen the big collie. Bobbie was devot-ed to Frank. The Braziers could only conclude that either something terrible had hap-pened to the collie or that someone was keeping him against his will.

The Braziers finally drove on to Bluffton, then days later, they sadly began the trip back to Oregon without Bobbie.

Meanwhile, Bobbie was left confused, shaken, and frightened. He was in completely unfamiliar territory. But while Bobbie's sense of direction may have been temporarily skewered, his ability to detect dog lovers among the Indiana populace remained in excellent working order. Time and time again, as he was nearing starvation, Bobbie arrived at the home of kind people who took him in and nurtured him back to good traveling condition.

> *Traveling ever westward back home to Oregon, he swam rivers, survived blizzards, endured hunger and thirst, and climbed over mountains.*

Traveling ever westward back home to Oregon, he swam rivers, survived blizzards, endured hunger and thirst, and climbed over mountains.

Nearly seven months later, Bobbie pushed past Mrs. Brazier and her daughter and dashed up the stairs to jump onto the bed where Frank Brazier lay sleeping after working the night shift at his restaurant. The startled man awakened to find his beloved collie licking his face. Bobbie refused to leave his master's bedroom that day, even to accept food and water.

When Colonel E. Hofer, president of the Oregon Humane Society, launched an investigation of Bobbie's fantastic journey, he received hundreds of letters from men and women who had assisted or befriended the dog on his amazing trek westward. People recalled Bobbie because of his bobbed tail, the prominent scar over his right eye (where a horse had kicked him), his mismatched hips (after being struck by a tractor), and his three missing front teeth (torn out by their roots while digging for a ground squirrel). Some of these kind strangers had tended to Bobbie when he was starving, when he was freezing to death, when the pads of his toes were worn away so badly that the bone was exposed in some places. It was from such accounts that Charles Alexander was able to document the fantastic story of the courageous dog's odyssey in his book, *Bobbie: A Great Collie of Oregon*.

While not enough can be said about the collie's incredible accomplishment of endurance and survival, after his initial period of confusion and misdirection, it seemed as though Bobbie somehow had been given a precise mental "map" that would take him home to his master. Remarkably, even after surviving that 3,000 mile trek through snow, freezing cold, and icy rivers to swim, Bobbie enjoyed another 12 years with his beloved family in Silverton, Oregon.

Clementine Finds Her Way from New York to Denver

We have all become familiar with the story of the dog that finds its way home while overcoming seemingly impossible odds—the "Lassie Come Home" stories—but few realize that cats are capable of accomplishing the same kind of feats in conquering the wilderness and coming home after walking great distances. Popular thinking holds that a cat is too aloof, too independent, too uncaring to wish to find its human family after it has been separated from them. In many remarkable cases, such feline indifference toward its owners is simply not the case.

When Clementine's human family moved to Denver in 1949, she was left behind on the farm outside Dunkirk, New York, because she was about to become a mother. Three months later, her coat rough and matted, her paws cracked and worn, her bushy tail dwindled to a rag, she arrived at the front door of the family's new home in Denver.

How the loving and loyal Clementine had managed to negotiate rivers, mountains, and prairies to find her way to a strange house in a city where she had never been remains a mystery.

Left in Boston, Rusty Finds His Own Way Home to Chicago

In 1949, Rusty the cat's human family somehow misplaced him while they were visiting Boston from their home in Chicago. After a desperate and tearful search for their missing pet, they gave up the hunt and returned to Chicago, a thousand miles away.

Eighty-three days later, Rusty was back home, scratching on the door to be let in.

Puzzled experts on such strange and unusual matters came to the conclusion that the cat had somehow managed to hitch an occasional ride on a train or a truck in order to traverse such a distance in so few days. But how did Rusty know which trains, trucks, or automobiles would take him in the direction of Chicago, Illinois—and not New Orleans, Louisiana or Albany, New York?

Skittles Was Very Hungry after He Found His Way Back Home

Charmin Sampson and her 16-year-old son, Jason, were heartbroken when they had to leave the Wisconsin Dells on their holiday in September 2001 and return home to Hibbing, Minnesota, without their orange tabby, Skittles. They had looked everywhere and called his name until they were nearly hoarse, but the cat was nowhere to be found.

On February 4, 2002, 140 days later, Skittles appeared at the Sampsons' home, suffering from severe malnutrition and needing a good, home-cooked meal, but not a great deal the worse for wear. The orange tabby with white paws had managed to find his way across two states and over 350 miles.

Sugar Hikes 1,400 Miles Back to Oklahoma

Early in 1950, the Stacy W. Woods family moved from Gage, Oklahoma, to Anderson, California, taking with them their yellow cat, Sugar. Then, in June 1951, the

Cats can prove to be just as loyal as dogs, and just as determined to stay with their owners, no matter how far away they may be.

Woodses made a decision to return to Gage. Not wishing to uproot Sugar a second time, they reluctantly left their pet with a friend with whom the cat had a good relationship.

In August 1952, 14 months after they had moved back to Gage, Oklahoma, a cat jumped through the open window of the barn in which they were milking cows and landed on Mrs. Woods' shoulder. To her astonishment, the animal began to rub itself against her neck in a familiar manner, all the while purring joyously. Taking the cat into both hands for a closer examination, she excitedly announced to her husband that the begrimed, battered, exhausted cat was their very own Sugar.

In an article in the April 1954 issue of *Frontiers: A Magazine of Natural History*, Woods said that he could not believe that a cat could find its way home over a distance of nearly 1,400 miles. Then he remembered that their Sugar had a peculiarly deformed hipbone that had been the result of a broken right rear leg sustained when she was a kitten. He ran his hand over the cat's flank and found the familiar deformity. There was no longer any question that Sugar had come home.

First Prize Goes to Tom—2,500 Miles to Find His Owners

Tom, a cat belonging to Mr. and Mrs. Charles B. Smith, may hold the feline record for traveling the greatest distance to find its owners' new home—2,500 miles from St. Petersburg, Florida, to San Gabriel, California.

In 1949 when the Smiths decided to move from St. Petersburg, they were concerned about the trauma such a long-distance journey might bring to their cat. Because they had once read that cats often develop an allegiance to a place, rather than to people, they were delighted when they noticed that Tom appeared to have developed a rapport with Robert Hanson, the purchaser of their home. Saddened to part company with Tom, but relieved that he would have a good home, the Smiths made the decision to leave the cat with Hanson.

Convincing themselves that they were acting humanely by not disrupting Tom's normal routine and bringing him all the way across the country, the Smiths bade their feline friend good-bye and left for California. Over and over they told themselves that they had done the right thing in leaving Tom in their former house with his new owner.

Two weeks after they had relocated to San Gabriel, however, they were saddened to receive a letter from Hanson informing them that Tom had run away. It seems quite likely at that point that the Smiths regretted their decision to leave their faithful friend behind. Now he had run off and would probably be run over by a car, mangled by dogs, or condemned to wander aimlessly until he starved.

On an August afternoon in 1951, two years and six weeks after their move to California, Mrs. Smith became annoyed by the sound of a cat wailing in the yard. Mr. Smith was given the assignment of chasing the noisy intruder out of their yard, but he was amazed when the cat ran toward him and leaped into his arms. It took him only a moment or two to recognize their old friend Tom.

Mrs. Smith was highly skeptical. They had left a sleek, well-fed cat with Robert Hanson. This scraggly creature was skinny, worn, frazzled, and so weak that it collapsed on the kitchen floor when Mr. Smith brought it into the house. Its fur was bleached by the sun and had come out in handfuls. Its paws were bloody and covered with scabs.

Then the Smiths thought of a sure test to determine whether or not the bedraggled cat was indeed their Tom. They had raised Tom on baby food, and he had developed an unusual fondness for pabulum.

Mrs. Smith went to the store and bought some, then put a saucer of it on the floor near the exhausted cat. As battered and beaten though he was, the cat got to his feet and dived into the saucer of baby food right up to his whiskers.

The Smiths were now convinced that their old Tom had found his way to their home in San Gabriel, California, from their former residence in St. Petersburg, Florida—a distance of 2,500 miles—to once again become a member of their family circle.

MEDICAL MIRACLES

Babies and Infants

Miracle of a 13-Month Pregnancy

In May 1970 Christine and her husband were elated with the news that they were to become parents. But in November, the couple from Chichester, England, was presented with the doctor's startling diagnosis that the baby had ceased growing.

Christine was devastated by the announcement, assuming at first that the fetus had died at sixth months. But the doctor assured her that there was a discernible heartbeat. It just seemed as though the little girl had stopped growing.

Every week Christine went back for tests, and after each session she was informed that for some strange reason, the status of Baby Tina remained static. She was the same size as the week before.

The original due date for Tina's delivery was February 2, 1971, but that momentous day came and went. Tina seemed in absolutely no hurry to enter the world. And she remained the same size as she had been at the sixth month of the pregnancy.

Dutifully, Christine continued to arrive punctually for her weekly appointment to monitor her baby's development.

Finally, weeks after the original date for Tina's emergence into life beyond the womb, Christine was told that the baby had begun to grow again.

At last, on May 22, 1971, Tina was born, weighing in at a very respectable seven and one half pounds. Christine had been pregnant for 13 months—101 days longer than the norm. Her unique term of gestation was verified by the *Guinness Book of Records* as the world's longest pregnancy on record.

As Tina was growing up, her mother said that the little girl who had slept so long in her womb would fall asleep while she was being held, bathed, or sitting idly for more than a few moments. Christine said that she could never leave Tina alone when she was giving her a bath for fear she would fall asleep and slip under the water.

When Tina was interviewed in 1994, the 23-year-old mother of twin girls, Abigail and Laura, said that she could easily sleep 12 hours a night if she forgot to set the alarm. She almost always dozed off whenever the family sat down to watch television.

Dr. Christopher Ruoss, an obstetrician at Worthing and Southlands Hospital in Chichester, commented that it was possible that Tina Houghton slept so much because of the extraordinary time that she had spent in the womb. One could not rule out such a connection, he noted, because Tina is certainly one of a kind.

Premature Baby Born Dead Comes to Life in Mother's Arms

The birth had been so sudden and unexpected that the doctor had not yet arrived in the delivery room. But when the nurses took her baby to a nearby table to check for vital signs, Deborah Goodwin experienced a moment of great concern. She could not hear her baby crying. And the nurses were far too quiet for things to be normal.

Then a nurse held one of Deborah's hands and sadly informed her that her premature baby had been born dead. With tears streaming down her face, Deborah asked to see the baby, to hold it. After the nurses had cleaned up the lifeless form, they brought it to the young mother.

Deborah reached out to take the still, tiny form of the girl that she had named Taryn. She wanted to embrace the daughter that she would never get to know for at least a few moments before she said good-bye.

Deborah and her husband, Brian, had been fearful of a tragic end to her pregnancy when in the twenty-second week she began to bleed. Doctors warned the Goodwins, who reside in Courtenay, British Columbia, that Deborah's life was in danger, as well as the child within her womb, but the young mother, who also had a four-year-old son, resolved to direct all her energy toward saving Taryn.

Deborah was rushed by helicopter to Victoria General Hospital, 150 miles from their home, and within one week's time she was given six transfusions, while losing half of her own blood. After carefully assessing the situation, doctors grimly pronounced that Deborah's chances of saving her baby would be zero to five percent.

At 8:00 A.M. on October 29, 1993, Deborah went into labor. The nurses wheeled her to the delivery room, but they didn't anticipate the baby for at least another two hours, so the doctor had not been called.

And then suddenly, Deborah began giving birth, but the tiny, premature baby had been born dead. It had weighed slightly more than a pound and was only 11.5 inches long.

As the saddened nurse placed the body of Taryn in her arms, Deborah remembers that she felt a great peace come over her. She understood that there was a plan for

That modern medicine saves so many premature babies today is already a miracle, but little Taryn Goodwin's story is more miraculous still.

everything in God's universe and a reason for every action that he took. She thanked God for allowing her to be able to hold her child and to see her lovely face.

It was at that moment when the miracle occurred.

Although Taryn Goodwin had been outside of her mother's womb for at least five minutes and had exhibited absolutely no signs of life, at the very second that Deborah completed her prayer of acceptance of God's will, Taryn's eyes opened wide and stared right at her. And then she raised her arms.

Deborah Goodwin felt shivers run down her spine, and she screamed out the joyous news that her baby was alive.

The nurses, awestruck and dumbfounded, rushed the premature infant into the special care nursery, where they set about applying their medical skills and knowledge to help tiny Taryn maintain her tenuous hold on life.

Two hours later, Brian Goodwin arrived at the hospital, not knowing what to expect about the conditions of both his wife and their unborn child. While Deborah had been transported the 150 miles by helicopter, Brian had been left to drive to Victoria General Hospital by car.

When he walked into the recovery room and saw his wife's radiant smile and learned that their new daughter was alive, he couldn't stop the tears from flowing.

Tiny Taryn was placed in an incubator and had to stay at the hospital for 99 days before her parents were able to take her home with them. Head nurse Wendy Amos, who had assisted in the birth, said that Taryn was a miracle baby. "There is no medical explanation for why she came to life in the arms of her loving mother."

She Put Her Trust in God and in New Surgical Procedure

In 1993, when Jill Crosland of Salt Lake City, Utah, was 20 weeks pregnant, a routine ultrasound scan revealed that her unborn baby had a noncancerous tumor the size of a lemon on his tiny chest. Doctors explained that the growth of the tumor would prevent the development of the baby's lungs and cause death. They suggested that she end the pregnancy.

But Jill just couldn't give her consent to terminate the pregnancy. She had felt little Ben moving around inside her; she had seen him on the ultrasound sucking his thumb. Somehow she knew that she had to save him.

Jill admitted that she was terrified, but she put her faith in God and in the skill of Dr. Harrison's surgical team.

Jill had heard of the work of Dr. Michael Harrison, a pediatric surgeon at the University of California—San Francisco, who had performed the first successful invasive fetal surgery at UCSF in 1989. During the pioneering surgery, Dr. Harrison had corrected a congenital diaphragmatic hernia which had been crowding the lungs of the unborn child and stunting its growth. When she contacted him in 1993, Dr. Harrison and his medical team had performed numerous successful surgeries on human fetuses.

Although Dr. Harrison agreed to perform the surgery on her unborn child, he advised Jill that Ben's chance of surviving the procedure was less than 50 percent.

Jill admitted that she was terrified, but she put her faith in God and in the skill of Dr. Harrison's surgical team.

When Jill Crosland was 24 weeks pregnant, she was given drugs to prevent her going into premature labor, and Dr. Harrison began the delicate three-hour surgical procedure. First, the surgeons carefully cut open the womb to expose the fetus, which weighed only about 24 ounces. The baby was partially removed so Dr. Harrison could raise Ben's tiny arm, cut into his chest just below the armpit, and remove the tumor. As soon as possible after the tumor had been excised from the fetus, the surgical team quickly stitched Ben up and replaced him in the womb. The amniotic fluid that had been lost due to the surgical procedure was replaced with a warm saline solution, and Jill was sutured together again.

After the operation, Jill remembered lying in the delivery room and receiving the good news from the nurses that the procedure had been a complete success. The joyful mother was able to hear little Ben's heartbeat on the monitor, and she recalled how thrilled she had been by the rhythmic sound of life and how she had thanked God for the miracle.

Five weeks later—and ten weeks before his due date—Ben was born, weighing only three pounds, seven ounces. Although he had undergone the surgical procedure and was premature, Ben survived. Every time Jill would looked at her little boy, she saw a living miracle.

Baby Born Dead Comes to Life
When Grandmother Holds Him to Say Good-bye

Logan Carroll was born on 4:42 P.M., April 6, 1995. Tragically, he was not breathing and his heart had stopped.

Tami Carroll, Logan's mother, a 28-year-old accountant from Nabb, Indiana, had been worried from the moment that she had gone into labor. She had lost a child at birth in 1993, but she kept reassuring herself that everything about her pregnancy with Logan had been normal. And just before the birth, Logan's heart rate had been monitored as normal.

Nothing should have gone wrong—but it had.

While Tami tried her best to remain calm and be positive, obstetrician Diana Okon began using all of her considerable skills as a physician to bring little Logan back to life.

But at 5:15 P.M., Dr. Okon and the obstetrics team at Clark Memorial Hospital in Jeffersonville, Indiana, ceased their efforts to revive Logan. He still showed no sign of a heartbeat, and his skin had turned a bluish-gray color.

Caring nurses wiped the baby clean, wrapped him in a blanket, put a little cloth on his head, and handed Logan to Tami so that she might say good-bye.

Tami remembered that tears had streamed down her face, and she felt overwhelming sadness. She had already lost one baby at birth. And now she had carried Logan nine months and had lost him at the very last moment.

The nurses abandoned their professional demeanor and began to weep along with the heartbroken mother. Tami's husband, Todd, and her sister and mother entered the delivery room to say their final good-byes to little Logan.

> *Tami's mother was the last to cradle Logan in her arms, and it was as she was holding him that she felt and saw that he had begun to breathe.*

Tami's mother was the last to cradle Logan in her arms, and it was as she was holding him that she felt and saw that he had begun to breathe.

In response to the grandmother's excited cries of joy, a nurse placed her finger on Logan's chest and verified, too, that she felt a heartbeat.

Dr. Okon was summoned, astonished that a full hour and 18 minutes had passed since the child had been born dead. When she entered the delivery room and saw that Logon's color had changed from lifeless blue-gray to a pink, glowing hue, she pronounced that he was, indeed, quite alive.

The word spread throughout the hospital, and within minutes the delivery room was crowded with wide-eyed doctors, each verifying that the baby born dead had a heartbeat and was breathing effortlessly.

Just to be certain, Logan was transferred to Kosair/Children's Hospital in nearby Louisville, Kentucky, for close monitoring. The baby was given some medication and oxygen, but he really required no special treatment. On May 10, Tami and Todd Carroll took their miracle baby home with them.

Tami told reporters that she and her husband recognized the reality that God had granted them a miracle in restoring their son to life and they gave daily thanks for the blessing.

Dr. Diana Okon said that there really was no medical explanation for a baby coming back to life after dying during childbirth and remaining dead for a full hour and 18 minutes. Dr. Okon agreed that Logan's resurrection was "an honest-to-God miracle."

The Healing Miracle of a Hug

Two tiny little lives made their earthly appearance 12 weeks before their due date, and in all likelihood, they and their worried parents were hardly aware of how famous they were about to become. Not only would a photo of the frail twin girls gain worldwide attention, they would set a precedent that very likely would save the lives of many other preemies through an innocent display of affection—one for the other—as the two made national headlines in newspapers throughout the world.

Kyrie and Brielle Jackson were born October 17, 1995, to Heidi and Paul Jackson at Memorial Hospital in Worcester, Massachusetts. Their little bodies were so small and underdeveloped that their very survival was tenuous at best, with Kyrie weighing in at a mere two pounds, three ounces, and Brielle at two pounds.

Premature babies born this early and at such a low weight are faced with the odds stacked against them when the trauma of birth forces their entire system into action when the organs are not yet fully formed in order to adequately perform their intricate functions. Often incapable of supporting life if left to their own resources, the stresses on the miniature heart, lungs, and kidneys can prove too burdensome to sustain and one by one they simply shut down. Even though in recent years the marvelous invention of highly sophisticated technical equipment, along with superb medical training and care, boosts the chance of survival by a large percentage, in many cases it still boils down to faith and prayer.

As soon as the twin girls were born, it was obvious they would need all the assistance and the best care available. They were each put into an individual incubator—a procedure that is routinely done to reduce the chance of infection and increase the monitoring capabilities for the good of each infant. Placed in the neonatal intensive care unit at the Medical Center of Central Massachusetts, surprisingly, the girls held their own, although struggling to survive.

Little Kyrie slowly but steadily gained in weight and strength, but for some reason Brielle's struggles proved too much for her and further signs of stress manifested. Immediately, she was put on a respirator, reducing the burden on her lungs, thereby allowing her to breathe with the assistance of the machine. This helped temporarily, but unfortunately did not last long.

Brielle began to exhibit a growing discomfort that soon mounted to incessant crying that would simply not be appeased by picking her up, feeding her, or by any other means. She seemed to be having trouble breathing, and although the nurse tried many things, including aspirating Brielle's breathing passages and increasing the flow of oxygen to her incubator, nothing seemed to be working. Suddenly a radical change caused alarm as her vital functions took an abrupt dive.

Brielle, gasping for air, began to turn blue. Her heart rate was erratic. It's little beat and rhythm were all over the place as none of the medical interventions were working. As Brielle's vital signs were failing and the prospects for survival looked grim, Brielle's mother and father helplessly stood by with a panic that few can understand without witnessing a moment in time so fragile and crucial.

With no immediate options apparent, perhaps it was good fortune or maybe destiny that sparked a thought in Gayle Kasparian, the attending nurse. Nurse Kasparian remembered hearing of an innovative technique tried with premature babies with some success. She recalled a colleague telling her of a *double-bedding* procedure used in Europe, but not yet at that time in the United States. The method consisted simply of putting multiple births, especially premature ones, together in the same bed, rather than separating them in different beds or incubators.

Amazingly, within seconds Kyrie reached out her little bitty arm and wrapped it around Brielle's shoulders.

Looking at the frail, pale Brielle, nurse Kasparian turned to mention her thoughts about the double-bedding idea to the Jacksons, who eagerly gave their permission to try it. So in desperation, the quick thinking, kind-hearted nurse picked Brielle up and put her into the incubator next to her twin sister whom she had not physically been near since their birth. The nurse had no sooner closed the door to the incubator when they all witnessed the girls already moving toward one another in a cuddling manner. Amazingly, within seconds Kyrie reached out her little bitty arm and wrapped it around Brielle's shoulders as if to welcome her back to a state of togetherness that should have never have been interrupted.

Miraculously, the comforting touch of Kyrie was the saving grace that turned Brielle's condition around. Fussy, weakened, and deteriorating, Brielle instantly calmed down and her vital signs returned to normal almost immediately! It was as though she was healed by the touch and love that bonded the twins together in the first-place.

So astounding was this radical physical turnaround and the changes in vitals so dramatic that at first nurse Kasparian could hardly believe her eyes. She thought the medical equipment providing the read-out of Brielle's heart rate, blood-oxygen, and other vitals might have been faulty and perhaps she should quickly hook up another unit. But seeing how peaceful Brielle now appeared gave further proof that something greater was at work.

Heidi and Paul Jackson could only burst into tears of joy as they experienced an overwhelming thankfulness that filled their hearts at the healing embrace of their infant daughters, the miracle twins, now out of danger.

The equipment had not been faulty at all. It was indeed an accurate read-out, and as they all observed little Brielle promptly falling asleep, wrapped in the arms of her twin, they all agreed that it was an astounding sight. In the comfort of her sister's presence, Brielle had rebounded. From that moment on, she gained in strength and weight, pulling through the crisis as though Kyrie was the medicine Brielle needed, as they continued to sleep side by side, arm in arm.

Chris Christo, then a photographer for the *Worcester Telegram and Gazette*, captured the moment of the twins' embrace as the preemies made history at Memorial Hospital as the first co-bedding in the United States. The article and photo were entitled "The Rescuing Hug," and the touching story and picture soon gained remarkable popularity. Appearing in *Life* magazine and *Reader's Digest*, the photo eventually found its way to the Internet as this picture truly is worth a thousand words.

A much relieved Heidi and Paul Jackson took their beautiful daughters home just before Christmas, when they were a little over two months old. The preemies were now just over five pounds each, but healthy enough to leave hospital care and were the best Christmas present imaginable to their parents. At home, the girls continued their togetherness, sleeping in the same crib, happily growing and thriving.

> *So far, what the research indicates is that co-bedded infants do ... develop at a faster rate.*

An interesting footnote to this story is that nurse Gayle Kasparian grew concerned that her decision to break protocol and place the premature twins in the same incubator might end up getting her in trouble—regardless of the successful outcome. Gayle Kasparian even wondered if, when her boss learned of the incident, she might lose her job. Kasparian's nurse manager, Susan Fitzback, would normally have had to give her approval before anything this unorthodox be carried out, but she was out of town at a conference. Fitzback was due back the very day after Brielle and Kyrie Jackson had been placed together in this manner.

Intriguingly, as fact is often stranger than fiction, the conference she was attending was about *double-bedding*! Linda M. Lutes gave a presentation at the conference on double-bedding. Lutes, of the Oklahoma Infant Transition Program, an affiliate of Oklahoma University, was the colleague from whom Kasparian had first heard of the procedure a year earlier. So, of course, when Susan Fitzback returned, she was hoping to implement this method.

In making her rounds as usual, another nurse pointed out to Fitzback how sweet the two preemies looked who were nestled together. Word had spread throughout the hospital and many of the employees and visitors peeked in the infant nursery window to view the teensy, adorable, cuddling babies. Fitzback was so surprised and pleased that she gave the nurse who had just directed her to the sight a hug right on the spot, as she expressed how beautiful she found that sight to be.

Since then, this *double-bedding*, or *co-bedding* as it is sometimes called, procedure has been tried at other hospitals around the country—and with great success. Scientific research at hospitals, schools, and institutions was undertaken and continues to officially determine the validity of the method.

So far, what the research indicates is that co-bedded infants do, in fact, develop at a faster rate. They have better feeding patterns and, in general, better vital signs. Being premature, the inability of undeveloped lungs to function properly often results in breathing problems—and even the cessation of breath altogether. But in keeping the preemies together, it seems that even the simple movement or squirming of one baby stimulates the other into taking a breath, somehow reactivating the system of the other. Therefore, co-bedding babies spend less time on oxygen. The overall effects are sufficient to decrease the average length of time a premature baby has to stay in the hospital in special care, which also adds the benefits of being cost effective and more efficient.

The Jacksons, however, don't need the research results. Having gone through an agonizing ordeal of giving birth to two two-pound babies, one or both of whom would probably not have survived without the wonderful advancements of hospital technology and care, it still came down to something more. When it came to the point where all the best equipment was not working and Brielle was not expected to live, the miracle of a risk-taking nurse, a rescuing hug, and cuddling between siblings worked.

Born with Her Heart outside Her Chest Cavity

On August 4, 1998, when she was only one day old, Jazmyn Hope Stumpf, who was born with her heart outside her body, underwent a five-hour operation to have the organ placed in her chest cavity. The team of surgeons at Children's Hospital of Wisconsin in Wauwatosa, led by Dr. Bert Litwin, had to move other organs around in Little Jazmyn's chest in order for her heart to fit into the place where it belonged.

In Jazmyn's case, her heart was free-floating, connected to her body by four major blood vessels—the aorta, pulmonary artery, and superior and inferior vena cava. Her heart was also rotated, with the apex pointing upward.

Jazmyn's parents, Marcie and Jeff Stumpf of Portage, Wisconsin, had been married for about two years when they learned that Marcie was pregnant. The Stumpfs had a 15-month-old daughter, and they each had children from previous marriages.

About halfway through 35-year-old Marcie's pregnancy, an ultrasound had disclosed the baby's heart condition, known as ectopia cordis. According to American Heart Association statistics, this rare condition occurs in only 5.5 to 7.9 of every one million live births.

On July 20, Marcie was hospitalized at Froedtert Memorial Lutheran Hospital in Wauwatosa. She was given medications to halt her labor, but when labor began again on August 3, the doctors decided to perform a Caesarean section because of the high risk to the fetus.

At 35 weeks—five weeks short of full-term—Jazmyn weighed five pounds, one ounce. Dr. Meg Autry performed the Caesarean section at Froedtert Memorial, and soon after birth, Jazmyn was brought to Children's Hospital for the delicate surgery by Dr. Bert Litwin and his team of four surgeons. Dr. Litwin had previously performed three such surgeries, two of which were at Children's Hospital.

Although risks are high in such operations Dr. Litwin felt that Jazmyn's heart was strong. He did advise that she would always have to be more careful than other children, however, for Jazmyn was also born without a sternum, the protective bone in front of her heart.

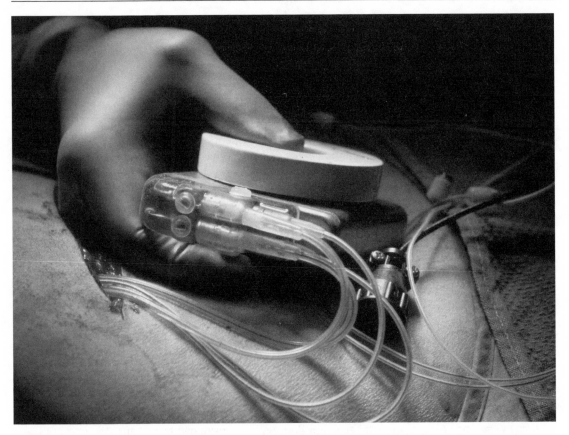

Implanting pacemakers into adults has become a fairly routine surgery for heart patients. Putting a tiny one called a "Microny" into a sick infant took the skill of a physician like Dr. Seshadri Balaji.

As remarkable as this story is, just two years later a similar case faced doctors. On August 16, 2000, Tyler Todd was born with his heart beating outside his chest and underwent intricate surgery at Rush-Presbyterian-St. Luke's Medical Center in Chicago. Although Tyler spent the first year of his life in the hospital, his surgeon Dr. Joseph Amato told the *Chicago Sun Times* that he believed the little boy would be able to lead a normal life.

Dr. Amato also explained that after Tyler's sixth birthday, he would have to undergo more surgery to build a breastbone to protect his heart. It would also be likely that Tyler would be required to undergo yet another such surgery later in his teen years.

Fitted with the World's Smallest Pacemaker

During the early summer of 2000, about four months into her pregnancy, Erin Schuck of Pendleton, Oregon, learned that her baby had a congenital heart condition. According to the doctors, the electrical charges in tiny Alexandra's heart weren't properly formed, so Erin was directed to Doernbecher Children's Hospital, where her baby could be monitored through the pregnancy.

At around 35 weeks, doctors became concerned when monitoring devices detected an accumulation of fluid around the baby's heart, and labor was induced. Alexandra Schuck was born in late September at Oregon Health Sciences University Hospital in Portland. Because of her heart condition, Alexandra was six weeks premature, and her chances for a normal life were predicted to be extremely small.

Dr. Seshadri Balaji, a pediatric cardiologist at OHSU, was aware of a new heart regulating device called a "Microny" that had been developed by St. Jude Medical in St. Paul, Minnesota. Dr. Balaji knew that the pacemaker was about a third the size of traditional models and that it was undergoing clinical trials by the Food and Drug Administration (FDA). Because early trials indicated that the tiny pacemaker worked effectively, Dr. Balaji appealed to the FDA to permit them to use the device on Alexandra.

Just a month after her birth, Alexandra was fitted with the world's smallest pacemaker, a device about the size of a quarter. The tiny instrument was fully capable of performing all the functions of a regular pacemaker and may not need to be replaced as Alexandra matures.

Dr. Balaji advised Alexandra's parents, Charles and Erin, that because of her heart problems, their daughter would always need a pacemaker, but that should have no adverse affect on her life.

At her six weeks checkup on November 8, OHSU made public the success of Alexandra having received the world's smallest pacemaker due to the exemption made by the FDA.

The Hand of Hope

In early 2000, an astonishing photograph circulated on the Internet with an accompanying caption that identified the picture as having been taken during a surgery on a 21-week-old fetus—and the fetus was holding the doctor's hand.

The photograph seemed too remarkable to be true, and many who received it in their email assumed that it had to be an urban legend or a hoax created by some Internet mischief maker.

However, as incredible as it may seem to many of those who have seen the inspiring photograph, it is no clever mock-up. The photograph was taken by Michael Clancy during fetal surgery being performed by Dr. Joseph Bruner on Samuel Armas, the unborn son of Julie and Alex Armas. According to Clancy, who owns the copyright on the picture, as he witnessed the procedure to correct spinal bifida, he had seen the uterus shake and the baby's hand emerge from the surgical opening. Clancy said that Dr. Bruner put his finger into the baby's hand, and the baby squeezed the finger.

The dramatic impact of Clancy's photograph of that miraculous moment was labeled by many as the "Hand of Hope," and some viewers suggested that the hand of

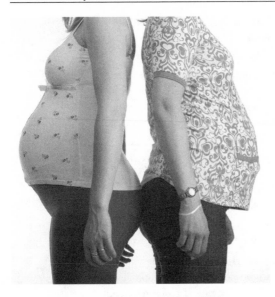

Researchers have found that twins, even those with little contact with each other, often experience interesting parallels. In one case, twin sisters had coinciding pregnancies.

little Samuel Alexander Armas had reached out to grasp Dr. Bruner's finger, as if to thank the surgeon for granting him the gift of life.

Samuel's mother, Julie Armas, was an obstetrics nurse in Atlanta, who learned that her unborn son was diagnosed with spinal bifida, a serious condition in which a baby's spine does not close properly during development. She knew that her baby would not survive if he were removed from her womb for any surgical procedure, but she was also aware of the remarkable work of Dr. Joseph Bruner of the Vanderbilt University in Nashville. Dr. Bruner has been internationally acclaimed for performing special operations on fetuses afflicted with spinal bifida while they were still in their mother's womb. The surgical procedure involves the medical team removing the uterus and making a small incision to operate on the baby. Dr. Bruner acknowledged that the procedure with a fetus as young as 21-weeks has its risks, because if anything should go wrong, the baby would not be able to survive on its own.

Although touched by the various accounts of the incident which described little Samuel's tiny hand reaching out to grab his finger, in an article in *USA Today* (May 2, 2000) Dr. Bruner commented that both the mother and the baby were under anesthesia and could not move. During the surgery when Samuel's hand suddenly emerged from the uterus, Dr. Bruner said that he instinctively offered his finger for the baby to hold. The little hand did not squeeze his finger, but merely rested upon it.

The fact that surgery on the 21-week-old fetus was successful was miracle enough for Julie and Alex Armus—with or without the optional dramatic moment of the finger squeeze. Samuel was born on December 2, 1999, and, according to his parents, was developing well.

Twins Give Birth on the Same Day—Half a World Apart

On November 15, 2002, 36-year-old twins Amanda and Meagan Baldwin each gave birth to a son. While this in itself is unique, it becomes even more bizarre when one considers that Amanda lives in Sydney, Australia, and Meagan resides in Belgium, approximately 12,000 miles away. And when one learns that Amanda's son, Truman, was scheduled to be born on November 4, while Meagan's son, Benjamin, was penciled in on the calendar to be born in early December, the births of the two cousins on the very same day becomes downright miraculous.

The chain of coincidences forged its first link when the twin sisters learned in late February that they were pregnant. Via emails and telephone calls, they joked about what a bizarre occurrence it would be if they happened to give birth on the same day. However, such a remarkable coincidence seemed unlikely when their pediatricians predicted due dates that were about a month apart.

Amanda had to be induced when she was about 11 days overdue; and after a 13-hour labor, she gave birth to Truman at 1:06 A.M. on Friday, November 15. Shortly after she had given birth, her husband sent Meagan an email informing her of the birth of her nephew.

And that's when things really got strange. As soon as Meagan in Belgium learned that Amanda in Australia had given birth, she began to feel nauseated. When she went to her doctor for a pre-natal examination later that morning, Meagan was told that her baby could come at any time. That afternoon her water broke, and she went to the hospital where, at 2:40 A.M. on Friday (the difference between time zones accounts for the fact that Meagan learned of Truman's birth), she gave birth to Benjamin, nearly a month before his due date.

When Meagan's husband called to tell Amanda and her family the news of Benjamin's birth, he could not resist saying that the two baby boys, though cousins in actuality, were really very much like twins. For, remarkably, those two first cousins, born 12,000 miles apart, will forever celebrate their birthdays on the same day, just as their mothers had always done.

Baby Growing in the "Wrong Place" Defies All Odds to Live

When Jayne Jones, 38, was 27 weeks pregnant, a routine ultrasound scan provided the tragic news that her baby was growing on the omentum, the layers of fat that cover the bowel. Only one such case had ever been reported in Great Britain, and in all available medical resources nearly all such fetuses had died within weeks, even days of conception.

Ten days after the scan, Mrs. Jones collapsed in pain, and her husband, Graham, rushed her to Derriford Hospital in Plymouth. At that time a groundbreaking decision was made to perform a surgery that had never before been undertaken in the Great Britain. Because of the great risk to both mother and child, Jayne and Graham were told frankly that the mother would have a one in five chance of dying in childbirth during the procedure.

On April 19, 2008, Billy Jones was born, weighing a tiny two-pounds, two ounces. The baby was immediately placed in an incubator to help keep his temperature up. His mother was placed in a High Dependency Unit where, upon her regaining consciousness, she was informed that she had delivered a miracle baby. Outside of a slightly malformed head from being squashed up against his mother's internal organs, Billy had developed very well.

Who Owns the Title for the World's Smallest Baby at Birth?

Who is the world's tiniest baby miracle? Interestingly, that crown must be placed upon at least two infant heads.

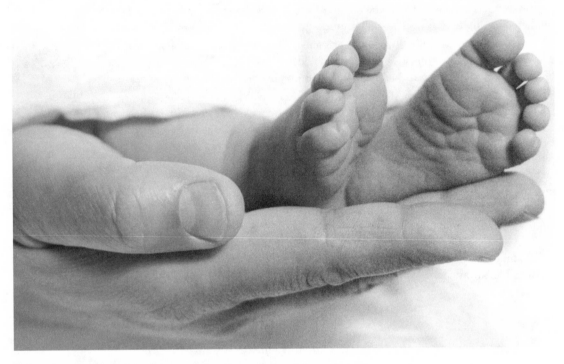

Babies have been surviving at extraordinarily small sizes in recent years.

When identical twin Tyler Davison was born on June 8, 1992, at Nottingham City Hospital in England, he entered the world three months premature, weighing a featherweight 11 ounces, and stretching out to just six inches. His twin, Stephen, was a hefty big brother at two pounds, two ounces.

The twins had to be brought into the world prematurely when doctors discovered during tests that they were not growing properly in the womb of their mom, 31-year-old Catrina Davison. Medical experts informed Catrina and her husband, Stephen, that Tyler was receiving less of the blood flow and was extremely small. The doctors told the Davisons that the only way to save the twins was to deliver them prematurely by a cesarean procedure.

After a week in a special incubator where oxygen equipment assisted his breathing, little Tyler was removed and was able to partake of his first meal of his mother's milk.

A spokesperson for *The Guinness Book of Records* said that Tyler would be included in a future edition of the book, replacing Marian Chapman as the world's smallest surviving baby. Chapman, also British, was born in 1938, weighing 10 ounces, one ounce less than Tyler. She was, however, 12 inches in length, twice Tyler's size.

Record keepers show that Madeline Mann was born at 9.9 ounces in Loyola Hospital in Chicago in 1989. Madeline was declared the world's smallest surviving baby.

On February 9, 1997, a contender for the crown of world's smallest baby was born in Iowa City, Iowa. Alicia Allen weighed only 12 ounces and was said by her parents, Lu Ann and Harry, to be smaller than a Barbie doll. When she was released by the University Hospitals in June, Alicia weighed five pounds, five ounces—seven times her birth weight.

While the average American baby is born after a gestation period of between 38 and 40 weeks, Drew McSweeney was born on April 15, 2001, after 23 weeks, five days in the womb. One of the smallest babies to survive in New Jersey, Drew weighed 15.6 ounces when he was born at Saint Barnabas Medical Center in Livingston. Drew remained in the hospital's Perinatal Center for four months, and he was released to his parents on August 5, just three days before his due date.

In February 2002, the world's smallest baby honor went to a baby girl nicknamed "Perla" by her medical team at the Careggi hospital in Florence, Italy. Perla weighed only 9.97 ounces and was 10 inches in length, thereby qualifying her as the smallest human on record to have survived so long.

Born two months premature, the miniscule baby girl spent three months in intensive care. According to her doctors, Perla suffered from breathing difficulties, anemia, hypothyroidism, hypoglycemia, and jaundice. When she was released to go home with her parents in May 2002, Perla weighed 4.4 pounds and was said to have an almost 100 percent chance of leading a normal life.

Perla's title lasted for two years. Then, in September 2004, Rumaisa Rahman was declared the smallest surviving baby in the world at a weight of 8.6 ounces, which is about the size of a cell phone. Her fraternal twin sister, Hiba, weighed one pound, four ounces at birth. The girls were born at the Loyola University Medical Center in Maywood, a suburb of Chicago.

In February 2007, Amillia Taylor weighed in at just under 10 ounces and measured only 9.5 inches long. As this book goes to publication, it would appear that Rumaisa Rahman wears the crown of world's smallest baby at birth, winning by less than a couple of ounces.

Christmas Morning Is a Good Time for Miracles

On Christmas morning, 1993, four-year-old Tyrel McAmmond gave his parents physical proof that God had answered their prayers when he showed the strength necessary to rip open his presents with gusto.

Just a few days before Christmas, Darren and Shelly McAmmond, had made funeral arrangements for their beloved son, because the doctors had sent Tyrel home from the hospital, sadly admitting that there was nothing more that they could do for him. The deadly, unmerciful cancer had spread through his body.

In June, Tyrel had been diagnosed with B-cell lymphoma in his liver and abdomen, and for the next five months, he underwent heavy doses of chemotherapy.

At first the exhaustive treatments appeared to be effective, and his doctors agreed that the tumors had shrunk completely. They cheerily informed the McAmmond that Tyrel could go home with them to Grande Cache, Alberta.

But the cure was not to be so easily won. Within a few weeks Tyrel had suffered a relapse.

When their little boy's temperature reached 105 degrees, the McAmmond frantically returned him to the care of the hospital technicians.

The revised diagnosis was not good. The cancer had spread through Tyrel's liver, spleen, and bone marrow.

On December 12, after an unsuccessful attempt with one more chemotherapy treatment, the dispirited physicians announced that the vicious, unyielding disease had beaten them. They somberly advised the McAmmonds to take their son home and try to make him as comfortable as possible for the little time that he had left.

> *On Christmas morning the McAmmonds gave heartfelt thanks to God when they saw that Tyrel was unmistakably getting stronger.*

Darren McAmmond later said that he and his wife had "cried their eyes out," but they decided to go ahead with Christmas plans so that little Tyrel would not think anything bad was going to happen to him.

But then Darren and Shelley made a positive decision not to give up. They had always been devout churchgoers and firm believers in the boundless mercies of God. And they most certainly believed in the power of prayer.

First they made an appeal to their church friends to pray for Tyrel. And then, spontaneously, a glorious grapevine of love began to spread to others of strong spiritual beliefs, and soon thousands of people across Canada and the United States were praying for the same little boy from Grande Cache.

On Christmas morning the McAmmonds gave heartfelt thanks to God when they saw that Tyrel was unmistakably getting stronger. They were elated to share the magic of Christmas with their beloved son, who ripped through the colorful presents with the enthusiasm and excitement envisioned in their prayers and dreams.

When they brought Tyrel in for tests after the holidays, the spirit of Christmas joy once again filled the hearts of the McAmmonds. The doctors were astonished to discover that the impossible had occurred: The cancer had disappeared from the four-year-old boy's body!

One of the doctors told the McAmmonds that only God could have healed their son. There was no medical explanation to account for such a healing.

On February 7, 1994, doctors drew bone marrow from Tyrel's one-year-old sister, Jenae, to perform a transplant to make sure the cancer wouldn't return.

In May 1994 Tyrel remained a picture of perfect health.

Dr. Bowen, head of the transplant unit at Alberta's Children's Hospital where Tyrel was treated, said that there was no doubt that when the boy had been sent home before Christmas, he was in a hopeless condition. However, the tests performed on Tyrel a few weeks later showed no evidence of cancer. The boy was in total remission.

While medical science can only record, not explain, such impossible cures, the McAmmonds know that God looked down on them and worked a miracle, a wondrous miracle for which they will thank him every day of their lives.

Comas—Coming Back to Life

Giving Birth to Her Baby Awakened Her after Five Months

Twenty-four-year-old Barbara Blodgett of Yakima, Washington, was three months pregnant when she was injured in a car accident on June 30, 1988. Although she survived the accident, Barbara was in a coma for five months, but still gave birth to Simon, a healthy baby boy, on December 9. The day after her son was born, she began emerging from the coma.

Doctors were uncertain why Barbara was able to regain consciousness, but they speculated that hormonal changes after the birth might have been responsible. While her complete recovery from the brain stem injuries suffered during the accident continued to handicap her to some degree, Barbara Blodgett spelled a message for readers of *USA Today* on February 14, 1989, when she pointed out the letters for the words: "Never give up."

A Masterpiece of Life

In January 1998, even though she had been in a coma for seven months, 21-year-old Ledy Minguzzi gave birth to a healthy baby girl at Lugo Hospital in Rome, Italy.

Ledy had suffered a brain hemorrhage when she was one month pregnant, and to prepare her for the delivery of her baby, neurosurgeons performed a complex surgery that brought her into a state called "vigilant coma." In this level of consciousness, Ledy remained paralyzed but could communicate with the doctors by blinking her eyes.

After the caesarean birth, Dr. Marco Mattucci placed the five-pound, four-ounce baby girl on Ledy's breast. According to the doctor, a single tear of joy ran down Ledy's cheek.

In Dr. Mattucci's opinion, this was a certain sign that Ledy understood what had happened. The Vatican's newspaper *Osservatore Romano* said that the surgery conducted by Dr. Mattucci and his staff was "a masterpiece of life."

She Gave Birth after Receiving Last Rites

On April 24, 1999, a pregnant Maria Lopez entered a coma after complaining of headaches and nausea. At first the doctors at the University of California Medical

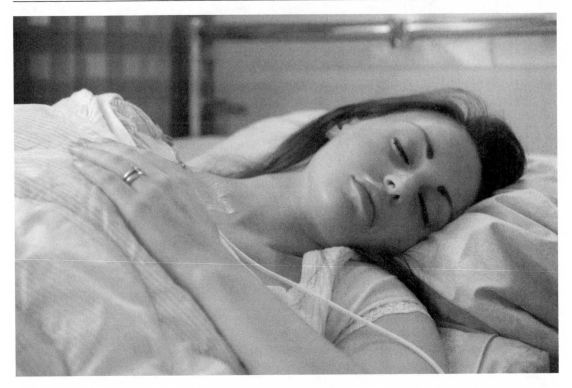

Patients have revived from very long comas, and there are even stories of women giving birth while in a coma.

Center assessed the symptoms as a result of the pregnancy, but upon closer examination of their patient they discovered that Maria had been born with arteriovenous malformation, a condition in which blood vessels in the brain are malformed or tangled.

Medical personnel sought to treat Maria Lopez's condition by a process called embolization, during which the blood flow to the brain is lessened. In spite of their concerted efforts, however, Maria remained in a coma.

After three weeks had passed with no signs of improvement, doctors at the UC medical center advised the Lopezes that they should consider withdrawing life support. Sadly, the decision was made to do as the doctors recommended for the sake of their comatose Maria. A priest was summoned to give her last rites.

Then, just as the priest was concluding the service, Maria Lopez coughed.

The attending physicians, not wishing to appear without compassion, nevertheless told the family gathered around Maria's bed for the last rites that her cough was only a kind of reflex.

However, the Lopez family saw the movement from their beloved Maria as a sign from God. Sylvia Hernandez, Maria's sister, said that it was sign that Maria was not ready to die, that she wanted the family to give her more time to come around.

A few days later, Dr. John Frazee, a vascular neurosurgeon at the UC Medical Center, was astonished when Maria awoke from her coma and responded to his commands. Dr.

Frazee commented that whether or not Maria's cough had been a sign from God, it had saved her life, because it had convinced the Lopez family to keep her on life-support.

Several days after Maria had communicated with Dr. Frazee, she slipped back into a coma. Once again, her family did not give up on her.

And it was a good thing that the Lopez family had a strong faith in God and in the eventuality of their daughter's recovery. Maria awakened again, this time for good, and six days later give birth to healthy twins.

While doctors at the Medical Center said that they could offer no explanation for Maria Lopez's recovery, Dr. Scott Strum commented that numerous studies in medical literature gave credence to the idea that a nurturing, loving, and supportive family is a great factor in the recovery process.

You Must Always Keep Faith

On January 14, 2001, Shannon Kranzberg delivered her daughter, Alexis, while in a coma incurred following a November 16, 2000, car crash in Dallas, Texas. Then, amazingly, a week later Mrs. Kranzberg awakened from the coma to find that she had given birth to a daughter.

"I just woke up, and the baby was there," Shannon told the *Dallas Morning News.* According to attending physicians, Alexis's birth was two months premature, evidently triggered by the staph infection that Shannon Kranzberg had contracted while in the hospital.

Michael Kranzberg had accepted the grim possibility that his daughter would never be born and that his wife would never regain consciousness. When Shannon and Alexis were released on March 15, Michael told the media that Shannon was his hero, and he offered their miracle as a testimony to everyone who might find themselves in a situation where they must always keep faith.

She Remained in Coma throughout the Entire Term of Pregnancy

On July 23, 2001, 24-year-old Chastity Cooper of Warsaw, Kentucky, gave birth to her daughter, Alexis, after having been in a coma since two weeks after conception. As far as is known, this was the first time that a woman remained in coma throughout the entire term of her pregnancy. Alexis Michelle Cooper was born a healthy seven pounds, seven ounces.

Chastity, who had previously given birth to two boys, ages four and three, received a severe head injury in an automobile accident on the rainy night of November 25, 2000. She had dropped off the boys at her sister's and was driving on U.S. 42 to meet her husband at a family gathering when her car slid into the path of another. Routine medical tests performed during Chastity's emergency treatment at University Hospital

> *Cooper also said that although his wife was not able to move or to talk, he was certain that she was aware of Alexis's birth.*

in Cincinnati, Ohio, indicated that she was pregnant. Since it was only two weeks after conception, even her husband, Steve, hadn't known that they were about to become parents again.

Dr. Michael Hnat, an obstetrician who specializes in high-risk pregnancies, said that the pregnancy did not appear to complicate Chastity Cooper's condition. Doctors had been aware of such potential problems as blood clots, and they had induced labor about a week prematurely to better manage the birth and the comatose patient's welfare.

Steve Cooper told the *Cincinnati Enquirer* that little Alexis, their newborn daughter, was precious. He said that Chastity and he had wanted a daughter for a long time. Cooper also said that although his wife was not able to move or to talk, he was certain that she was aware of Alexis's birth. He said that he had placed the baby on Chastity's side and she had smiled and established eye contact with her daughter. Cooper was convinced that a bond had been established between mother and baby.

Pronounced Clinically Dead, Miracle Brings Brenda Back to Life

On January 21, 1996, Brenda, a mother of two, was at home in Grand Prairie, Texas, when she began to experience chest pains. At his insistence, she got in her fiancé Jim's truck and he set out for the hospital, about 15 minutes away.

They had not gone far when Brenda, complaining of dizziness, fell forward onto the dashboard. Jim stopped his truck and reached for Brenda. Her eyes were open and dilated. He could feel no pulse, and she was not breathing. Brenda appeared to be dead. Desperately praying that his layman's analysis was wrong, Jim continued to the hospital.

When medical personnel brought Brenda's body into the emergency room, the attending physician, Dr. Chavda, concurred with Jim's tearful diagnosis. Brenda had no vital signs. She had gone into cardiac arrest and was pronounced clinically dead.

Dedicated to the preservation of life, Dr. Chavda placed heart paddles on Brenda's chest in an attempt to shock her heart into starting. Even as he performed CPR, the physician was concerned that even if Brenda could be resuscitated, she would suffer brain damage. If a brain is deprived of oxygen for more than two to three minutes, the patient is likely to experience severe impairment—and Brenda had been clinically dead for far longer than three minutes before she was brought into the emergency room.

The doctor was about to give up all hope for Brenda when one of the nurses detected a tear coming from one of Brenda's eyes. The emergency room became electrified with hope. Brenda was fighting to come back to life.

After 48 minutes of intense efforts on the part of the medical team, Brenda's heart was once again beating. Although she remained unconscious for a week, when she awakened she had no brain damage at all. Nor did she have any memories of her ordeal from the moment she slumped forward in Jim's truck until she returned to consciousness in the hospital a week later.

A Miracle of Miracles When Terry Awakened after 19 Years

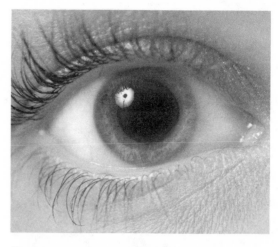

I t wasn't the fact that the first spoken words from her son in over 19 years were those asking for a particular choice of soft drink that startled Angilee Wallis, it was the miracle of miracles that Terry Wallis spoke at all! It was simply ironic that after 19 years in a coma, Terry's first uttered words on June 12, 2003, were those requesting something so mundane and routine, as though no time had passed at all. And perhaps in his mind, it hadn't.

Her eyes were fixed and dilated and she had no vital signs for 48 minutes, yet Brenda was brought back to life.

This extraordinary span of missing time might in itself be considered a grace—to wake up after 19 years of sleep as though it had been nothing more than a night's rest.

Time had *not* stood still for Terry's brother, mother, father, wife, and daughter. The whole family had maintained a nearly two-decade-long vigilance of faith and hope as they continued to visit Terry in the hospital, then eventually in the nursing and rehab center, never knowing if he was to ever awaken from this paralyzing perversion of life that had impacted all of their lives in one fateful evening.

On July 13, 1984, Terry Wallis and a friend were involved in a severe auto accident that had catapulted their car off the road into the river below, ultimately coming to rest under the bridge. The crash was not discovered until the next day when the two young men's bodies were found. Tragically, the driver, Terry's friend, died on impact. Terry's injuries were so severe that he was left a comatose quadriplegic.

In spite of what they had been told by doctors and medical personnel, Angilee and Jerry Wallis's undying love for their son never wavered. The trauma's impact was magnified by the fact that Terry and his bride, Sandi, had just had a baby girl, Amber, born only six weeks before the tragic accident occurred. As Terry lay in a comatose state, he may have had little or no awareness that he had left behind a daughter who grew up viewing her daddy only in a seemingly petrified state and a wife who could do no more than offer a one-way communication about the joy this little girl had brought to her life.

Eerily, almost exactly 19 years later, as Angilee devotedly sat by her son's bedside in Stone County Nursing and Rehabilitation Center in Mountain View, Arkansas, she was quite literally shocked by the sound of Terry's voice saying, "Mom." One can only imagine the elation she experienced as her son suddenly and miraculously awakened from the coma ... and asked her for a Pepsi!

From then on, Terry's improvement has been slow but sure. His vocabulary and awareness gradually increased and he was considered inexplicably "fully emerged" from the cocoon-like coma state in which he existed for so long. In 2006, doctors and

One of a father's proudest moments is walking their daughter down the wedding aisle, and for one man it was a doubly wondrous occasion.

researchers said that the tiny nerve connections in Wallis's brain were slowly beginning to rewire. At that time, doctors stated that Wallis was the only person in the United States to have recovered so dramatically after such a severe brain injury and such a long time in an unconscious state.

A speech therapist worked with Terry three days a week, and nurses are encouraged to communicate constantly with him in sentences that help him to think and to give answers requiring more than a "yes" or "no". Dr. James Zini, Terry's physician, explained that Terry had never been expected to regain a full awareness or cognitive level to any degree. Terry's continued improvement will involve a great deal of effort from a team of doctors and therapists and will also require immense patience and persistence from him.

Although Terry doesn't seem to understand the vast amount of missing time since the accident, Dr. Zini made the observation that Terry is beginning to realize he's in a very different world now. His baby daughter is 19 years old. Ronald Reagan is no longer President of the United States. A whole new technology has come into being, including cell phones, the Internet, and satellite dishes.

But Terry's long-term memory seems to be acute. Unaware that his grandmother had passed away, Terry asked to see her, even reciting her phone number that the rest of the family had long-since forgotten. Step by step, his healing miracle is coming more clearly into focus.

After His Life Support Was Shut Off, He Recovered to Walk His Daughter Down the Aisle

In February 2006, Brian Paolo's doctors told his family to prepare for the worst. His emphysema had won the hard-fought battle.

Anne-Marie, his daughter who was to be married in a few days, became distraught that her father would not walk her down the aisle and give her away. The church in Handforth, near Wilmslow, Cheshire, would not be merry on her wedding day without her father.

Brian Paolo had entered a coma. As the grieving family watched, the doctors pulled the tubes from his neck and shut off his life support. The physicians explained that his lungs were just too badly damaged and his immune system had run its course.

Then, astonishingly, after all the machines were shut off, Brian Paolo began to breathe on his own.

Within days, he was sitting up and boldly announcing that he would be at Anne-Marie's wedding and walk her down the aisle.

The doctors and nurses were astounded. They had never seen anyone look so grey and drifting away as when they pulled the tubes from his neck.

They were even more astounded when, just three hours after Brian Paolo was discharged from the hospital, Anne-Marie came by in her car to pick him up to take him to her wedding, which would now be the happiest she could imagine.

After 19 Years in a Coma, He Awakened to Give the Credit to His Wife

When Jan Grzebski, 65, woke up in June 2007, he found that a great deal had changed since he was struck by a train in 1988. Among the greater changes he discovered was that the Communist Party was no longer in power in Poland and that food no longer had to be rationed.

Immediately after the accident, doctors gave Grzebski, a railway worker, two or three years to live. Amazingly, Grzebski remained in a comatose state for 19 years.

The newly awakened man was quick to give the credit for his survival to his wife, Gertruda. According to hospital personnel, Mrs. Grzebski was at her husband's bedside to move him every hour to prevent bed sores.

Gertruda admitted that she cried and prayed a lot during the ordeal that lasted nearly two decades.

Jan Grzebski told Polsat television interviewers that it was his beloved Gertruda who had saved him and brought him back to life.

> *The newly awakened man was quick to give the credit for his survival to his wife, Gertruda.*

The Miracles of Audrey Santo

Audrey Santo was in a comatose state for nearly 20 years before she succumbed to cardio-pulmonary failure on April 14, 2007. Audrey had spent nearly all of her life in a bed in her parents' home in Worcester, Massachusetts. Although Audrey never did awaken from her coma, miracles took place around her during this sad time.

As a toddler, Audrey suffered an accident which was aggravated by unfortunate medical errors that left her in a condition known as akinetic mutism. Soon after she entered a comatose state, friends and family came by the Santo home to pray at the little child's bedside. After a time, individuals began to notice a great deal of supernatural phenomena occurring in Audrey's bedroom. Various statues of saints began to exude oil. Some visitors noticed that the scent of roses permeated the bedroom.

Over the years, thousands of visitors came to pray at the silent girl's bedside and went away reporting their own mystical experiences. As time passed, the events claimed by the pilgrims to the shrine of a little girl's bedroom began to grow in number. There were reports of bleeding Hosts, the oil that flowed from religious statuary, and always the scent of roses, said by some to signify the presence of Mother Mary.

Officials of the local diocese investigated the hundreds of reports of spiritual phenomena, but did not issue any definite conclusion regarding their authenticity.

When Bishop Robert McManus learned of Audrey Santo's death, he remarked that thousands of individuals who had visited the Santos' home had come away impressed by their devotion to life. God, the bishop observed, worked through individual men and women to make his love available to those who are most in need.

A funeral mass was held for Audrey Santo, the woman of silence who appeared somehow to generate extraordinary events, on April 18, 2007.

It Takes Brains

In Spite of the Old Medical Myth,
We Do Use More than 10 Percent of Our Brain

One of the most pervasive myths about the human brain is the assertion that we only use about 10 percent of our brain capacity. It is likely that this myth arose during research in the 1930s when scientists were uncertain regarding the functions of large areas of the cortex. In recent years, thanks to increasingly sophisticated brain scan technology, researchers have been able to "map" the functions of different areas of the brain. While there appears to be some redundancy, there are high degrees of specialization in some areas, especially those governing speech and abstract thinking.

For its small size with a weight of about three pounds, the human brain is a wonderful instrument and harbors many mysteries yet to be solved. The neocortex, the outer layer of the brain, by which we perform higher thinking, consists of a thin sheet of cells about 2.5 millimeters in thickness. In addition to containing our "thinking tissue," the neocortex is also made up of cortical blood vessels and supportive cells for the neuronal (nerve) matrix. If the neocortex is damaged in humans and the higher mammals, the result is a condition known as decorticate rigidity in which the thinking processes are shut down.

From the perspective of human evolution, the neocortex is built upon the older brain in the cerebellum and brain stem which perform the autonomic functions, such as posture, heart rate, blood pressure, and the onset of sleep. The brain stem is a primitive area of the brain that merges the lower brain into the spinal cord. Without the neocortex, consciousness as we understand it would not exist. However, the neocortex can't even stay awake to perform the simplest of tasks without constant stimulation from the brain stem.

Although the neocortex is the crowning achievement of human evolution, it does contain large cavities without any brain cells, as well as considerable amounts of cerebrospinal fluid, white matter, blood vessels, blood, and "non-thinking cells." And while scientists caution against suggesting that these areas constitute the mythical unused 90 percent of the brain, they do admit that some individuals have been able to function with only a tiny fraction of the brain—or no brain at all.

The French Tax Official Who Did Just Fine without a Brain

On July 20, 2007, neurologists at the University of Marseille revealed the remarkable case of the 44-year-old French tax official who had been managing just fine with a fluid-filled cavity taking up most of the space where his brain should have been. Writing in the medical journal *Lancet*, doctors described how the civil servant had gone to the hospital in 2003 because he had been complaining of a slight weakness in his left leg. When the doctors scanned his brain to see if the problem lay there, they found mostly a black hole.

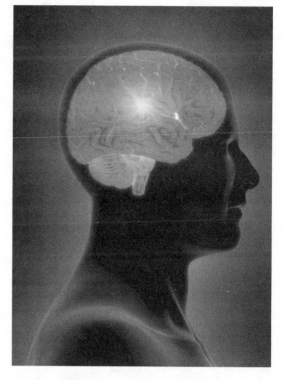

The human brain is a truly remarkable organ capable of feats even medical professionals have never imagined possible.

The patient told the attending physicians that as a six-month-old baby he had suffered from hydrocephalus (commonly known as "water on the brain") and that a shunt had been inserted to drain away the fluid. Dr. Lionel Fuilet ordered a tomography scan (CT) and an MRI (magnetic resonance imaging scan) and discovered that the lateral ventricles, chambers that hold and cushion the brain, were extremely enlarged. In a normal brain, these ventricles are very small.

Upon close examination, Dr. Fuilet and his team found that a massive cavity had built up in the man's skull and that it had filled with fluid and a thin sheet of functioning brain tissue, which was pushed back against the inner walls of his cranium.

Tests by the medical team revealed that the tax official was neither physically nor mentally disabled by his strange condition and that it had not hindered his socialization. The man was married with two children and carried out his duties at the tax office without difficulty. IQ tests indicated the man's score to be 75 (average IQ is around 100).

Der Spiegel quoted Florian Heinen, a brain development expert at the Dr. von Hauner's Children Hospital at Munich University, who explained that while the French tax official's case was extremely rare, his was one of a number of cases in which individuals had functioned quite well with a very small amount of brain matter. The most striking observation Heinen made was that "these few brain cells can achieve just as much as the millions more cells that other people have."

Born without a Brain?

When Leah Church was born in 1985, her mother said that she could not help thinking that her baby looked like a little alien visitor from Mars. At six pounds, four ounces, most of Leah's weight was in her head—which was nearly 19 inches around, just a fraction more than her total body length.

To make matters even worse, the attending physicians' initial diagnosis of Leah was that she was blind, deaf, and born with no brain at all, only a brain stem. The prognosis was that the little girl would be unable to live for more than a few weeks or months.

A sympathetic nurse told the parents, Tim and Sandy Church, to insist that the doctors drain the fluid from Leah's skull. The doctors knew that the little girl was also afflicted with hydrocephalus, a condition in which the cerebrospinal fluid, instead of circulating around the brain, becomes dammed up inside the cranium and leaves no space for the brain to develop normally. The doctors told the Churches that draining the fluid from Leah's cranium would not help their daughter in any way. Without wishing to appear cruel or indifferent to their anguish, the doctors once again explained to the Churches that no brain at all had been allowed to develop in Leah's cranium because of the enormous buildup of fluid.

> *The doctors told the Churches that draining the fluid from Leah's cranium would not help their daughter in any way.*

Sandy pleaded that while the procedure might be pointless from the medical perspective, perhaps it might at least ease little Leah's suffering.

The doctors yielded on the basis of compassion and after the procedure were astonished to discover that Leah did have a brain. The pressure from the buildup of spinal fluid in her skull had so compressed her brain that it had not shown up on the previous CAT scan.

Prior to the advent of computerized axial tomography (CAT scans), a physician's prognosis for the one in 500 children born with hydrocephalus was quite bleak. Generally doctors predicted a brief life span, plagued by numerous complications, and little hope of the child developing normally in either intellectual or physical capacities. With the increased reliance upon the CAT scan and advances in diagnostic imaging technology, most parents may expect the likelihood of normal longevity with little or no intellectual or physical deficiencies.

For four months, the Churches continued to return to the hospital in Billings, Montana, to have Leah's head drained with a syringe. Eventually, her doctors installed a valve under her scalp so that her parents might pump out the buildup of fluid.

By the age of five, Leah knew the alphabet and could write her name, so the Churches enrolled her in school. Although their daughter had been left with poor eyesight, she was able to progress throughout school with relatively few problems. She even competed in a track meet—a miracle for a child who was said to have been born without a brain.

Some People Have Functioned Very Well without a Brain

As dramatic as Leah's case in the previous story may be, there have been instances in which people have lived with only cerebrospinal fluid in their craniums—and some of them have done very well. Dr. John Lorber acquired a remarkable set of data regarding people who seemed to get along just fine without a brain.

A neurology professor at the University of Sheffield in the United Kingdom, Lorber recalled the time in the 1970s when the campus doctor asked him to examine a student whose head was a bit larger than normal. Lorber gave the student a CAT scan and found that he had virtually no brain at all. Instead of the normal 4.5-centimeter thickness of brain tissue between the ventricles and the cortical surface, Lorber discovered that the student had only a thin layer of mantle measuring about a millimeter and his cranium was filled mainly with cerebrospinal fluid.

> *Conventional medicine would state that such individuals would be completely unable to function.*

The young man had hydrocephalus, a condition in which the cerebrospinal fluid, instead of circulating around the brain, becomes dammed up inside the cranium and leaves no space for the brain to develop normally. Such a condition is usually fatal within the first few months of life. If individuals with hydrocephalus should survive beyond infancy, they are usually severely retarded. In the case of the math major from the University of Sheffield, he had an IQ of 126 and graduated with honors.

Professor Lorber collected research data concerning several hundred people who functioned quite well with practically no brains at all. Upon careful examination, he described some of the subjects has having no "detectable brains." Conventional medicine would state that such individuals would be completely unable to function on any mental level at all, yet many scored up to 120 in IQ tests.

Lorber's discovery of people thriving without brains was not unprecedented. In 1970, an autopsy performed on a building janitor who died at the age of 35 revealed that he had hardly any brain at all. Although he wasn't considered an intellectual by those who knew him, the man was known to read a newspaper daily and was regarded as a popular personality by all those in his neighborhood who were acquainted with him.

Dr. Patrick Wall, professor of anatomy at University College, London, stated that there existed "scores" of accounts of people existing without discernable brains. The importance of Lorber's work, Wall said, was that he had conducted a long series of systematic scanning, rather than simply collecting anecdotal material. Lorber had gathered an astonishing set of data that challenged scientists to explain how people lived without brains.

Lorber and other scientists theorized there may be such a high level of redundancy in normal brain function that the minute bits of brain that these people have may be able to assume the essential activities of a normal-sized brain.

David Bower, professor of neurophysiology at Liverpool University, England, stated that although Lorber's research did not indicate that the brain was unnecessary, but it did demonstrate that the brain could work in conditions that conventional medical science would have thought impossible.

Guns and Bullets

Shot Point-Blank, Bullet Bounced Off His Head

On September 29, 1993, Mohammed Jafari, 30, was opening one of three conven-ience markets that he owned with his brother in Memphis. At 8:30 A.M., a masked gunman ran into the store brandishing a pistol. He demanded the money from the cash register, but when Jafari complied and handed him the key, the thug clumsily knocked it to the floor. In anger and frustration, the thief began pounding at the register and demanding that Jafari open it.

When Jafari tried to explain that he could not open it without the key that the thief had knocked somewhere out of sight, the man flew into a rage, cursed Jafari, and put the pistol to his head.

Jafari saw a bright flash, felt a terrible pain between his eyes, and felt blood pouring down his face. But somehow the bullet had bounced off. As Jafari would state later, his hard head saved his life.

The gunman stood astonished that the storekeeper didn't drop to the floor, and Jafari took advantage of the man's confusion to grab his gun and begin to wrestle with him. The gun fired again, this time tearing into the thug's forearm, causing him to flee the convenience store.

Amazingly, Mohammed Jafari had been shot point-blank in the head and suffered only a few powder burns and nine stitches.

The Taxi Driver Took Three Slugs to the Head
but Still Managed to Leave the Thug Empty-Handed

Taxi driver Bill Cornett kept praying to God to spare him for the sake of his seven children as the carjacker fired two .22 bullets point-blank into his skull. The teenaged thief continued to order Cornett out of the cab, shouting that all he wanted was the car.

On that night in May 1996, the carjacker had ordered Cornett to a remote area and had shot him when the taxi driver refused to leave his vehicle. Cornett passed out when the two bullets ripped into his head and slumped over on the steering. When he regained consciousness, the teenaged thug was outside the car and had reloaded. That was when he fired the third bullet into Cornett's head.

Still unable to open the doors of the cab, the gunman left when it appeared Cornett was dead. When he saw the thief leave, Cornett used his cell phone to call police.

For one man, a Bible not only protected his soul but also deflected a bullet!

The taxi driver spent nine days in the hospital. One bullet was removed from inside his skull. Another had entered above his left eye and had come out just above his left ear. The third slammed into the back of his head and also exited near his left ear. But God had answered his prayers and spared his life for his children. Police later arrested the 18-year-old responsible for pumping three slugs into Cornett's head.

Thieves' Bullets Were Deflected by Bible

Tony Schrouf was on his way to Bible class in Oklahoma City in November 1996 when two thugs approached him on the driveway of his home and demanded his wallet. Startled, Schrouf could only attempt to explain that he had only three dollars in his wallet.

Without uttering another word, one of the thieves shot Schrouf twice at point-blank range and ran off. Schrouf's father, who was in the house, called the police and an ambulance.

Tony Schrouf was in the hospital for 10 days. One of the bullets had struck him in the abdomen, but the potentially fatal shot, the one the robber had fired point-blank at his heart, had struck the Bible that Schrouf was holding near his chest. The slug that would have penetrated his heart, simply ricocheted off the Good Book.

Shot in the Face, Bullet Slides down Throat—and Is Swallowed

In December 1997, professional boxer James Shipp was minding his own business and walking toward a gas station when a gunman suddenly blocked his path and shot him in the face at point-blank range with a .22 pistol.

Shipp uttered a prayer, then, to his astonishment, he felt the slug slide into his throat, and he swallowed it.

Doctors at Western Medical Center in Santa Ana, California, were baffled. The bullet should have blown Shipp's brains out and killed him, but, amazingly, it had stopped at the back of his nose and slid down his throat. After a day or so in Shipp's stomach, the slug passed naturally through his digestive system. Valaida Shipp, the boxer's mother, declared that her son was alive because of the power of God's will.

The "Cyst" in His Shoulder Turned Out to Be a Slug from 1938

Faustino Olivera, an 88-year-old veteran of the Spanish Civil War, had felt a lump in his left shoulder sometime in 2006. He thought it was a cyst of some kind and paid little attention to it until it started growing and becoming painful.

In February 2008, Olivera entered the hospital in Barbastro, in northern Spain, with the intention of having doctors remove the painful lump on his left shoulder. Surgeons were taken aback when they extracted a slug that had been fired from a Mauser 98 rifle.

When he was shown the bizarre souvenir that he had carried for 70 years, Olivera remembered being a lad of 18 conscripted to General Francisco Franco's Nationalist troops. On November 11, 1938, Olivera recalled a jolt to his shoulder when he was holed up in a farmhouse during the Battle of the Ebro.

His Wedding Ring Deflected a Bullet and Saved His Life

When two men entered the antique shop of Donnie Register in Jackson, Mississippi, in early December 2007, they asked to see a coin collection. Register brought out the coins, but the two men suddenly brought out a gun and demanded the coins and whatever cash was in the register.

Although the antique dealer complied with the thieves' every request, as the thugs turned to leave, the one with the pistol fired at Donnie.

Instinctively, Donnie Register put up his left hand to shield his face, and the bullet was deflected by his wedding ring.

Police investigators stated that the ring saved the store owner's life, but Donnie Register did not escape uninjured. A portion of the bullet pierced his middle finger, and another fragment penetrated the muscle tissue of his neck. Neither injury was serious.

Register's wife, Darlene, gave God all the credit—God, and the fact that Donnie had married her and wore his wedding band to ward off bullets.

Witness to a Gun Fight Finds a Slug Lodged in a DVD in His Pocket

Barry McRoy, an off-duty firefighter, was leaving a fast food restaurant in Walterboro, South Carolina, on February 22, 2008, when two men, struggling for control of a gun, pushed their way inside.

Before anyone could attempt to intervene, the pistol discharged accidentally and struck one of the troublemakers, thereby ending the fight.

Later, as police were taking McRoy's statement, the firefighter noticed a bullet hole in his jacket. When he looked inside, he found a bullet lodged in the DVD that he was carrying. Before that astonishing discovery, McRoy had no idea that he had been hit by the stray bullet.

A wedding ring saved one man from a thief's bullet.

According to the police investigation, when the gun fired, it hit one of the miscreants, passed through him, shattered a glass window, and lodged in the DVD in the inside coat pocket of McRoy, who had just stepped out of the restaurant.

Little Angel Takes Seven Bullets Intended for Her Mother—and Survives

December 1, 2007, began for seven-year-old Alexis Goggins and her mother, Seliethia Parker, 32, with the bad news that their furnace had gone out on a cold Detroit day. On December 2, their bad luck would transform into the miracle of Alexis surviving seven point-blank bullet wounds.

Shortly after midnight, Seliethia called her friend Aisha Ford and asked her to pick them up so they could attend a late-night birthday party for Aisha's mother. As they were getting into Aisha's SUV, Calvin Tillie, Seliethia's ex-boyfriend appeared in a very bad mood. He had been standing for hours in the cold outside Alexis and Seliethia's apartment. He drew a pistol, ordered Seliethia and Alexis into the back seat, and demanded that Aisha drive him to an address that he gave her.

Stalling for time and trying to think of a way to get help, Aisha Ford said that she needed to get gas. When she went inside the station to pay for gas, she called the police. The station attendant noticed her crying and asked what was wrong.

That was the terrible moment that they heard gun shots coming from the SUV.

In a fit of rage, Tillie had fired two shots from his 9mm at Seliethia. One bullet grazed her forehead, and the other slammed into her chest, stopping just short of an artery.

It was at that moment that seven-year-old Alexis shouted at Calvin Tillie not to hurt her mother. Alexis threw herself across her mother and took the next seven bullets from the pistol into her own little body. She was hit in her left temple, chin, cheek, right eye, and arm.

At the sound of the shots, the gas station attendant put in another call to the police.

Seliethia Parker staggered from the SUV, screaming for help. Police, responding to Aisha's first call for help, approached the vehicle and found little Alexis in a pool of blood in the front seat. They arrested Calvin Tillie on the scene.

For no reason that Marie and her party could determine, the occupants of the two cars seemed furious at them.

Through her tears, Seliethia said that she had been thinking how she might save her child and herself when Tillie pointed the 9mm at them. She did not have the remotest thought that little Alexis would throw herself in front of the spray of bullets and be the one to save her. Seliethia hailed her daughter as an angel, an angel who would sacrifice herself for another without giving such action a moment's thought.

Incredibly, the little angel with seven bullet wounds in her tiny body was not yet ready to return to heaven. After an almost three-month stay in Children's Hospital of Michigan and enduring multiple surgeries, Alexis was fitted with a prosthetic right eye and returned to first grade. The Detroit Police Department hailed Alexis as a hero—praise that is echoed throughout the nation.

Shot between the Eyes, She Requires Only Stitches and Walks Out of ER

Everybody in Tampa was calling it "Marie's Miracle." On April 12, 2008, Marie arrived at the emergency room at Tampa General Hospital with a .44 bullet wound behind the eyes. Not only was Marie alive, she was not unconscious or even complaining of any pain.

Marie, 42, her boyfriend, and her 22-year-old daughter were returning home after a pleasant evening out when two cars pulled alongside them when they stopped at a traffic light. For no reason that Marie and her party could determine, the occupants of the two cars seemed furious at them, shouting obscenities and making crude hand gestures. Even more startling was the threat made by one of the men that he was going to kill Marie.

When the light changed, the two hostile vehicles drove on either side of Marie's boyfriend's pickup truck. At the next traffic light, one of the occupants of the other cars stood up and rose through the open sunroof. He pointed a pistol at Marie and fired three times. One of the bullets struck Marie directly between the eyes.

Blood was pouring from the wound, and Marie thought that she was going to die. Strangely, though, she felt no pain. When they wheeled her into the ER, Marie was sitting up and talking to medical personnel.

Doctors determined that the bullet had shattered into three pieces when it struck her skull. The fragments had exited through her cheek on one side of her head and beside her ear on the other. All Marie needed was some stitches, and after that minor medical function was completed, she walked out of the hospital, truly the recipient of a miracle.

Shot Close to the Spine in an Accident, He Coughs Up the Bullet

In September 2007, teenaged Austin Askins was shot in the mouth during an accident at a house party in Boise, Idaho. Because the bullet had lodged too close to his spine, doctors decided against the risk of surgery.

On October 11, after an airplane flight, Askins began to cough. The coughing continued uncontrollably until the teenager felt a sharp pain in his mouth. Another bout of coughing, and Askins coughed up the bullet.

Stabbings and Foreign Objects

Doctor Finds Patient Had a Rusty Nail in His Skull for 22 Years

In January 1997, Robin Hanshaw, 52, an engineer from Stoke Poges, England, went to the doctor to see about a stubborn cold. When the doctor asked Hanshaw about the lump on his face, the engineer said that it had been there for a time, but didn't pay any attention to it.

An X-ray revealed an inch-long rusty nail stuck between Hanshaw's eye and his ear, and emergency surgery removed the nail that had been in his head for 22 years. Hanshaw recalled the day over two decades before when he had stepped on a plank while working in his garden. He didn't realize the board had a nail in it that was driven into his skull.

Charity Worker Lives after Psycho Drives Knife into Her Brain

In March 1998, 28-year-old charity worker Alison sat alone in a deserted London train car. Skinhead Robert Buckland walked by, smiled at her, then turned and savagely drove a five-inch knife through her head.

You would think you would notice a nail going into your head, but one man went about his life for decades without complaints about one inside his skull.

Alison staggered down the train car, the handle of the knife protruding from her skull, until a man comforted her and summoned help.

Surgeon Adrian Casey said that he had never seen such a shocking injury in 13 years of medicine. The knife had gone straight in at the back of Alison's head and right through the middle of her brain. Incredibly, the blade did not strike a major artery and there was only minor bleeding. It was also a miracle that the blade very narrowly missed the brain stem at the top of the spine. If it had pierced the brain stem, Alison would likely have died at once.

Although she cannot see things to her left and all feeling was lost to her left arm, Alison was looking forward to getting on with her life. Her 18-year-old psychopathic attacker was convicted of attempted murder.

Pencil Was in Her Skull for 55 Years

In 1954, four-year-old Margret was running with a pencil in her hand. She fell, drove the pencil through her hand and into her head.

Fortunately, the pencil missed vital parts of her brain, but at the time no surgeon dared to operate. After suffering headaches and nose bleeds for nearly her whole life, in 2007, Margret Wegner was told by surgeons that technology had improved sufficiently to allow them to remove the pencil. On August 26, nearly all of the pencil, three inches long, was extricated from Margret's skull after 55 years. Only the very tip of the pencil remained. It had grown in so firmly that it could not be removed.

His "Weeping" Eye Caused by Shard of Glass
Unseen during Earlier Surgery

It probably had not been his finest hour, but Xiao Zhu, 22, of Jinjiang, China, was struck across the head with a beer bottle during a fight in 2001. His right eye was injured, and he had a successful operation to fix a torn tear duct. The wound appeared to heal perfectly, but Xiao seemed to bothered by a seemingly endless flow of tears.

Early in 2007, his right eye became very painful, and he went to a number of different hospitals to have it checked. Always the diagnosis was the same: Nothing is abnormal. Everything is fine.

At last the pain became so much that Xiao Zhu appealed to surgeons at Dongnan Eye Hospital in Fuzhou to have another very careful look at his right eye. On this occasion, the surgeons found a shard of glass 1.4 inches long embedded 2.4 inches deep that had been overlooked by previous surgeons.

Amazing Recoveries

Car Crash Ends 22 Years of Paralysis

In 1974, after surviving a terrible car crash near her mother's home in Manchester, England, 32-year-old Sandra was told that she had suffered severe injuries to her spine. She was paralyzed and would never walk again.

Sandra's great passion had been ballroom dancing with her husband, Albert, and the couple had taken their kids to dancing classes four times a week. Accepting the doctor's decree that she was condemned to a wheelchair for life, she settled into the day-to-day chores and challenges that came with trying her best to be a good mother to her children while she was handicapped.

Almost at once, Sandra began to experience sporadic pains and sensations in her legs. She told her doctors that she was able to wiggle her toes, but they patiently informed her that she was having an occasional muscle spasm. When she asked to be given braces and physical therapy, the doctors explained that she was undergoing denial of her condition. She must accept the reality of a life in a wheelchair. And Sandra did accept that unhappy reality for 22 years.

Doctors at the hospital couldn't understand why a paralyzed woman was experiencing so much pain.

Then, in 1996, while she was seated in her wheelchair in the back of their van, Sandra was thrown onto the floor when Albert suddenly braked to avoid hitting a car that had pulled out in front of them. Sandra's right leg snapped, and she screamed out in pain.

Doctors at the hospital couldn't understand why a paralyzed woman was experiencing so much pain. Curious, they ordered an ultrasound examination of Sandra's spinal cord and discovered that the injuries had not been as severe as the physicians had believed in 1974.

After 22 years in a wheelchair, Sandra was prescribed physical therapy to help restore weakened muscles. Soon, she was able to stand up and slowly walk the length of her hallway. Sandra could now look forward to playtimes with her grandchildren and, perhaps, an occasional slow dance with Albert.

Legally Blind, His Sight Came Back after a Punch to the Head

Lee, 44, awakened to his miracle of sight after a thug punched him in the head. One night in the winter of 1994, a brutish intruder burst into his home in northern England home, looking for someone who owed him money. When the hoodlum realized that he had the wrong house, he took out his anger on the blind father of four who tried to stand up to him despite his handicap.

After the invader fled their home, Lee began to feel dizzy and ill, and he went upstairs to the bedroom to lie down. He fell asleep and awoke about an hour later to the initial stages of a healing miracle. He was able to see patches of color.

Lee, a former truck driver, had been declared totally blind in 1990. His adjustment to being blind had been made even more difficult by the fact that Lee was unable to see his youngest son, who was born after the onset of his sightlessness.

By morning, Lee was able to distinguish shapes. By the end of the day, he was able to recognize his wife and three children—and to see his youngest son for the first time. The first thing that Lee did was to take his children to the park and play catch with them.

Lee's physician couldn't explain why Lee's sight had been returned by a thug's punch to the head. Both the doctor and Lee were satisfied to call it a miracle.

Blind in One Eye for 53 Years, Walking Smack into a Pole Restored His Sight

When Verne, who had been blind in his left eye for 53 years, walked into his optometrist's office in Grand Rapids, Michigan, the doctor exclaimed that he had just witnessed his first miracle.

Then 10-year-old Verne had lost his sight in 1944 when one of his buddies accidentally hit him in the left eye with a clump of dirt. In January 1997, the 63-year-old advertising salesman was walking through a mall with some friends when he walked right into a pole. Verne shook his head, a bit stunned by the accident, then was astonished that he could see out of his left eye.

Verne's optometrist discovered that the blow had apparently jarred loose a cataract that had been clouding the lens of the eye. After 53 years of sightlessness in his left eye, Verne was now able to read with a pair of trifocal glasses. A regimen of exercises to improve his hand-eye coordination strengthened eye muscles that hadn't been used since he was 10.

Verne believed that divine intervention caused him to hit the pole on that day. He said that he had always believed in a divine being and that miracles do happen.

She Regained Her Sight through the Miracle of Childbirth

An astonishing report in the November 14, 2002, issue of the Norwegian newspaper *Aftenposten* told of a woman who regained her sight through the miracle of childbirth.

Mona Ramdal, 29, was born with toxoplasmosis, an infection which can cause eye or brain damage in infants. Because of the infection, Mona's right eye has always been afflicted with limited vision; and when she turned 13, her left eye also began to fail. Gradually, Mona had only 15 percent vision remaining in her left eye and scarcely any in her right eye.

But when she became pregnant, a wonderful series of miracles appeared to be set in order. The sight in Mona's left eye began to return. By the time her daughter Anne-Marthe was born in 2001, Mona could see. Within a few months after Anne-Marthe's birth, Mona applied for a driver's license and passed the tests on her first attempt.

Dr. Per Hvamstad, who has treated Mona Ramdal since the late 1970s when she was a little girl, said that he had never read or heard of a similar case of loss of eyesight restored through pregnancy. Since the retina is by medical definition a part of the brain, Dr. Hvamstad explained, once it is destroyed, it is gone forever. That is why, in his opinion, the restoration of vision in someone such as Mona Ramdal, who was terribly visually impaired, must be considered a miracle.

One blind man recovered his sight after accidentally walking into a pole.

Spinal Treatment Restores Sight in Eye after 12 Years

On January 3, 2008, Doug Harkey, 30, from Dubuque, Iowa, arrived for another chiropractic treatment at the office of Dr. Tim Stackis. Harkey was skeptical of the value of chiropractic, but his fiancée, Gina Connolly, had talked into trying the procedure to help a spinal bone spur problem.

After the session, Harkey's eye began to water, and the moisture continued to flow for 45 minutes. Then, after he wiped his right eye, he noticed an astonishing development in his left eye, the eye that had been completely devoid of sight for 12 years. Somehow, the spinal treatment that he had just received from Dr. Stackis had restored his sight.

Dr. Stackis said that the chiropractic adjustment that had corrected the spinal problem had performed the miracle of restoring his patient's sight. Chiropractors believe that the nervous system controls and regulates every function of the body, but Dr. Stackis said that he was also very open to a miracle.

A checkup with Dr. Lester, an eye doctor, verified that Harkey now had 20/100 vision in his left eye (20/20 is considered normal) and that the eye could attain 20/30 with corrective lenses.

Can a mere handshake offer more than friendship? For one man, it had great healing powers.

A Healing Handshake

Even a chance meeting may lead to a miracle.

Mark Gurrieri, 36, was working at a restaurant when a friend introduced him to his dinner partner, General Practitioner Chris Britt. As the two men shook hands, Dr. Britt recognized Gurrieri's large spongy hand and his larger than normal facial features as symptoms of acromegaly, a tumor at the base of brain.

Dr. Britt, 46, Woodford Green, Essex, hadn't seen a case of acromegaly since he was a medical student. Such a condition is extremely rare, and most doctors would not have seen patients with it, but Dr. Britt had never forgotten the demonstration in a medical classroom when he was a student decades ago.

Upon Dr. Britt's urging, Gurrieri went for an examination in June 2008, and the doctors found a two-centimeter tumor which confirmed Britt's suspicions.

Gurrieri and his family are convinced that Chris Britt is a guardian angel in disguise as a medical doctor. Mark Gurrieri has said that he owes his life to Dr. Britt.

Handicapable Heroes

Over 2,000 Miles of Hiking while Blind

If you should accept the challenge to hike the entire length of the Appalachian Trail—a total of 2,144 tough miles through thick forests, waterfalls, rivers, mountain ranges—everything that you will need for daily necessities on the grueling trek must be stuffed into a 90-pound pack on your back.

When 51-year-old Bill Irwin accepted the wilderness challenge, he had never hiked or camped before in his life, and his only companion was his seeing-eye dog, Orient— for Bill Irwin is blind.

In March 1990, in perhaps one of the most astounding self-imposed challenges ever undertaken by a physically challenged person, Irwin strapped a 90-pound pack to his 210-pound frame and set out on the trail from Georgia to Maine. For the entire length of the arduous march, his only teammate would be his faithful German shepherd guide dog, thus proclaiming Irwin's confidence and trust in Orient's intelligence and resourcefulness.

The two adventurers began their trek in Dahlonega, Georgia, on a day when a driving rain sent a chill through them. When they made camp on the first night, Irwin had no way of determining if they were lost or on the correct path.

With only Orient to guide him and no other human to read a map or to confirm directions, Irwin knew that he had no choice but to continue walking with firm determination.

That first night Orient curled up next to him, barking or growling whenever he heard the strange night sounds of wild animals in the forest. The big dog would continue to lie protectively next to his owner on every subsequent night of the wilderness journey.

On the third day of their trek, they chanced upon some hikers, who, much to Irwin's joy and peace of mind, assured him that they were, indeed, following the Appalachian Trail.

To some degree, Irwin had been able to prepare himself for the ordeal by listening to cassette tapes which described the wonders of the famous trail. Friends who had some familiarity with the area also did their best to paint substantial word pictures of the various terrains that they would encounter.

Irwin and Orient had not been on the trail too long before the German shepherd developed painful, running sores on his back from carrying a supplementary pack. Irwin knew that Orient needed time to heal, so he added the dog's pack to his own.

For three weeks, he recalled, he lugged Orient's pack, struggling along, stumbling, being tripped by roots and knocked down by low tree branches.

Irwin admitted that he had felt genuine fear when a late-season hurricane came roaring inland from the Atlantic Ocean.

He remembered the wind howling, tearing branches from the trees, and ripping the trees themselves from the ground. While the lightning and thunder seemed to shake the very ground around them, the adventurer and his loyal canine companion huddled under Irwin's poncho.

Weeks turned into months as the stalwart duo maintained a steady pace along the trail. Occasionally, they would meet other hikers, who would confirm or deny the correctness of their course.

According to a prearranged plan established with friends, Irwin and Orient would leave the forest every five days to pick up food that had been shipped to designated post offices.

About halfway on the 2,144-mile hike, a misstep on a slippery rock in a river bed sent Irwin sprawling. The awful snapping sounds and the sharp pains in his torso provided him with the unwelcome news that he had broken several ribs.

For the next two weeks, Irwin said, each step, each breath brought him severe pain. To make matters worse, he had already lost all of his toenails from rubbing against his boots while edging his way down long, steep stretches on the trail.

There were some days, Irwin concedes, when he assessed his broken ribs, his painful feet, the discomfort of cold, wet weather, and began to laugh at himself. But he refused to quit.

He had known at the outset that he would face pain, hardships, and many days of inclement weather.

He also knew that he would never give up.

Perhaps one of his most harrowing experiences occurred in November, when he and Orient had nearly achieved their goal of conquering the Appalachian Trail. Irwin lost his footing in a stream swollen by heavy rains, and he was dragged by the swift-moving current toward what he would later learn was a 40-foot waterfall.

Somehow, he managed to grab hold of a rock, and then, moving from rock to rock, he pulled himself out of the stream.

When Irwin and Orient finally reached the pathway's end in November, it had taken them eight exhausting and painful months to attain their goal of hiking the entire 2,144-mile length of the Appalachian Trail.

Their remarkable achievement marked the first time that a blind person had ever completed the trek, a heroic effort that was accomplished through the mutually supportive partnership of a man and his dog.

Blind at Two, He Learned to "See" with His Ears

Thomas Johannesen of Askoy, Norway, lost his eyesight to cancer when he was only two years old. After he had received radiation therapy, the doctors conferred and decided it was best to remove Thomas's eyes to halt any chance of the disease spreading.

Then, remarkably, little Thomas began to make strange, high-pitched clicking sounds as he moved about the house. At first his parents, Vigdis and Geir, were puzzled, but then, as Thomas continued the procedure day after day, it occurred to them that he was employing his own kind of sonar technique to enable him to avoid running into things.

In 1997, at age 14, Thomas had learned to "see" with his ears so well, that he could easily identify objects in his path and distinguish between people, animals, trees, bushes, automobiles, traffic signs, and anything else that might present itself to him. Thomas was able to ride his bicycle around his neighborhood, as well as go boating and swimming. He had even joined the Boy Scouts to be able to keep up with his friends.

Thomas was confident that he was able to do almost anything that his classmates could do—only slower.

> *Thomas began to make strange, high-pitched clicking sounds as he moved about the house.*

Scientists explained that when Thomas sent out the high frequency clicking sounds with his tongue, the clicks bounced off objects and echoed back to him, telling him precisely what was in his path. Thomas had created his own radar. By experimenting since he was just a toddler, he had learned to identify the echoes that various objects made and even to judge their distance from him. He literally used the airwaves to navigate his way through the darkness that had surrounded him since he was a child of two.

Five Years after Losing 40 Percent of His Skull, He Was Named as One of the Top Sculptors of Western American Art

The very fact that Ivan Schultz survived the brutal accident is in itself a miracle. In 1990, Schultz, then 28, was a pilot flying out of Vance Brandt Airport in Longmont, Colorado. He was working on an airplane engine when he bumped a piece of equipment and that caused the propeller suddenly to lurch forward and strike him on the head.

Schultz was thrown 20 feet by the blow. The left side of his skull was broken into four pieces—one large forehead section and three smaller ones that lodged in his brain. Remarkably, Schultz remained conscious throughout the horrible ordeal.

After a week in the hospital, he was sent home with his right side paralyzed and his skull stitched together with hundreds of tiny threads. The day before the accident, Schultz had been considering accepting one of the offers that he had received from several major airlines. Now he was faced with years in rehabilitation just learning how to walk, talk, and read again. He would never pilot another airplane.

As one of the therapeutic exercises designed to strengthen his right hand, Schultz was given a small ball of clay to squeeze. In time, the lumps of clay became recognizable objects. Excited by his newly exhibited creativity, Schultz's wife, Dena, encouraged him to take a class with Fritz White, one of the top Western artists in the nation and senior sculptor for Cowboy Artists of America. With White as his mentor, Schultz began sculpting tribal figures and symbols.

In 1995, five years after the terrible accident that had sliced away 40 percent of his skull, Schultz was named by *Art of the West* magazine as one of the top sculptors of

Native American art in America. His piece "Spirit Seeker" received an honorable mention from the Plains Artists National Competition, and it was purchased for the city of Loveland, Colorado, in 1997. Today, Ivan Schultz's works are in great demand, and he is famous for his anatomically accurate depictions of Native Americans.

After 20 Years of Being Paralyzed, Israeli Paratrooper Becomes Real-Life "Iron Man"

Radi Kalof, 41, a former Israeli paratrooper, was paralyzed for 20 years. On August 25, 2008, Kalof began walking the streets of Haifa, Israel, in an electronic exoskeleton called ReWalk, the invention of engineer Amit Goffer, founder of Argo Medical Technologies. The ReWalk is now in clinical trials in Tel Aviv's Sheba Medical Center and consists of motorized leg supports, body sensors, and a back pack with a computerized control box and rechargeable batteries. Some have described the device as a combination of the exoskeleton of a crustacean and the suit worn by the comic book hero Iron Man.

ReWalk does require the use of crutches to help with balance. A remote control wristband allows the individual to stand, sit, walk, descend, or climb. Ironically, Goffer, the creator of the mechanism that will enable thousands to rise out of their wheelchairs, cannot benefit from his own brainchild. Goffer was paralyzed in an accident in 1997 and does not have full function of his arms.

After 28 Years without Hands, She Becomes the First Woman to Receive a Double Hand Transplant

After 28 years without hands, Alba Lucia, 47, originally from Columbia, became the first woman in the world to receive a double hand transplant. The 10-hour surgery took place on November 30, 2006, and was conducted by Dr. Pedro Cavadas and a team of 10 medical professionals at Hospital La Fe in Valencia, Spain. Six double-hand transplants had been carried out on men—the first being a 33-year-old man in France in 2000.

The highly ranked medical team carried out both transplants simultaneously. First, Lucia's forearms had to be adjusted to match the donor's, a woman who was pronounced brain dead after an accident. Bonex had to be fixed with metal plates and screws. Microscopic surgery was used to attached the arteries, veins, and nerves.

Dr. Cavadas said that it would be five to six months before the patient had any feeling, but Alba Lucia said it would be worth the wait to have beautiful hands that would allow her a far more independent life than any prosthesis.

He Set a New World Land Speed Record—While Blind

In October 2005, Mike Newman, 43, from Sale, Cheshire, hoped to break the 200-mile-per-hour barrier on the track at Elvington Airfield near York, but he ran out of room on the track. Newman did break his previous record of 144 miles per hour, however, and set a new world land speed record by reaching 167.32 miles per hour in a specially crafted BMW M5.

Mike, the father of two, is blind, and he set the record to raise awareness that a person can achieve anything that he or she wants.

Legless Climber Conquers Mt. Everest

Mark Inglis, 47, from New Zealand, was trapped in a storm and nearly died while climbing Mt. Cook, the country's highest peak, in 1982. Due to severe frostbite, Inglis lost both of his legs beneath the knees.

Fitted with carbon fiber false legs, he went on to become a ski guide and won a silver medal for cycling in the Sydney Paralympics.

In May 2006, Mark Inglis conquered Mt. Everest, the world's highest peak. One of his artificial legs broke during the intense 40-day climb, but he had brought along a spare set of limbs and parts just in case of such an event.

Celebrating the remarkable victory of a legless climber mastering Mt. Everest, Mark's wife, Anne, said that he had dreamed of reaching the peak of the world's highest mountain all of his life.

Skiing Enthusiast Breaks Two
World Speed Records—after Being Blinded

When Kevin Alderton interrupted two thugs attacking a woman near his home in Islington, North London, the blows to his head that he received for his act of heroism cost him his eyesight. Since Kevin was a skiing enthusiast who had participated successfully in numerous racing contests, it seemed as though that part of his life had come to a sad and depressing close.

Kevin Alderton, however, was not a man to surrender to a negative act of fate so easily. He refused to allow his disability to end his career as a speed racer.

He devised a helmet with a two-way radio enclosed so he might be guided by someone sending him feedback about the course ahead. His guide could advise him if he were veering too far to either side.

Climbing Mt. Everest is a daunting task for even the most rugged, healthy individuals. But one man did it without the use of his legs.

He trained hard for three months—in his living room, rather than on the slopes. Most of that time, he explained, was invested in perfecting his familiarity with the helmet.

In addition, his partner, Susan, would take pictures of Kevin working out of the ski machine, then email them to his trainer in Scotland. After analyzing the photos, the trainer would email feedback concerning Kevin's technique.

In 2006, Kevin Alderton, 35, broke two world ski records. Nicknamed "the Cannonball," Kevin scorched the course in Les Arcs, France, by attaining a speed of 105 miles per hour.

In early November 2006, he set an indoor record in Landgraaf, Holland, where he pushed himself to reach more than 56 miles per hour.

By demonstrating that a blind man could break two world records, Alderton hoped to set an example to all those who suffered from one handicap or another that one should never allow a disability to hold them back.

One-Armed Guitar Player Makes the Finals in World Competition

Marc Playle was born without his lower left arm, but that disability didn't prevent him from wanting to play the guitar. When he was 14, he received an artificial limb, attached a guitar pick at the end, and began to strum the strings.

In July 2008, Marc, 22, made it to the finals of the International Guitar Idol competition in London. By the time that Marc faced off against the remaining 12 competitors, he had outplayed 750 two-handed competitors from all over the world.

Although he lost to a Brazilian in the final play-off, the judges acknowledged Marc Playle's remarkable skill and talent. One of the panel of judges told Marc that he was definitely in his top two acts.

Declaring that a disability should never affect a person's goals, Marc Playle announced his plans to release an album with his band, Minnikin.

Quadriplegic Becomes Accomplished Professional Artist

When Barry Reed, 25, of Casper, Wyoming, climbed into the saddle that day in September 1981, he probably had no thoughts other than staying on the bronco and picking up a little rodeo money. The bronco threw him, and Reed was hurt. In fact, he was hurt very badly. He wasn't even able to speak for a year.

Left a quadriplegic by the accident, Reed began to paint to have something to do to pass the time. At first, he held a brush in his mouthpiece and painted by numbers. His mother would mix the paints for him, and he would follow the instructions.

One day Betty Downing, a professional artist, was visiting the Reeds, and Barry's father asked if she would show Barry how to mix the paints for himself. Downing was pleased to comply, and she said that she would come by from time to time to critique his work—if he would stop painting by numbers.

Over the years, Betty has seen Barry Reed become a professional artist, specializing in Wyoming scenery and wild life. Barry had traveled to all parts of Wyoming before his accident, and he enjoyed bringing his memories of so many beautiful areas into life on the canvas. All of his paintings are done with acrylics, and they are popular at area county fairs—and as far away as the Kennedy Center in Washington, D.C.

Although Barry cannot breathe on his own, he jokes that he can do anything else—other than ride a horse.

Among his accomplishments in addition to his beautiful paintings, Barry runs his own website on the computer and works as a career development specialist for Casper College. Reed earned his associate's degree in social work from Casper College in 1990 and received a bachelor's degree in social work in 1993.

In June 2007, in response to a request from Nicole Mussen, an occupational therapist, at the Wyoming Medical Center, Reed began a support group for people with spinal cord injuries. Mussen commented that Barry Reed had the knack of convincing young people that to suffer a disability is not to reach the end of one's life.

Heart Transplant Recipient Climbs Mountains All over the World

In 1992, after Kelly Perkins and her husband, Craig, returned from a back-packing trip in Europe to their home in Lake Tahoe, she suddenly became so weak that she could not even walk around the house. Diagnosed with cardiomyopathy, which inflames heart muscles, Kelly received a new heart at the UCLA Medical Center in November 1995.

Transplanted hearts usually lack nerves that link them to the brain, which means that the heart may not receive adequate information when the muscles need more oxygen. Five-foot-two, 103-pound Kelly Perkins underwent a strenuous exercise program and made demands on her donor heart that required a sheer effort of will.

Ten months out of surgery, Kelly completed the first of numerous post-transplant climbs by hiking up the easier side of Half Dome, Yosemite National Park's famous granite monolith.

> *"What should she do? Roll over and play dead?" She intends to live her life to the fullest.*

Since 1996, Kelly Perkins has reached the summit of Mount Whitney, California; the Matterhorn, Switzerland; Mount Fuji, Japan; Mount Kilimanjaro, Tanzania; Mount Rolling Pin, New Zealand; El Capitan, Yosemite; and a remote peak in the Andes, near Argentina's border with Chile.

On June 26, 2008, Kelly, 46, and her husband, Craig, led by a guide, began a precarious two-and-a-half day climb up the sheer, 2,000-foot face of the harder side of Half Dome in Yosemite. On Saturday afternoon, they reached the top of the 8,842-foot dome.

When asked why she underwent such incredibly strenuous climbs—especially with a heart transplant—Kelly Perkins just smiles and answers her interrogators with another question: "What should she do? Roll over and play dead?" She intends to live her life to the fullest.

However, Kelly does have to tote something up to those summits that no other climbers need carry—a backpack filled with prescription drugs, medical supplies, and blood-pressure monitors.

First Legally Blind Runner to
Qualify for the U.S. Olympic Team—Twice

In 2000, Marla Runyon became the first legally blind runner to qualify for the United States Olympic team. Entered in the 1,500-meter race at the Sydney Summer Olympics, Marla finished eighth. In the 2002 New York City Marathon, she finished fifth among the fastest runners in the world with a time of 2:27:10.

In 2004, she qualified for the U.S. Olympic team in Athens in the 5,000 meter event and finished with a time of 14:59.20, making her the number five all-time U.S. runner.

When she is racing, Marla requires no special treatment or accommodations. And, interestingly, she has never collided with another runner.

When she runs in marathons, her husband, Matt Lonergan, whom she married in 2002, directs her around the potholes and street signs. Other times, a race official rides a bicycle beside her to warn her of any obstacles in her path.

In 2001, Marla took the time to co-write an autobiography, *No Finish Line: My Life as I See It*, and in 2005, she skipped some training time to give birth on September 1 to her daughter, Anna Lee. The Lonergans live in Eugene, Oregon, where Marla is a crowd favorite at Hayward Field and Matt runs a track club called Team Eugene.

Marla was diagnosed with Stargardt's disease when she was nine years old. The disease, a form of macular degeneration, will continue to worsen as she grows older. She has degrees in teaching the blind and deaf, a life-path that she is likely to follow when she decides to end her competitive running career.

In September 2006, Marla became a two-time U.S. champion at 20 kilometers, and although she was 39 for the 2008 Olympics in Beijing, she must have felt tempted to try out when she learned that the U.S. Olympic Field Trials would be held on her home territory at Hayward Field. However, in May 2007, she underwent lower back surgery to repair a lumbar disc tear.

Marla would not say that she was finished with running. When asked once if running was difficult for a sightless person, she replied that running was the easiest thing that she did. Running felt safe to her, far safer than the effort she had to put forth to get through an ordinary day.

SPIRITUAL EXPERIENCES

Angelic Interventions

Millions of People Believe in Angels

There is a rich Jewish tradition that envisions angels carrying human prayers to heaven, and there is a belief that the entreaties of the righteous can more effectively intercede with God than ordinary mortals. As in the Christian and Islamic traditions, there are strict warnings against worshipping the angelic intercessors. God alone must be the sole and ultimate focus of all prayer.

The results of a poll taken in Israel and released in March 2008 revealed that 38 percent of the population believed in God and 45 percent professed that they believed in the reality of angels. Perhaps many individuals felt that angels were more accessible than God. Dr. Martin Jaeger, who directed the survey, also discovered that 16 percent admitted to a belief in spirits.

A joint study conducted by Scripps Howard News Service and the EW Scripps School of Journalism, along with Ohio University, revealed in December 2003 that 77 percent of those adults polled said that they believed in angels.

On October 28, 2005, FOX news released the results of their survey that 84 percent of Americans believed in miracles and 79 percent believed in God.

According to an AP-AOL polled released on December 25, Christmas Day, 2006, more than 50 percent of those individuals with no religious affiliation believed that angels were real. Overall, the survey found that 81 percent believed in angels.

Police Officer's Guardian Angel Saved Her from Drowning

In 1995, Officer Christa Evans had been diving in murky waters in search of a woman who had driven her car off a ramp into the river. She quickly found the dazed motorist, pulled her free of the submerged car, and dragged her alive and sputtering to the surface. A waiting ambulance sped away to an emergency room with the fortunate woman, and it seemed as though the police rescue squad had successfully averted a tragic drowning.

> "I pulled the driver out from an air pocket trapped near the roof of the car."

But then a witness claimed that he had seen a passenger in the car with the driver before it sank.

"We had no prior report of another person in the car," said Officer Brian Curtis, Christa's partner. "Do you think this guy knows what he's talking about?"

"We can't take any chances," Christa answered. "I pulled the driver out from an air pocket trapped near the roof of the car. She was lucky I was able to get to her so fast. I didn't see anyone else down there."

"If there was," Officer Curtis observed solemnly, "he would surely have drowned by now."

Christa nodded in silent agreement. "Either way, I had better check it out. We can't risk leaving someone who might still be alive down there to drown. And in any event, it's my job to bring the victim to the surface."

"I wish the lady you just pulled out were still here to question," Officer Curtis said. "I hate to see you go down again so soon."

"She was dazed and in pretty bad shape," Christa reminded him. "I don't think we could have relied on her memory. If there's any chance of anyone being left down there, I'd better dive immediately."

After several minutes of circling the submerged automobile, Christa satisfied herself that there had been no other victim—alive or drowned—but she suddenly found herself in trouble. When a sudden shift in water pressure swirled against her, it had slammed the car door on the little finger of her left hand.

With only a few minutes of air left in her tank, she frantically tried to open the door, but it would not budge.

With her oxygen nearly gone, she knew that she must cut off her finger or drown.

"Please, dear God," she prayed, thinking especially of her two small children. "Please don't let me die like this."

According to Officer Evans, that was when a benevolent being appeared to rescue her: "A bright light approached me. It came within arm's length … and then it disappeared. But my finger was free! I rose to the surface and was pulled into a boat by two other members of the rescue squad. Neither of them had entered the water.

"I am convinced that it was my guardian angel that saved me from drowning."

Many people believe in guardian angels who protect them from danger. Whether or not this is true, such thoughts offer a lot of comfort in times of stress.

Baby Falls Seven Floors and Survives

She may not have believed in miracles before that fateful day in 1996, but when Michelle Markotan's 23-month-old son David fell from a seventh-floor window and survived, she knew the sky had to have been filled with angels.

Little David had been playing near an open, screened window when he suddenly leaned against the mesh and it gave way. Becky, his three-year-old sister, came running into the kitchen where their mother was working and screamed that the baby had just fallen out the window.

Michelle was "scared to death" when she entered the room and saw the ripped screen. Then, when she rushed to the window to look down, she was horrified when she saw David lying on the ground seven floors below. Instinctively, she asked God not to take their son from them.

David Sr., who was outside working on their car, was puzzled by the sound of a "thud" about 30 feet away from him. When he investigated and saw his precious son lying motionless, blood trickling from his mouth, he picked David up and began crying.

Miraculously, little David was still breathing. There was at least some hope that he might live if he were rushed to a hospital and received immediate medical treatment—and most likely, serious surgery.

A trauma team was standing by when the ambulance arrived at Pittsburgh's Children's Hospital, ready to rush David into surgery—but the miracle was not yet complete.

Dr. Edward Barksdale Jr., a pediatric surgeon, had expected to face a tragic death of a child or, at the least, a child who had suffered severe life-threatening injuries. However, when he examined David, Dr. Barksdale found that neither possibility presented itself. The little boy who had fallen seven stories to the ground below had suffered only a slight concussion, a few fractured ribs, and some bruises.

David's father expressed his gratitude to his son's guardian angels, and his mother said she now believes that miracles do most certainly occur.

Dr. Barksdale agreed, stating that it was a miracle that David was alive.

A Vision of Angels Restored a Boy's Wish to Live

A physician who practices pediatrics in the Omaha, Nebraska, area, told of a potentially tragic case involving a 10-year-old boy that had a happy resolution.

"Jimmy Ludke had been involved in a hunting accident in which he had been wounded and his older brother, Samuel, had been killed," the doctor said. "Tragically, Sam had fallen on the 12-gauge shotgun that he had been cradling as he crawled over a fence. The blast had blown away a large portion of his face, and numerous pellets of shot had traveled behind him to strike Jimmy in his face and neck. He had lost a lot of blood and was in a coma-like state before he was brought to an emergency room."

Jimmy remained mute and withdrawn. He would not even speak to his parents.

"It quickly became apparent that he had worshipped his 17-year-old brother. Samuel had taken Jimmy along hunting pheasants, and it was the first time that the two brothers had been allowed to go hunting alone without their father or uncle. Jimmy was absolutely devastated by the loss of his brother. He was unable to attend the funeral, and even though it was a closed-casket ceremony, it was just as well that he was not subject to the additional trauma."

Even after a week in the hospital, Jimmy was showing no improvement. His wounds had not been that bad. It was as if he had simply lost the will to live.

"One day as I was doing my rounds, I noticed that Jimmy had been doodling on the back of a get-well card that someone had sent him. When his parents came for visiting hours, I found out that Jimmy had always liked to sketch and draw. I instructed one of the nurses to leave a sketch pad and some colored pencils at his bedside table. Perhaps he would begin to 'talk' to us through his drawings."

The next afternoon the doctor was rather distressed to discover a drawing that he considered quite dark and morbid. Two young men or boys, covered with bloody wounds, were lying in a ditch while vultures circled overhead. Insects, worms, and snakes were crawling over the bodies of the two boys. Jimmy had entitled his drawing, "Sammy and Jimmy Go to Hell."

They had been feeding Jimmy intravenously, because he refused to eat. That night around midnight he began to run a very high fever and lost consciousness.

A pheasant hunt turned tragic for two unsupervised brothers, but the grief and guilt was eased by one boy's vision of heaven.

"One of the nurses on duty called me at home to report that it appeared as though little Jimmy Ludke had decided to pull the plug on himself. All of his vital signs were suddenly nose-diving. I told her to call his parents. Since visiting hours had been over for quite some time, I knew that they would be back home. I said that I would be there as soon as I could."

The crisis didn't pass for Jimmy Ludke until about 4:30 that morning.

He suddenly opened his eyes and began to cry. He clutched his mother's hand and spoke for the first time since before the accident: "Mom! Dad! I saw Sammy, and he's all right. He's in heaven with the angels, and he's okay. He didn't go to hell, after all. "

The Ludkes wept openly and hugged their son and each other in warm embraces. "We didn't want to lose both our boys," they told the doctor and the attending nurse, as if having to explain their open and unrestrained emotion. "Thank God, Jimmy has come back to us."

Jimmy's assertion that he had seen Sammy in heaven was overlooked in the Ludkes' rejoicing and the medical personnel's triumph over death.

It wasn't until a couple of days later that the physician really paid much attention to Jimmy's new pieces of artwork. In one drawing he had used bright colors to depict a taller boy shaking hands with a smaller one. A half dozen angels in white robes and bright golden halos stood around the two, smiling and singing in obvious approval.

"I really saw him, the doctor," Jimmy told him, his expansive smile a welcome replacement for the expressionless mask of the previous days. "I saw Sammy and talked to him, and he told me that he was all right. He didn't have to go to hell. Even the angels told me that Sammy could stay with them."

The doctor wanted to know why Jimmy had been so concerned about his older brother going to hell.

"Just because" was all that the doctor could get out of Jimmy before he went back to drawing another picture of a being that he said was Sammy's special guardian angel.

Later, Jimmy revealed that he had seen his brother drinking beer and joking that it would be all right to go to hell because the devil gives out free beer.

Near-Death Experiences

Millions Experience NDEs and Believe in an Afterlife

A Gallup Poll conducted in 1992 indicated that around 13 million American adults claimed to have undergone at least one near-death experience, or NDE.

A survey by *U.S. News* magazine revealed that a total of 18 percent (approximately 50 million adults) of the U.S. population had undergone a near-death experience.

In a special report on spirituality, the August 29/September 6, 2005, issue of *Newsweek* released survey results which included the statistic that 67 percent of Americans believe in an afterlife, a heaven or hell to which souls ascend or descend.

On March 7, 2006, Scripps Howard News Service released the results of their survey in which 72 percent of Americans said that they believe in an afterlife in which they will have "some sort of consciousness."

While Out-of-Body in Extreme Pain,
He Encountered an Angel

A rnold Sandeen of Utah added this account of his near-death encounter when he returned his "Steiger Questionnaire of Mystical, Paranormal, and UFO Experience": "When I was 13, back in the mid-1940s, I awakened one evening with what I thought was a terrible case of indigestion as a result of having eaten too much at a school picnic.

"Although I tried not to disturb my sleeping parents, the absolutely unbearable pain caused me to moan and cry out, and soon my mother was at my bedside. She diagnosed the symptoms as being indicative of appendicitis and she called Dr. Radnich."

As he lay thrashing about in agony, Arnold's thoughts began to fixate on the possibility of being somehow able to escape the pain that seemed to fill every corner of his being. How wonderful it would be to be able to leave his torment, he said mentally.

"Just then a spasm of pain doubled me over, and the reflex action seemed to shoot the *thinking part of me* up to the ceiling. I thought, 'Oh, no! I wanted to be able to escape the pain, but I didn't want to die!'"

Arnold was completely astonished. He could actually see his mother fussing about, and he could clearly perceive himself tossing about on the bed, moaning and groaning.

"My body seemed to be like some kind of puppet, just going through the motions of awful sickness. But I—the *real* me—could no longer feel a thing. Incredibly, the pain remained down below with my physical body on the bed.

"Then I started feeling kind of ashamed about the way my physical body was behaving like such a baby. I mean, the pain was awful and all; but I was whimpering and moaning like a wimp. I decided that I really should go back and act like a man."

And just like that, Arnold said that he was back in his physical body and howling in pain.

Extreme nighttime pain initiated a bizarre out-of-body experience for one teenage boy. But was it just the excruciating pain causing him to hallucinate?

"If it hurt so bad to be in my body—and there was absolutely no pain when I was outside of my body—then it didn't take a genius like me very long to decide where I wanted to be."

Arnold was surprised to discover how quickly the *Real Arnold* was able to be back up floating near the ceiling.

He wondered when Doc Radnich was going to get there—and suddenly he was inside the doctor's car as he traveled to the Sandeen home.

After he had ridden with the doctor for a few minutes, Arnold thought once again of his mother's anxiety, and he was back in his room.

"Mom was crying, and when I looked at my body, I could see why. I looked hideous. My face was gray and my mouth was hanging open—and I didn't seem to be breathing!"

Arnold experienced just a moment of panic when it occurred to him that he might truly have died.

"But then I looked behind me and saw this really beautiful being of pure light that seemed to be waiting for me on the other side of a crystal clear river. Somehow I understood that all I had to do was to cross over the bridge and join the Light Being—and that would be all there was to it.

"I guess like so many kids I had never really thought much about dying. And I certainly had never thought that it could happen to me. At least not until I was an old guy, like fifty or so. But if this was all there was to it, then it was hard to understand why people always made such a big deal about dying. You just 'pop' out of your body, maybe float around the ceiling for a while, then meet some beautiful angel who's waiting for you on the other side of the bridge between life and death. It's really no big deal at all!"

> *Arnold seemed to be being drawn away from the crystal river, the bridge, and the Light Being and pulled toward his physical body.*

And then, all of a sudden, Arnold seemed to be being drawn away from the crystal river, the bridge, and the Light Being and pulled toward his physical body.

"I seemed to land hard on something, and I opened my eyes to see Dad standing with his arm around Mom's shoulder. Doc Radnich's face seemed to be really close to my eyes, and I could hear Dad cussing him out for having taken so long to get there.

"Everything went out of focus, then black for a while; and when I opened my eyes again, I could hear Mom crying and praying and thanking God that I had come back to life.

"I was sick for three or four more days. Doc said it was probably some spoiled meat that I ate at the school picnic. I know now that death is not such a terrible thing," Arnold concluded his account, "but I really am not in any hurry to cross that bridge, either."

Marine Sergeant Views His Body in Foxhole, Never Fears Death Again

In 1942 the First Marine Division was ashore on Guadalcanal, digging in at Henderson Field against the mounting Japanese attacks on the perimeter.

Sergeant Ted Snowden recalled that they had been under unusually heavy fire for days and that during the worst of the bombardment the ground shook like an earthquake. Some of the marines had been bruised from the vibrations alone, for they were rattled from side to side in their foxholes "like dice in a cup."

At night battleships with 14-inch guns shelled them, and the entrenched marines would pray for daylight. When first light came, the Japanese planes zoomed in and bombed them until nightfall.

"The rare times when the bombers didn't come and the ships were silent, there was an artillery piece we called 'Pistol Pete' perched on a hill not far away that took potshots at us," Snowden wrote in the November-December 1951, issue of *Fate* magazine.

In spite of the heavy Japanese bombardment, little actual damage was done. All of the important equipment was kept well-hidden in the jungle, and often when a U.S. plane landed it could be successfully refueled in the thick undergrowth even in the face of an attack.

On the particular day when Snowden's remarkable experience occurred, Pistol Pete had begun to rake its daily target practice, opening fire here and there, but not seriously affecting the airfield.

One of the fiercest battles of World War II was between the Japanese and Americans at Guadalcanal. Many harrowing, life-or-death tales have been told as a result, some bordering on the mysterious.

The Japanese artillery piece with the colorful nickname was actually a howitzer that fired a high-trajectory, low-velocity shell, and it was more of a nuisance than a real threat since it seldom hit anything of consequence. Because it traveled so high in the air to get to where it was supposed to be going, it could always be heard-and the marines would simply hit the dirt and hope for it to land far away.

By nightfall of that day, the men were secure in newly dug foxholes. Danger from falling trees the night before had caused them to move their foxholes from the forest onto a grassy meadow. The moon was full, shining down on the embattled men with unpretentious simplicity.

As the men talked among themselves to keep up morale, the *whee-whee-whee-whee* sound of the howitzer informed them that Pistol Pete was at it again.

A shell exploded one hundred yards from the foxholes, and some of the men grew apprehensive. Pistol Pete was getting too close.

Snowden had hoped that he might be able to get some sleep that night, but Pistol Pete had other plans. Having registered on target, the howitzer proceeded to bombard the Yanks in their foxholes.

"The shells came in regularly," Snowden recalled, "about a minute apart and ranged all through our foxholes."

The men had time after each explosion to rise up and see where it had hit. Shallow craters about eight feet apart were appearing throughout the meadow—some quite close to foxholes with marines in them.

Snowden felt apprehensive. "Pistol Pete had never been that good before."

As he sought to relax in his foxhole, Sergeant Snowden heard Pistol Pete's noise and suddenly knew with a certainty that this particular shell could not get any closer.

"This is it!" he thought to himself.

The shell came screaming toward him, louder and louder, until the shrill screech had engulfed his entire universe.

Snowden heard the thud into the left side of his foxhole.

Then, suddenly, without knowing how or why it happened, Snowden—or *some part of him*—was standing in the moon-shade of a large tree watching his physical body in the foxhole.

"The outline of my helmet and body was plainly visible to me, as I—or this *other* part of me—stood there waiting for the explosion to wipe the picture away.

"I remember the bright moonlight, the pattern of our foxholes, and the fresh over-pattern of the shell scars. I saw this impression only—as I didn't take my eyes off my body.

"I remember anticipation, but mainly I felt calm—a calm such as I had never known before. It was calmness that nothing could shake."

Snowden clearly saw the white blast of the explosion and its deadly red core. He watched as his foxhole erupted and widened to the crater of a shell hole.

> *The shell came screaming toward him, louder and louder, until the shrill screech had engulfed his entire universe.*

All of this his Real Self viewed from a height of about thirty yards; and though he saw it, he neither heard the blast nor felt the heat.

"The next thing I knew, I was back with my body again, lying on my left side, facing what had been the side of the foxhole, but was now only a loose rubble of smoking, hot clods of dirt."

Snowden knew that he was completely exposed except for his back, which was pressed against what remained of the other side of his foxhole.

Miraculously, he had somehow escaped injury.

He made a quick check of legs, arms, back.

He felt nothing mangled or destroyed.

But he was aware of a whirring sensation in the top of his head and a feeling of being cramped for space inside his body.

This restricted sensation, by comparison, brought back a sharp memory of the lightness and freedom that he had experienced while floating outside of his body. Other than that, he seemed to be all right.

"My God, they got the sarge!" he heard a voice shout.

"Like hell they did!" he yelled, without moving. "You men keep your heads down!"

As if to complete some bizarre series of experiences, Snowden never heard another shell that entire night—although it was a matter of record that one of his men caught a splinter in his chest and lung and was evacuated the next morning.

But Snowden never stirred from his foxhole, and he slept peacefully for the rest of the night.

"I still do not understand this incredible experience," Snowden concluded a decade later. "But I do know that it has removed all fear of dying from my mind.

"I now believe death—or transition—is accomplished with far greater ease than the opening of a door into another room."

Deer-Hunter Succumbs to the
Sleep of the Snows, Encounters a Very Special Rescuer

Rick Kremer, 34, had somehow managed to become separated from his friends when they were deer hunting in northwest Iowa in December 1995.

"You think of Iowa as a bunch of interconnected farms, cornfields, and friendly little towns, but in certain areas of the state there are still a lot of woods and places where someone unfamiliar with the countryside can get lost," Rick said. "And after two or three hours of hopelessly searching for my friends, I realized that I was thoroughly lost and confused.

"The temperature dropped well below zero when the sun went down, and I figured the wind-chill factor was at least 20 below. I didn't even have any matches with me to light a fire. It was my first time ever deer hunting, and I had really relied totally on my more experienced friends to provide all the essentials for survival in the field."

Earlier that day, he had fired most of his shells in an attempt to attract the attention of his buddies Ike, Bill, and Paul. He tried firing one of his last 12-gauge, solid-slug shotgun shells into a pile of leaves and sticks, hoping that the muzzle blast would ignite the dry tinder, but he only succeeded in scattering the would-be bonfire into the wind.

"I leaned back against a tree and started to pray," Kremer continued. "I had always been pretty religious, even before my confirmation. But lately, with marriage and work and three kids, I had become more or less an Easter and Christmas Christian. But I always prayed and felt right with Jesus, regardless of whether or not I was a regular churchgoer."

The last time Rick glanced at the luminous dial on his wristwatch, it was nearly ten o'clock. He had been out in the field since early morning. He felt himself growing numb with cold. His hooded parka and insulated coveralls had kept him plenty warm while he had been hiking through freshly fallen snow in the bright sunlight, but now he felt as though he could hardly move.

"Then I started getting really sleepy. I knew that I should stay awake and jump around to keep warm, but I started to feel real groggy and tired. I was soon feeling almost indifferent to my dangerous situation. I was drifting into what they call the 'sleep of the snows:'; I was freezing to death."

Although Rick Kremer had always been highly skeptical of accounts of out-of-body and near-death experiences, he testified in his report that he suddenly felt as though he had left his physical body and was standing a short distance away viewing his frozen corpse.

"I looked terrible, leaning against that tree all hunched over. My normally ruddy complexion was ashen. My beard was covered with ice particles. I looked like Jack Frost."

When a deer hunter got separated from his friends during a winter hunt, he almost succumbed to the "sleep of the snows."

Rick said that he next experienced the tunnel effect that so many near-death survivors have reported.

"I seemed to be moving down this dark tunnel. Up ahead I could see a brilliant light, so I kept moving toward it."

After an undetermined length of time, Rick said that he seemed to step into the light and emerge into a beautiful garden and bright sunshine.

"It reminded me of a garden that my Aunt Glenda used to have on their farm in southern Iowa. She used to fuss so over her plants, and she always had more kinds of beautiful flowers than anyone else I have ever known. This was like Aunt Glenda's garden in mid-June—only more so."

After a few moments of luxuriating in the lovely flower garden, Rick said that he became aware of another presence that was standing off to his side.

"At first I couldn't believe my eyes! It was Jesus himself. He looked just the way that he did in the mural above the altar back in my old home church. He had shoulder-length, reddish-brown hair and beard, and he was dressed in a white gown with a blue hood or mantle over his shoulders. He was smiling at me, and I felt tears come to my eyes. I knew that I was in spirit, but I still felt like crying when I saw Jesus face-to-face.

"Then I thought about that old hymn that we used to sing about coming to the garden when the dew was still on the roses and then seeing that Jesus was also there and walking and talking with him. I don't actually remember seeing his lips move, but I heard his words inside me.

"'Some day,' he told me, 'you will come home again to this garden and be with me in my kingdom. But your time is not yet now. You must go back and be a good person and a solid husband and a loving father.'"

Rick remembered that Jesus bade him to look into a still pond in the garden.

"On the surface of the water I could see my buddies heading in the direction of my body, just as if I was seeing it all happen in some kind of movie screen. My thoughts were kind of mixed. I certainly wanted to return to life and be with Judy and the kids, but I also felt so peaceful and at home with Jesus in the garden."

As Jesus and he watched the search from the strange vantage point of the pool in the garden, Rick saw Ike open his mouth to shout out his grim discovery when his flashlight beam fell upon the severely chilled body of his friend.

"I couldn't hear anything that any of them said, but I could see Ike yelling and waving his flashlight in the air. At the same time, like watching a split-screen motion picture, I saw Bill and Paul pointing their flashlights in the direction of Ike and me."

Rick watched as the three men gathered around his physical body.

"Bill started building a fire, and Ike was kneeling beside me with his flask, trying to get some whiskey past my lips and down my throat. Paul had removed my gloves and was rubbing my hands and fingers."

As Rick watched his physical self start to choke on the whiskey, he felt his spirit presence in the garden with Jesus begin to waver.

"It was like every time that the physical me sputtered and choked, the spiritual me in the garden experienced a tug back toward Earth. I turned to say something to Jesus—you know, about how much I had always really loved him ever since I was a little kid—and all of a sudden I was being sucked back into the dark tunnel.

"The last thing that I remember seeing before I seemed to slam back into my body was the peaceful countenance of Jesus that emanated the most wonderful kind of love."

Rick suffered severe frostbite, and for a time the doctors felt that several toes and fingers would have to be amputated. Fortunately, his three friends had found him just a few degrees short of the crisis point and had carried him to their van, which, ironically, was parked near a clump of trees less than a hundred yards away. After Rick had become separated from the others, he had walked in circles for hours before he became exhausted in the subzero weather.

"Not everyone believes me when I tell them that I saw Jesus in that beautiful garden," Rick Kremer said. "Most people assume that I was hallucinating with the cold.

"But I am convinced that I had a genuine near-death experience and that my soul left my body and was greeted by Jesus in a garden in heaven. I don't really care what others think. Lord willing, they will have their own opportunity to walk in the garden with Jesus when their souls are called home."

Frozen, Reverend Bertrand
Finds Proof of Life after Death

In a classic case from the previous century, Reverend L.J. Bertrand, a Huguenot minister, went on a mountain-climbing vacation in the Alps with a group of his students—and found proof of his lifelong preaching when he experienced the process of the soul's capacity to leave the physical body.

Bertrand's energy advanced him far ahead of the rest of his lagging party. The students accompanying him—their physical ability unable to match their exuberance—straggled behind with the local guide. The clergyman became impatient for them to catch up with him, for they were carrying his lunch.

He found a rock to sit on, and he made himself as comfortable as possible and resigned himself to wait with as much patience as he could muster. Soon after, however, he found himself drifting into the "sleep of the snows." He began to lose all mobility, and he realized with a sudden shock that he was freezing to death.

The fatal freezing process had been gradual and unnoticed, but now Bertrand suddenly felt a moment of intense pain, which he interpreted as the throes of physical death.

The scenic beauty of the Alps can easily blind people to the dangers of climbing trips in these mountains.

When the spasm ended, Bertrand was bobbing above his body as if he were a helium-filled balloon on a silver string. Below him, he could see the near-frozen hulk of his physical body.

The clergyman's thoughts turned toward his students, and immediately he was with them, watching with great annoyance as they repeatedly made wrong turns. He was also horrified with the particularly amateurish climbing techniques of most of them.

Bertrand felt a special surge of irritation when he saw the guide duck behind a rock and partake of the very lunch that he was supposed to be bringing to him.

The minister next thought of his wife, who was to join him in Lucerne within three days.

To his astonishment, he perceived her arriving in the Swiss city at that very moment in a carriage with four other travelers. His beloved wife was three days ahead of schedule.

Bertrand continued to hover near her in spirit form, actually observing her go through the procedure of registering at the hotel.

It was at that time that his laggard students and the local guide came upon his frozen body.

Immediately the guide set about employing the old folk remedy of rubbing Bertrand's body with snow in an effort to stimulate sluggish circulation.

The clergyman's soul, his essential self, however, hovered above the alpine scene on the silver cord, feeling very loath to return to the cold, empty shell that had housed it for so many years.

But the final choice was not that of Reverend Bertrand. Within minutes he was back in his frostbitten body, hearing the guide's sigh of relief and the cheers of his students.

He rose with difficulty to his feet, shuddering at the cold. Then, turning to his students, he scolded them for not following his instructions and for so clumsily missing so many correct turns.

Whispering among themselves, the startled students cast frightened glances at their pastor. What powers of mind did he possess that he could spy on them from a distance?

Bertrand then turned to the hungry guide and thoroughly berated him for having dipped into his lunch uninvited.

The awestruck man stammered his guilt and offered his apologies to "the man who sees everything."

> *What powers of mind did he possess that he could spy on them from a distance?*

The clergyman nodded, then offered the guide a warm smile of absolution. "Well, the food probably gave you the energy to save my life—and for that, my friend, I shall be everlastingly grateful."

Many hours later, at the base of the mountain, Bertrand's wife experienced amazement when her husband was not surprised by her early arrival. What was more, he went on to describe the carriage in which she had arrived as well as the other four passengers who had accompanied her.

Bertrand himself had no easy explanation for his near-death experience. It sufficed for him that he had been granted a remarkable demonstration of the immortal soul's capacity to survive physical death.

Two Young Girls United in Heaven before One of Them Dies

Dr. David Smith, associate professor of pediatrics at the University of British Columbia, reported the case of four-year-old Sandra and three-year-old Chrissy, two young cancer victims who were reunited in the spirit world.

According to Dr. Smith, the two girls met while they were being treated for leukemia in a hospital cancer ward. Sandra was sent home to spend her final days with her family, and she was unaware that Chrissy had died.

Two days after Chrissy's death, Sandra fell into a deep coma, and when she regained consciousness, she told her mother that she had seen Chrissy in heaven. Sandra had at first been frightened in the celestial surroundings, but her friend had told her not to be afraid; she was there to guide her.

Dr. Smith said that it was impossible for Sandra to know of Chrissy's death. The two little friends were miles apart and had been separated for months without any contact.

After her near-death visit to heaven, Sandra became "calm and peaceful," stated Dr. Smith, who treated both girls at Vancouver General Hospital. Sandra told him that she had gone to a place of beautiful white light, and she knew that everything would be all right, because Chrissy was there waiting for her.

The man was obsessed by a dream of a bright light and a woman he felt he knew and needed to talk to but could not.

Sandra gradually lost consciousness and died the following day.

"She had no fear of dying," Dr. Smith commented. "Chrissy's death took on special meaning—she was to guide another troubled child who was to die soon after."

Dream Triggers Memory of Near-Death Experience at Birth

As incredible as it may seem, John Lione of Brooklyn, New York, recalled a near-death experience that occurred to him during his birth.

"My mother said my birth was a difficult one," Lione told us. "I was what they call a 'blue baby.' They didn't bring me to her for two days. My face was all black and blue, and I had two black eyes. She said it looked like the skin had been pulled off my face. That was where the forceps had cut me up. They had to give me a tracheotomy so I could breathe. I am also completely deaf in my right ear. As if all that was not enough, I came down with measles when I was about six months old."

From his earliest childhood, John could remember a recurring dream that always began and ended in the same way.

"I would be kneeling down, all bent over. I am frantically trying to untie knots in some kind of rope. I am just starting to get free of the rope when I get punched in the face."

At first little John would wake up crying. Later, as he became conditioned to the nightmare, he would be able to sleep through the part with the knots, the rope, and the punch.

"The dream would then go on to the part where I can see this bright light coming at me from my right. Then, when I look to my left, I see this woman in a long, flowing gown. I cannot see her features clearly, but I know that she is not my mother. At the same time, I know that I know her. I also feel a great urgency to reach her. I call and call to her, but I can't seem to get to her. And that's where the dream would end."

For years John told the repetitive dream to friends and to health care professionals. No one seemed to have a clue as to what particular meaning the dream held for him.

In 1986 he had his gall bladder removed, and John experienced the bizarre dream again.

John had decided that the nightmare of ropes and knots and floating women in gowns and bright lights would always remain one of his personal mysteries when he chanced across—in a most peculiar way—a copy of Dr. Melvin Morse's book *Closer to the Light*..

"I was walking to work on a rainy day when I saw this book lying on the ground, dry, like someone had just dropped it," John said. "I didn't see anyone around who might be its owner, so I picked it up.

"That night when I started reading it, I was amazed to find stories of children who had had weird dreams somewhat similar to mine. My wife said that maybe I hadn't been dreaming after all. Maybe I had been having a memory of a near-death experience. The rope with the knots was when I struggled in the womb with the umbilical cord. Getting punched in the face is when the doctor grabbed me with the forceps. Then I believe that I died—and after that I went into the light."

Sometime later, John attended a conference at which Betty Eadie, author of *Embraced by the Light*, was speaking and relating her own near-death experiences.

"Afterward, when I was speaking to Betty, she mentioned seeing heavenly beings spinning material out of some bright substance," John said. "Dr. P. M. H. Atwater was there, and she said that she believed the substance to be 'spun light.' That's when I knew what the woman in the long, flowing gown had been wearing. It was a gown made of spun light."

Missing Teenager Tells Uncle in a Dream Where She Can Be Found

When 16-year-old Darcy Braden's car plunged down an embankment next to a county highway, she spent nearly 36 hours lying at the bottom of a ditch, fading in and out of a coma.

Police conducted a massive search for the missing teenager, but no one was able to locate her until her uncle, Fred Anderson, saw her in a dream and told the authorities exactly where she was.

Darcy and her family lived in a heavily wooded area near a small town in the Ozark region of northern Arkansas. She had been elected a cheerleader for the high school athletic teams the previous spring, and in September 1988, with football season going full steam ahead, she had talked her parents, Howard and Mae Braden, into buying her a used car so that she could drive to cheerleading practice and the home games.

On that terrible night in mid-September when Darcy had not returned by 1:00 A.M., the Bradens were wishing that they had not yielded to their daughter's entreaties regarding her own automobile. There had been rain earlier that evening, and then a dense fog had settled in.

By 2:00 A.M. Mae Braden feared the worst. Darcy never stayed out late without permission, and she always called if something unforeseen had come up to delay her arrival back home.

Mae Braden's mother's intuition was being activated for a very good reason. The dense fog that shrouded the country roads had made Darcy nervous, and she left her

A thick fog led to a car crash that left Darcy fading into a coma, but she still managed to contact her family through mysterious means.

friends almost immediately after the football game had ended. She hadn't even stayed for the after-game dance in the school gym.

The young and inexperienced driver became confused and anxious driving the eerie country roads. She was reaching down to turn on the radio to help her not feel so alone when she misjudged a sharp curve. Inappropriate acceleration sent her car off the road, completely clearing a guard rail and rolling down a steep embankment that was thick with small trees and dense foliage.

Darcy struck her head on the steering wheel several times as the car caromed down the embankment. Her seat belt was disengaged, and she was thrown from her car and into a ditch.

First thing the next morning, the Bradens called all of Darcy's friends to see if anyone had a clue to her whereabouts.

"My blood literally froze in my veins when we were told time and time again that Darcy had left early the night before to head straight home," Mrs. Braden said.

After they checked with local hospitals to see if anyone had been admitted after an automobile accident, the Bradens called the county sheriff's department to report their daughter missing.

"Within a few hours the deputies had driven all the possible routes that Darcy could have taken to our farm home," Howard Braden said. "We were now really getting frightened. And although we tried our best to be positive, you know, parents just can't help thinking about awful things like kidnappings, abductions, and even murder."

Darcy lay battered, bruised, and only occasionally conscious near her wrecked automobile. Her clothing had been ripped and torn when she had been thrown into the dense foliage, and her body was covered with cuts.

"Once I saw Cheryl Green, one of my mom's best friends, come walking up to me," Darcy recalled in her report of the incident. "She told me that I looked lonely and she would just sit and keep me company for a time. We talked for quite a while, and then I said, 'Hey, wait, Cheryl, you died three summers ago from stomach cancer. You can't be here talking to me now. I mean, you're dead and all.'"

> *"I just kind of floated around in his room, and when I heard him start to snore, this voice spoke to me."*

The image of the woman remained with her, and Darcy became convinced that either she herself was also dead—or she soon would be.

"And then I just seemed to stand up and leave my body," Darcy said. "Pretty soon I was looking down on my bloody and battered corpse, just lying there covered with dirt and broken branches. I just seemed to fly through space. It was neat. I could see the town below me and all the different farms and stuff."

Then, as she passed above the farm of her uncle, Fred Anderson, she suddenly felt herself being pulled downward.

"I heard my aunt Zoe telling Uncle Fred that there was nothing more he could do until he got some rest. She scolded him that if he didn't get some sleep, he might drive in the ditch and that wouldn't help get Darcy back. And then I realized that Uncle Fred had been out looking for me.

"I wanted to hug him and give him a kiss. Fred and Zoe never had any kids of their own, and he had always seemed to treat me so special and loving. My mom said that Fred and I had some kind of special bond.

"Something told me that it was important for me to stick around while he took a nap. I remember turning my head when he shucked down to his underwear and crawled under the covers.

"I just kind of floated around in his room, and when I heard him start to snore, this voice spoke to me. It said, 'You can talk to him now. He can hear you now.'"

Darcy said that she wasted no time informing her uncle exactly where her body lay.

"A few minutes later, old Fred snorted, got out of bed, and yelled to Aunt Zoe: 'I know where Darcy is. She came and told me in a dream. Her car went way down an embankment, and the deputies haven't been able to see it 'cause it's down in a ditch.'"

Darcy watched while Fred rang up her mother and father and told them to get in their cars, and then she felt her Real Self being pulled back to her body.

Mae Braden didn't argue with her older brother. "Fred is as hardheaded as they come. He has never been the least bit mystical. So when he told us that Darcy had just appeared to him in a dream and told him where she lay still alive, we chose not to doubt him for a minute."

When the Andersons and the Bradens met at the revealed curve where the dream had said Darcy went off the road, a few elements of doubt surfaced.

"There were no skid marks, the guard rail was untouched, and we knew that the deputies—and we ourselves—had been by here a dozen times," Howard Braden recalled. "But Fred said, 'Come on, damn it! Darcy told me she's way down there in a ditch.'"

Thankfully for Darcy, her parents and her aunt and uncle managed to keep their faith in her manifestation in Fred's unusual dream.

The 16-year-old was found just where her spirit image had said the physical representation of Darcy Braden would be lying, desperately needing help.

Mae Braden called 911 from the nearest farm home, and minutes later an ambulance arrived to take Darcy to the local hospital.

For nearly a week her condition was listed as critical. In addition to dozens of bumps, bruises, and scratches, she had sustained a severe concussion, a fractured leg bone, and three broken ribs.

Fred Anderson still does not claim to possess any special psychic abilities. He just knows that he has always thought the world of his niece, and he agrees with his sister Mae that he and the child have always enjoyed some special bond. This time that special love connection and Darcy's out-of-body projection into Fred's dream saved her life.

The Power of Prayer

Discovering the "Perfect" Prayers

For Christians worldwide the "perfect prayer" is the one that Jesus gave to his apostles and which has been known for centuries as the Lord's Prayer: "And … as [Jesus] was praying in a certain place, when he ceased, one of his disciples said unto him, Lord, teach us to pray as John [the Baptist] also taught his disciples. And he said unto them, When ye pray, say, Our Father which art in heaven, Hallowed be thy name. Thy kingdom come. Thy will be done, as in heaven, so in earth. Give us this day our daily bread. And forgive us our sins; for we also forgive everyone that is indebted to us. And lead us not into temptation; but deliver us from evil." (Luke 11:1–4, King James Version [Matthew 6:13 adds: "For thine is the kingdom and the power and the glory, forever. Amen."])

Jesus prayed a great deal. He prayed at his baptism (Luke 3:21), before he chose the Twelve (Luke 6:12), before his invitation to all humankind to "come unto" him (Matthew 11:25–27), at the feeding of the 5,000 (John 6:11), before his Transfiguration (Luke 9:28–29), for little children (Matthew 19:13), at the Last Supper (Matthew 26:26–27), in Gethsemane (Matthew 26:36–44), and on the Cross (Luke 24:30) to name only some of the most significant prayers recorded by the gospel writers.

But as often as Jesus declared that prayer could work mysteries and wonders, he also admonished his followers concerning the secret nature of the act of praying: "When thou prayest, thou shalt not be as the hypocrites are, for they love to pray standing in the synagogues and in the corners of the streets that they may be seen of men.… But thou, when thou prayest, enter into thy closet, and when thou hast shut thy door, pray to the Father which is in secret; and thy Father which seeth in secret shall reward thee openly." (Matthew 6:5–8)

Jesus frequently prayed and instructed his followers how to pray. The faithful of other religions all find comfort in prayer, too, and many testify as to the power of prayer in their lives.

In Islam prayer, *salat,* is one of the five Pillars of Islam, and the true believer must say his prayers (*salla*) five times a day, as well as on special occasions. The set schedule of prayers—dawn, noon, afternoon, sunset, and nighttime—are strictly prescribed and regulated. There is another category of prayer, the *du'a,* which permits spontaneous expressions of supplication, petition, and intercession. The du'a may also be allowed after the uttering of the formal salat.

While many religions suggest that their supplicants fold their hands, bow their head, close their eyes, and so forth, the followers of Islam have many exact procedures that must be observed in their prayers. Before prayer, there is the ritual purification (*tahara*) which at the very least requires washing the face and the hands to the elbows, rubbing the head with water, and bathing the feet to the ankles. In addition, the mouth, nose, and teeth must receive a thorough cleansing. If water should be unavailable to someone on a journey or away from home, clean earth or sand may be substituted in an abbreviated ritual exercise of cleansing.

In a city or village, the call to prayer (*Adhan*) is announced from a minaret or tall building by a muezzin, a crier. When the worshippers have assembled, another crier issues the *iqama* in a rapid, but more subdued voice, announcing that it is now time to begin the prayers. If the worshippers should be away from a city, a mosque, and a muezzin, they themselves may call out the two summons to prayer.

While it is desirable to pray in a mosque, when the supplicants find themselves away from a formal place of worship, they must attempt to find as clean an area as possible. Prayer rugs (*saijada*) are carried by many Muslims, but they are not an essential aspect of the ritual. It is essential to properly cover the body: males, at least from the navel to the knees; females, the entire body except for face, hands, and feet. It is also of utmost importance that wherever they may be, they face the *Qiblah*, the precise direction of Mecca. And while it is always preferable to perform the salat in the company of others, it is permissible under certain conditions to pray in private—except for the Friday congregational salat which may never be performed alone.

Before kneeling on their prayer rugs, however, it is of the utmost importance that the supplicants perform a required number of bending and bowing postures (*rak'as*) with the appropriate accompanying phrases. There must be two rak'as at dawn, four at noon, four in the afternoon, three at sunset, and four at night.

Jewish liturgy did not begin to achieve its fixed form until the centuries after the destruction of the second temple, and the prayer book did not appear in its classical form until the Middle Ages. But spontaneous prayers are found throughout the tenakh, the Hebrew Bible, and the Old Testament in the Christian Bible.

To list only a very few, there are the prayers of Abraham (Genesis 15:2–3), Isaac (Genesis 25:21–23), and Hannah (I Samuel 1:9–13) petitioning God for an heir. There are Moses' prayers for plagues on the Egyptians (Exodus 8:12), for the Red Sea to part its waters (Exodus 14:21), for a glimpse of God's glory (Exodus 33:18), and for Aaron's forgiveness after his sin of making the gold calf (Deuteronomy 9:20). Also there is Samson's prayer for strength to bring the columns down upon the Philistines (Judges 16:28–31); David's prayer to be forgiven for his immorality with Bathsheba (Psalms 51); Job's prayer to be forgiven for pride (Job 40:3–4; 42:6); Solomon's prayer for wisdom (I Kings 3:5–9); Elijah's prayer for fire to consume the altars of Baal (I Kings 18:36–37); and Jabez's prayer for prosperity in his work (I Chronicles 4:10).

Surveys Discover that Americans Are Great Practitioners of Prayer

Prayer is a basic element within all forms of religious expression. According to a survey taken by Lutheran Brotherhood reported in *USA Today* (February 7, 1997), Americans are great practitioners of prayer: 24 percent of those polled said that they prayed more than once a day; 31 percent pray every day; 16 percent several times a week; 10 percent several times a month; 9 percent several times a year.

From May through August 2007, Pew's Religious Landscape Survey questioned 35,000 Americans, nearly 3 in 10 of whom professed no denominational religious identity. This major survey found that U.S. adults believe overwhelmingly in God (92 percent) and 58 percent stated that they prayed at least once a day.

Many Americans enjoy the prayer experience in group settings.

On November 29, 2007, the Harris Poll released their findings of U.S. adults conducted between November 7 and 13, 2007. In their survey, they found that 82 percent believed in God, 74 percent in angels, and 79 percent in miracles.

Are prayers answered? According to an Arizona State University study published in the March 2007 journal *Research on Social Work Practice*, the answer is "yes." David R. Hodge, assistant professor of social work at Arizona State University, conducted a comprehensive analysis of 17 major studies on the effects of prayer that is offered for the benefit of another person (intercessory prayer) and found a positive effect.

Hodge stated that when the effects of prayer were averaged across all 17 of these major studies, controlling for differences in sample sizes, "a net positive effect for the prayer group is produced."

While offering cautions that prayer alone should not be used in certain medical cases, such as depression, Hodge wrote in the journal, "Overall, the meta-analysis indicates that prayer is effective."

Praying Is Beneficial for Your Health

In June 2000, researchers at Duke University Medical Center in Durham, North Carolina, presented the results of a six-year study in the *Journal of Gerontology* in which nearly 4,000 mostly Christian men and women, 65 and older, were asked about health problems and whether they prayed, meditated, or read the Bible. Dr. Harold Koenig, one of the researchers, stated that this was one of the first studies showing that people who pray live longer. Relatively healthy seniors who said that they rarely or never prayed, ran about a 50 percent greater risk of dying during the six-year study compared with those who prayed at least once a month. People who prayed even once a month appeared to get the same protection as those who prayed more often.

A 1999 CBS News poll found that 80 percent of adult Americans believe prayer improves recovery from disease.

Critics of such studies accuse the researchers of making subjective judgments concerning patients or of injecting hope into the equation. Others say that the results of people praying for the sick are no greater than random chance.

But in general, Americans believe that the power of prayer is beneficial for their health. A 1999 CBS News poll found that 80 percent of adult Americans believe prayer improves recovery from disease. In June 2001, a national Gallup poll revealed that 54 percent of adult Americans believed in spiritual healing.

In a poll conducted by Princeton Survey Research Associates, 84 percent of U.S. adults believe that God can perform miracles; 77 percent that God can heal through miracles; 65 percent have prayed for a miracle; and 48 percent have experienced a miracle.

Increasing Numbers of Medical Doctors Take Prayer Seriously

In recent years, more and more doctors and scientists have begun to study the power that many religious men and women claim may be achieved by focusing their prayers upon God and asking healing for themselves or others.

Dr. Larry Dossey, author of *Healing Words: The Power of Prayer and the Practice of Medicine* recalled when he was doing his residency at Parkland Memorial Hospital in Dallas, Texas, and had his first patient with a terminal case of cancer. Whenever he would stop by the man's hospital room, Dr. Dossey found him surrounded by visitors from his church, praying and singing. Dr. Dossey thought this was appropriate since they would soon be singing and praying at the man's funeral, because the cancer had spread throughout both lungs.

A year later, when he was working elsewhere, Dr. Dossey learned from a colleague that the terminally-ill patient was alive and well. When he had an opportunity to examine the man's X-rays, Dr. Dossey was stunned to see that his lungs were completely clear. There was no trace of cancer. Although Dr. Dossey had long since given up the faith of his childhood, it seemed to him that prayer had healed this man of his terminal cancer.

Intrigued, but devoted to the power of modern medicine, Dr. Dossey became chief of staff at a large urban hospital. He observed that many of his patients prayed, but he put little trust in the practice.

It wasn't until Dr. Dossey came across a study done in 1983 by Dr. Randolph Byrd, a cardiologist at San Francisco General Hospital, in which half of a group of cardiac patients were prayed for and half were not, that he started to change his mind. Those who were prayed for did better in a significant number of ways. Dr. Dossey could no longer ignore the evidence. The Byrd study had been designed according to rigid criteria. It had been a randomized, double-blind experiment—neither the patients, nurses, nor doctors knew which group the patients were in.

Inspired to search for other such experiments, Dr. Dossey was astonished to find more than 100 serious and well-conducted studies exhibiting the criteria of good science. About half demonstrated that prayer could bring about significant changes in those suffering from a variety of illnesses.

Medical doctors may be men and women of science, but that does not prevent them from having faith in a higher power.

Dr. Dossey has since given up the practice of medicine to devote himself full-time to writing and researching about prayer and how it affects human health. His extensive studies have produced such discoveries as the following:

1. The power of prayer does not diminish with distance. It can be as effective from the other side of the world as it is from the next room.

2. There is no right way to pray. There is no difference in the effectiveness of the various religious methods of praying.

3. Rather than asking for a specific healing for a particular health problem, the non-specific prayer, "Thy will be done," works as well or better as attempting to specify the outcome.

4. Love added to prayer increases its power.

5. Prayer is outside of time. It can be answered even before it is made.

6. Prayer is a reminder that we are never alone.

Boy Comes Back to Life in Morgue When Family Prays for Miracle

On July 8, 2002, 14-year-old Luis Alfredo Pinilla of Santiago, Chile, was accidentally strangled while playing a game with some friends. Although he was rushed to the Padre Hurtado Hospital in Santiago, Dr. Ernesto Behnke declared Luis dead upon arrival. Dr. Behnke, the hospital's director, said that Luis's heart had stopped and that he was unresponsive to cardiac massage, medication, or resuscitation procedures. In addition, the PH of the teenager's blood was 6.7, which is incompatible with life.

Luis's parents could not accept the tragic death of their young son. They gathered their family, friends, and neighbors and formed a prayer circle that began praying for a

> *Their 14-year-old son had awakened in a morgue after medical doctors had declared him dead.*

miracle from the Virgin at Lourdes. They believed that the Virgin would spare Luis because he was an altar boy and because he wanted to become a priest.

Later that evening, staff members at the hospital heard strange sounds coming from the morgue. After investigating, they found Luis Alfredo Pinilla breathing and very much alive.

Completely baffled, Dr. Behnke told the Santiago media that there had been no mistake. Luis was clinically dead when he was placed in the mortuary.

The Pinilla family and their friends rejoiced that their miracle had been granted. Their 14-year-old son had awakened in a morgue after medical doctors had declared him dead.

Her Baby Was Healed after Prayer to Mother Mary

Barbara May shared a beautiful story of the healing of her infant daughter's viral pneumonia through the grace of Mother Mary.

"It was in January 1960 that my four-month-old daughter, Laura, was admitted to the City of Hope Hospital in Duarte, California," Barbara said. "At that time it seemed as though most admissions were done with the understanding that there was little hope of the patient recovering. Laura was admitted with viral pneumonia in both lungs, and we were given little promise that she could be saved."

The infant was placed on the critical list for six days with private nurses in attendance around the clock.

On the afternoon of the sixth day, Barbara felt that she needed a break from the stress of being at her daughter's bedside and went to see her mother-in-law.

"She suggested that we walk to her local parish church in Sierra Madre to pray," Barbara recalled. "She remained at the back in one of the pews, and I went up to the front, to the Our Lady side of the church. I lit a candle and began to pray."

Laura is Barbara's second daughter, and she could not bear to accept the reality of her dying.

"I was asking for grace and understanding," she said. "I remember looking up at the statue of Our Lady and thinking that it must be because of my lack of sleep that the statue appeared to be expanding and glowing."

At the same time, Barbara remembered, the church was suddenly filled with an overwhelming scent of roses that became so powerful that it was nearly sickening.

"I thought at first that only I noticed the scent, but as I walked toward the back of the church, my mother-in-law asked me where the roses were, and she began looking around to see where they might be," Barbara said.

Barbara told us that she can still recall the hush of the church, the afternoon light falling right where they stood, and the strong, enveloping scent of roses.

"My mother-in-law told me that St. Teresa of Liseux had the identical experience with the scent of roses when she prayed to the Virgin Mary," Barbara said.

"I did not see the Virgin, but the smell of roses stayed with me until the next morning, when the hospital called and told me that a miracle had occurred: Laura's fever had broken, and she no longer had any trace of a virus or any pneumonia."

When Barbara returned to the hospital that she had left only ten hours before, she found a rosy-checked, healthy baby "whose light-brown baby fuzz had turned completely white during the night."

Barbara was so excited that Laura was going to live that it was some time before her mother-in-law reminded her of what had happened that day in church.

"It gave me goose bumps then, and it still does, because I believe that the Virgin Mary answered my prayers that day. I know what I experienced, and I had a witness in my mother-in-law. Most of all, in Laura's miraculous recovery I have a result that is undeniable and documented."

Many Christians, especially Catholics, pray to the Virgin Mary because they see her as an intercessor who then speaks to God on the behalf of humanity.

Little Hannah's Survival Proved the Power of Prayer

When Robert Gessner, coroner of Kankakee County, Illinois, was asked on June 16, 2007, if he believed in miracles and the power of prayer, he replied that he did now after a five-year-old girl who had been given up for dead came walking out of the woods near the Kankakee River.

Little Hannah Klamecki and her grandfather David Klamecki, 62, were last seen on Wednesday, June 13, on the river near Momence, about 45 miles south of Chicago. The Klameckis owned a cottage near the river, and Hannah enjoyed exploring the forest and the river with her grandfather.

Hannah's father, Mike Klamecki, was senior pastor at New Hope Community Church in Villa Park. When his father and his daughter had not returned by Wednesday evening, the Klameckis and some of their friends met for prayer.

On Thursday night, more than 100 members of the church joined the Klamecki family in group prayer, asking for the safe return of Hannah and her grandfather.

On Friday morning, June 15, searchers found the body of David Klamecki in a part of the river that is known locally as "Whirlpool Bend." There is a small island at the place where two tributaries join in the river to create a strong whirlpool current.

From the evidence that searchers located, it appeared that the two had walked out on a beach and entered the river to have a swim. The footprints of the girl were very much in evidence on a small island where the two had apparently stopped to rest before they resumed swimming. It must have been somewhere near the island where the two were swept away by the strong current.

Later on Friday morning, a group of searchers, including Kankakee Undersheriff Brad O'Keefe, were discussing where next they should search for Hannah's body when a small girl, smeared with dirt and grime, came walking out of the woods.

Chief Deputy Ken McCabe remembered how people were wondering who she was and why she was there, so he finally approached the little waif and asked who she was.

> *The object of their massive search had just come walking out of a wilderness area in which there were no homes, but plenty of coyotes.*

She was Hannah Klamecki, she answered. And she was looking for her grandparents' cottage. She had been walking and walking through the woods, but it was so hard for her to see above all the thick brush.

The rescue workers were astounded. The object of their massive search had just come walking out of a wilderness area in which there were no homes, but plenty of coyotes.

Someone gave her a banana and some water. Hannah asked for a chocolate cookie. There were none available, but one of the rescue workers suggested that they might have some cookies at the hospital where they were about to take her for an examination.

The Klamecki gave all the glory to God for the return of their beloved Hannah.

Later, Hannah explained that she had been wearing floats on her arms which kept her above the water when the river pulled her away. After being carried along by the river for quite some distance, she had managed to grab hold of an overhanging branch and pull herself to shore.

The joy of Hannah's survival was clouded by the death of her grandfather, but the Klamecki family once again acknowledged the mystery of God's will and the heavenly survival of Hannah Klamecki.

His Mother's Prayers Saved Him from Japanese Bayonets

The defeat of the Japanese forces at Guadalcanal at the end of January 1943 dealt them a major blow from which they never recovered. However, in December 1942, during the earlier days of fierce fighting in the Pacific, the U.S. Marines and Infantry were on the defensive from crack Japanese troops.

On the night of December 23, 1942, Private First Class Howard Grady experienced a miracle that saved his life. He had been mired in his muddy foxhole for hours when he was ordered by his squad leader to deliver a message to company headquarters. As he slithered his way across the battlefield, all of his thoughts and senses were occupied solely with the business of survival.

The soldier had a vision of his mother, who was praying in church, warning him of imminent danger from Japanese shell fire.

The young soldier managed to deliver the dispatch, and on his way back to his fox-hole, he stopped to enter a dugout in which several Marines were clustered around a battered coffeepot. The men offered to share their java, and Grady gratefully accepted, letting the steaming brew in the tin cup nestle snugly in his mud-caked hands.

As he leaned back against a damp earthen wall to relax for at least a few minutes before he returned to the grim reality of staying alive, his thoughts began to drift to images of his family back home in Missouri. Sitting there in a muddy dugout on a steamy, malaria-ridden, rain-soaked island, fighting a bloody battle that had already claimed hundreds of American lives and thousands of other casualties, it was hard to believe that it was the Christmas season back home in the states.

And then, so clearly in his mind's eye, he saw his mother kneeling at prayer in their home church. Beside her were his father, kid sister, and his sweetheart, Mary Alice. His inner vision lingered longingly on the scene, and his physical body was suffused with a mixture of warmth, love, and terrible homesickness.

Suddenly, it was as if he could truly hear his mother's voice. In his vision, she had ceased praying and had turned to face him and seemed to be speaking directly to him. He was positive that it was her voice, but he couldn't make out what she was saying. There was something unnerving about her tone, and she was frowning, as if she were terribly upset about something. And then he got the distinct impression that she was trying to warn him of danger.

On a sudden impulse, Grady threw down the tin cup, picked up his rifle, and ran out of the dugout, leaving the startled Marines staring after him in surprise.

The soldier began crawling back to his squadron's position, elbowing his way through the mud, convinced that his mother was warning him to get back to his foxhole as soon as possible.

He had managed to get no more than 20 feet from the dugout when the earth trembled and exploded with light, and the air around him was filled with the agonized cries of men in pain. A Japanese shell had scored a direct hit on the dugout, and when Grady crawled back to investigate, he discovered to his horror that every one of the Marines had been killed.

He lay still on the ground in the midst of the debris from the explosion, trying to blot out the faces of the Marines that he had seen about the coffee pot just minutes before. A violent trembling seized his body as he lay face down in the mud of bloody Guadalcanal.

At this unlikely moment, Grady again pictured the image of his mother kneeling in prayer at church. Once more, even though he still could not distinguish her exact words, he felt that she was praying that he be protected and watched over by God's all-abiding love.

At the same time, the image of his loving mother praying for him became very soothing and comforting to the distressed soldier. The more he thought of being at home at Christmas time with his family, his sweetheart, and his mother's Southern fried chicken, the more relaxed his body became and his muscles ceased their involuntary trembling.

Then, as he lay quietly face down in the mud amidst the huge chunks of earth churned up by the violent explosion that had destroyed the dugout and the men within, a squad of Japanese Sendai marines came running in his direction. As they jogged past him, bayonets fixed and ready, Grady did not move a muscle. He did not even breathe.

Had it not been for the second vision of his beloved mother and being home on Christmas that had so completely relaxed him, Grady's quivering, distressed body would certainly have been noticed by the Japanese marines and he would have been killed.

Three years later, the war was over, and Howard Grady had safely returned home. He married his childhood sweetheart in the same church which he had seen so clearly during that fateful December day on Guadalcanal. Had it not been for the miracle that had shown him the vision of his mother, who actually had been kneeling in the church praying for his safe return at the very same time that he lay in the mud of that faraway Pacific island, Grady might never have returned home to claim his bride or to celebrate another Christmas with his family.

Family Keeps Praying Loved One
Will Recover after Heart Stops Three Times

At 1:30 A.M. on Saturday, May 17, 2008, Val Thomas, 59, stopped breathing. Certain members of her family tried to revive her, while others began to pray for her recovery.

By the time help arrived to transport Mrs. Thomas to a Charleston, West Virginia hospital, rescue workers estimated that she had been without a heartbeat or oxygen for as long as 20 minutes before she was put on a ventilator. Her son Jim said her skin had already begun to harden and her fingers had curled. He assumed that his mother had died.

Doctors at the hospital put her on a machine that would induce hypothermia and lower her body temperature. Val Thomas began to breathe, but then her heart stopped again.

The Thomas family, who had come to the hospital, began to pray for her recovery, and Val's heart started again. It appeared that prayer would continue to pull their beloved family member out of the valley of the shadow of death.

She had been kept on life support for nearly 18 hours. Her heart had stopped for a third time, and doctors quietly informed her family that Val Thomas's chances of recovery were less than 10 percent. In fact, the doctors spoke frankly, she had gone over 17 hours without any sign of brain waves. To put it in medical terms, she had no neurological function.

> *The Thomas family, who had come to the hospital, began to pray for her recovery, and Val's heart started again.*

Although several of the Thomas family continued to pray for a miracle, others urged them to allow their blessed mother, aunt, sister, or cousin to go to be with God. After a brief family discussion, all those assembled said their good-byes, and a nurse began to remove the tubes from various machines that had been sustaining some semblance of life in Mrs. Thomas.

While the nearest of kin remained in the room to discuss the issue of whether or not there should be any organ donation, the ventilator had been left running. A nurse, noticing the oversight, reached down to disconnect the last of the tubes that had been employed in an effort to sustain life for the patient.

The nurse was still in the room when Val Thomas opened her eyes and began speaking with the caregiver.

The nurse apologized for having shut off all the life support systems. Mrs. Thomas gave her a warm smile and told her that that was all right. She was just fine now.

The Thomas family was elated that God had granted them the miracle for which they had been so earnestly praying.

Val Thomas's baffled doctors were called back to the room to examine her. The recovery of a woman who had no neurological function for nearly 18 hours could only be defined as a miracle.

On May 21, Mrs. Thomas was brought to the Cleveland Clinic to be checked out by a heart specialist to determine any damage that might have been gone to her heart. It had, after all, stopped three times.

The astonished specialists at the Cleveland Clinic found no blockage or damage.

The Thomas family feels that they were blessed by the power of prayer. Val Thomas agreed and said that she knew that God must have something special in mind that she must do before she truly goes home to heaven. She admitted that she had no idea what that purpose might be, but she was certain that he would let her know in due time.

Shrines and Sacred Places

Many people of faith find that a pilgrimage to a holy shrine or icon, such as the one in Knock, Ireland, or Medugorje in Bosnia and Herzegovina, can accomplish miracles of healing. There are many such places around the world, and pilgrims of all religious denominations may journey to these shrines and sacred places with the expectation of receiving a miracle.

What follows are descriptions of some of the more prominent sacred places in the world, and a few remarkable tales associated with them.

Allahabad, India

Each year since the eighth century Hindu pilgrims have traveled to one of the four sacred cities—Hardvar, Prayag, Ujjain, and Nasik—each located on a different sacred river—to seek forgiveness of sins as they bathe in the holy waters. According to Hindu mythology, the four cities became consecrated by the four drops of the nectar of immortality that fell upon them from the vessel that the gods used to carry the elixir of life away to heaven.

The ancient city of Prayag, now known as Allahabad, is a city of about 900,000 located on the Ganges River in southeast Uttar Pradesh in North India. Allahabad is called the Titharaja, "King of Tithras" (King of the Holy Cities), for it is located where three sacred rivers meet—the Ganges, the Yamuna, and the mythical Sarasvati, known as Sangam. (The Sarasvati, according to tradition, flowed from the Himalayas before it transferred its magical powers to the Ganges and disappeared into the north Indian desert). The very act of bathing at the confluence (the Triveni) is believed to bestow a triple blessing upon the Hindu pilgrim.

The annual pilgrimage to Allahabad, the *Magh Mela*, allows the pilgrims to visit a number of temples, as well as bathe in the confluence of the sacred rivers. Pilgrims are welcomed at such places of worship as the Mankameshar Temple, dedicated to Shiva; Hanuman Temple, dedicated to Lord Hanuman; and Alop Devi Temple, devoted to Lalita Devi, an incarnation of Shiva's consort Parvati. Every 12 years, the pilgrimage to Allahabad is made particularly significant because of a series of astrological conjunctions which occur at that time.

Pilgrims camp by the Ganges River near Allahabad, India.

Bayside, New York

From 1970 until her death in 1995, the "Bayside Seeress," Veronica Lueken, issued pronouncements from Mother Mary against the spiritual abuses of contemporary society. A Sunday Holy Hour is still conducted on the very spot where Veronica Lueken first received her visions. Her work is continued by St. Michael's World Apostolate under the direction of Michael Mangen, who joined the mission in 1978 and who promised Veronica that he would maintain the integrity of her teachings.

Chartres, France

The magnificent gothic cathedral that stands on the hill in the French town of Chartres is the sixth church or cathedral that has been constructed on that site over a period of 1,500 years. Although the cathedral that exists today is among the most venerated of all places for Christian pilgrimage, it is also one of the most enigmatic—for no one knows exactly who built it or how the unknown architects and master builders were able to construct such an architectural masterpiece.

Tradition says that the hill on which the cathedral was built was considered a holy place even in prehistoric times. Even before the Gauls inhabited this region on the River Eure about 60 miles southwest of present-day Paris, some ancient priests of an unknown religion constructed a dolmen (two or more large upright stones with a space in between and covered by a large horizontal rock) and a well within a mound. The chamber fashioned by such a structure is believed by many to create a point of power by which earth energies will be focused on all those who enter the space between the large stones.

Centuries later, the Druids, Celtic priests of Gaul and Britain, made the mound and dolmen a center for the study of their religion. It was here that a Druid priest had a vision of a virgin that would bear a child. To honor the vision, an image of the virgin with the babe resting on her knee was carved from a peach tree and placed next to the well and the power point within the dolmen.

> *It was here that a Druid priest had a vision of a virgin that would bear a child.*

When the Christians first appropriated the area in the third century, they immediately identified the age-darkened image of virgin and child that they found at the dolmen with their veneration of the Virgin Mary and worshipped her as the Black Virgin. Within a few years of their arrival in the area, they built the first church dedicated to Our Lady on the site of the dolmen, mound, and well and placed the image of the Black Virgin in the church's crypt.

The first church was burned by the Duke of Aquitania in 743 C.E., and marauding Vikings destroyed the second in 858. The third and fourth churches were also burned in 962 and 1020, and the first of the cathedrals erected on the site was destroyed by fire in 1194. Each time the place of worship was burned or crumbled, large numbers of vigorous and faithful Christian townspeople, builders, and architects appeared to rebuild the edifice, but the identity of the master builders who constructed the majestic Chartres Cathedral that stands there today, which is generally regarded as one of the great architectural masterpieces of the world, remains unknown.

Some have theorized that Bernard of Clairvaux, founder of the Cistercian monastic order and mentor of the secret order of Knights Templar, discovered the remains of the Ark of the Covenant in the ruins of King Solomon's temple and returned to France with the priceless treasure in 1128. Perhaps Cistercian scholars managed to decipher some of the secrets of the Ark regarding the principles of sacred geometry and the law of holy numbers, weights, and measures. Somehow, an unknown someone—Cistercian scholar, Knight Templar, or enlightened architect—was able to employ architectural principles greatly in advance of the time, and within 30 years after the former cathedral was burned in 1194, the remarkable Chartres Cathedral, considered an exemplar of the High Gothic style, was completed.

Those who visit the place today perpetuate the centuries-old claims that Chartres Cathedral has the power to transform individuals and to elevate them to a higher spiritual state. One of the artifacts within the cathedral which contributes to a sense of transformation is the great labyrinth that was built into the floor to serve as a maze wherein the pilgrim might walk on a spiritual journey to God. Others envision it as a pilgrimage to Jerusalem, walking the "Chemin de Jerusalem," the Road of Jerusalem. The labyrinth itself is an eleven-circuit design divided into four quadrants. The center consists of a rosette design, symbolizing enlightenment. The four arms of the cross are easily distinguished in the overall design of the labyrinth and represent the cross of Christ.

The tower of Fatima in Portugal.

Conyers, Georgia

Beginning in 1987, Nancy Fowler began receiving daily messages from Mother Mary. On the thirteenth of each month, beginning in 1990, apparitions of Mary and Jesus began to appear. By 1993 as many as 50,000 pilgrims could be expected to gather for each month's demonstration of the divine. In 1998, Nancy Fowler announced that she would no longer receive visions, but pilgrims still gather on the farm to pray, drink water from a well blessed by priests, and, hopefully, to receive healings.

Fatima, Portugal

Mother Mary appeared to three children near Fatima, instructing them to say their rosary frequently. During her six visits between May 13 and October 13, 1917, Mary issued a number of prophecies, many of which are said to be held secret by the Vatican.

Garabandal, Spain

A series of ecstatic visions of Mother Mary began for four children one Sunday after Mass in 1961. The visitations continued until 1965 and produced numerous accurate prophecies and astonishing miracles.

Guadalupe, Mexico

In 1531, a Native American named Juan Diego saw Mother Mary four times and was given a miraculously created serape as evidence of her heavenly visitation. Each year pilgrimages are conducted and miraculous healings are reported.

Jerusalem, Israel

Jerusalem stands in the middle of the nation of Israel, a holy city to three of the world's great religions—Judaism, Christianity, and Islam. Before Muslims underwent pilgrimages to Mecca, the most venerated holy place in all of Islam was the Dome of the Rock, a magnificent mosque built over the sacred rock where Abraham prepared to sacrifice his son Isaac to the Lord and where the Prophet Muhammad ascended to Paradise. For the Jews, Jerusalem is the site of King David's ancient capital of Judea and a massive wall, called the Wailing Wall, is all that remains of the great Temple that was destroyed by the Romans in 70 C.E. Christian pilgrims revere the city as the place where Jesus was crucified and rose from the dead, and for over 1,600 years they have visited the most revered of all Christian holy places, the Church of the Holy Sepulchre, which was built over Christ's tomb.

> *According to tradition, King David established Jerusalem as Israel's national capital in about 1000 B.C.E.*

According to Hebrew tradition, Jerusalem was chosen to be the earthly headquarters for the Lord's work among humankind in very ancient times, for Melchizedek, a priest, a survivor of the pre-flood world, the oldest living human at that time, was living there as King of Salem even before Father Abraham set out on his quest for the Promised Land. Obeying a commandment of the Lord, Melchizedek had come out of Babylonia to south central Canaan to build a city on the summit of the watershed between the Jordan River and the Mediterranean. Salem was constructed on the southeast hill of a mountain ridge with deep valleys on its east, south, and west sides. With the spring of Gihon at its feet to provide fresh water easily available for its inhabitants even during times of siege, the location of Salem made it a naturally impregnable fortress.

According to tradition, King David established Jerusalem as Israel's national capital in about 1000 B.C.E., and in about 950 B.C.E. his son Solomon built the magnificent temple which housed the Ark of the Covenant. The city and the temple were destroyed by the Babylonians in 586 B.C.E., but by the time that Jesus walked its streets in about 29 C.E., Jerusalem had been restored to its former glory. In 70 C.E., a series of Jewish revolts against Rome brought the imperial army to the walls of Jerusalem on the day of Passover. After a five-month siege, the city walls were brought down, the Temple of Herod destroyed, and Jerusalem was left in ruins and desolation.

In 326, after the Roman Emperor Constantine converted to Christianity, he traveled to the Holy Land to view the sacred sites for himself. Helena, his mother,

A view of the old city of Jerusalem with the Dome of the Rock in the foreground. The city has many sacred sites for Jews, Muslims, and Christians alike.

received a vision that showed her the exact spot where Joseph of Arimathea, a wealthy follower of Jesus, had buried him after his crucifixion. The site lay beneath a temple to Venus that had been erected by a Roman army of occupation, but Constantine perceived the edifice as only a minor impediment. He ordered the temple of the goddess torn down and replaced by the Basilica of Constantine, the original Church of the Holy Sepulchre, near the Tomb Rotunda, which covered the tomb of Christ. In time, the Basilica, the tomb, and Calvary, the site of the crucifixion, were all brought under the roof of a vast Romanesque cathedral. For the next three centuries, Jerusalem remained a Christian city, and in the fifth century, it dominated Christendom as one of the seats of the Five Patriarchs, along with Rome, Constantinople, Antioch, and Alexandria.

In 638, a Muslim army under Caliph Omar Ibn al-Khattab conquered Jerusalem. A devout follower of the Prophet Muhammad, the Caliph was also tolerant of other religions. He ordered that the Church of the Holy Sepulchre be respected as a Christian place of worship and forbade it to be converted into a mosque. When he was taken to the Temple Mount, he was shocked to discover that the holy rock where Abraham had taken Isaac to be sacrificed, the place that had held the Ark of the Covenant in Solomon's Temple, and the spot where Muhammad had ascended to Paradise lay exposed to the elements. After the area had been purified by prayers and a rainfall, the Caliph ordered the Dome of the Rock to be built to shelter the sacred rock. The shrine with its massive dome gilded with gold mosaics was completed in 691.

The golden dome collapsed in 1016, but it was soon rebuilt. In 1099, Christian Crusaders converted the Dome of the Rock to a Christian shrine, replacing the crescent on the top of the dome with a cross and constructing an altar on the rock. The shrine returned to Muslim possession in 1187 when the great Muslim military genius Salah al-Din, known to the Crusaders as Saladin, captured Jerusalem. In 1537, the Ottoman Turks replaced the gold mosaics on the outside of the dome with 45,000 Persian tiles. The Dome of the Rock was completely restored from 1956 to 1962.

The Dome of the Rock plays a significant role in the End-Time beliefs of Christian, Jewish, and Muslim Fundamentalists. Jews and Christians envision the site as one of the places in which Armageddon, the last great struggle between the forces of good and evil, will begin before the Messiah appears—or for the Christians, returns in a Second Coming. For the Muslims, it is here that Jesus will conquer the Antichrist and the Mahdi (Guided One) will appear to help destroy the forces of evil and to bring about the conversions of all Jews and Christians to Islam.

Knock, Ireland

In the late 1870s, the village of Knock in County Mayo, Ireland, was in the midst of a terrible famine. In desperation, 15 devout villagers gathered in the little Catholic church to ask for deliverance from the unrelenting pangs of hunger that had weakened them all.

As they prayed for divine help, they were amazed to see a glowing light beginning to form at one end of the small church. As the astonished villagers gazed spellbound at the brilliant light, they were able to distinguish the figures of Mother Mary, St. Joseph, and St. John standing at the altar, looking upward at a lamb surrounded by golden stars.

A short time after the villagers had reported their vision, many ill, diseased, or crippled people who visited the church began to claim miraculous cures as they knelt at the statue of Mary.

In 1879, clerical authorities from the Roman Catholic Church were sent to Knock to investigate the alleged vision and the numerous cures ascribed to the holy visitation. After the clerics had spent several days interrogating the villagers who had witnessed the apparition and the people who had received miracle healings, they stated their official conclusion that an authentic manifestation of the Blessed Mother had occurred.

Since that time the small village of Knock has come to be called the "Irish Lourdes," and medical authorities continue to be astounded by the number of healings that have taken place at the little church's shrine. In 1979, on the centennial of the apparition, Pope John Paul II visited Knock. While he was there, he, together with the crowds that had gathered to welcome him, experienced a visitation of Mary.

Miracles Associated with Knock, Ireland

Bridie Hopkins, a Leeds teenager who suffered from a diseased leg bone, testified that after she had received the blessing at the shrine in Knock, the numbness in her leg disappeared and there came a strange kind of prickling sensation.

Four months later, doctors pronounced Bridie's leg completely healed.

* * *

In 1994, Dr. Patrick O'Mara stated that his observation of the miraculous recovery of Marion Carroll from multiple sclerosis defied the laws of science and medicine as he had previously understood them.

Although Mrs. Carroll, a resident of Athlone, Ireland, began having symptoms of multiple sclerosis in 1972, the disease wasn't diagnosed in the young mother until 1978. By then she had lost the use of both of her legs.

> *Marion felt a strange sensation moving over her. She knew that some unseen force was urging her to walk.*

Her husband, Jimmy, got her an electric wheelchair, but her hands soon became too weak to work the control button. Then the muscles in her throat were stricken, and she couldn't speak or swallow properly. She had to drink with a straw, and she was unable to hold her head up without a neck brace. When it seemed that her physical condition could not be worse, Marion developed epilepsy and kidney infections. Her husband and her two children took turns washing, changing, and feeding her.

Then, on September 3, 1989, 41-year-old Marion agreed to allow some friends to take her by ambulance to the statue of Mary at Knock. After all, what did she have to lose? She had heard the priest say that he was already choosing the kind words that he would say at her funeral.

Marion Carroll was carried into the church on a stretcher and placed under the statue. Later, she told journalist Fleur Brennan that she didn't have the will to pray and beseech the Blessed Mother for a healing. She simply said to Mary that she, too, had been a mother. She would know how Marion felt about leaving her husband and children.

A few minutes later, during a religious service in the village church, Marion felt a strange sensation moving over her. She knew that some unseen force was urging her to walk.

She didn't want to make a spectacle of herself before the statue of the Blessed Mother, so she waited until she had been carried out of the church before she convinced her nurse to undo the straps on her stretcher.

Immediately Marion was propelled to her feet by that same unseen force. She felt herself completely filled with love, and she rose from the stretcher and began to cry tears of joy.

When Marion Carroll returned home and showed her husband and children that she could walk, there were many more tears of joy and thanksgiving. Jimmy told her that he had been earnestly praying that she would receive a cure.

Dr. Patrick O'Mara, the Carrolls' regular physician, together with a physical therapist, conducted a thorough examination of Marion and declared that the muscles which had been shriveled for 11 years were now totally normal. In addition, the epilepsy and kidney problems that had so afflicted her had also disappeared.

Although patients suffering from multiple sclerosis do have remissions, they generally take place over a period of time. Dr. O'Mara told Fleur Brennan in November 1994 that Marion Carroll's case was different because she had regained her full health instantly. Dr. O'Mara reinforced his earlier diagnosis and treatment and stated that Marion Carroll's multiple sclerosis had been as bad as any that he had ever seen, and she did not have long to live. He simply could not explain what happened. It appeared that Our Lady of Knock had worked another miracle.

* * *

When he was just a boy of 10 in the 1960s, Nicholas Doyle of Bray County was stricken with rheumatic fever. Doctors said that the boy's heart had been so severely affected that, in addition to being forbidden to participate in even the mildest forms of exercise, Nicholas had to be confined to his bed. He was denied even the mild exertion of knitting as a means to pass the time.

Just a few days after he had been blessed before the statue of the Blessed Mother in the tiny village church in Knock, Nicholas was riding his bicycle. The Doyles' family doctor found himself completely at a loss to explain the miraculous cure.

Lourdes, France

The healing Grotto of Bernadette at Lourdes, France, was constructed on the site where 14-year-old Bernadette Soubrious conversed with Mother Mary in 1858. Since the time that the miracle occurred to the young miller's daughter, pilgrims have journeyed to Lourdes to seek healing from the waters of the natural spring that appeared in the grotto next to the Gave de Pau River. Consistently, for decades, an average of 200,000 people visited the shrine each year. The celebration of the 100th anniversary of Lourdes in 1958 brought more than two million people into the small community in southern France. In the 1990s, annual attendance rose to over five million a year.

> *Since the 1860s, thousands of pilgrims have left their crutches and canes at the shrine.*

The full story goes like this: On February 11, 1858, Bernadette Soubrious and her two sisters were gathering firewood outside Lourdes when she fell behind the younger girls. That was the first time that Bernadette saw the apparition of a lady dressed in white with a blue sash and a yellow rose on each foot standing in a grotto next to the river. The lady did not speak, but made the sign of the cross before she disappeared.

Bernadette returned to the grotto a second time, but it was not until the lady's third appearance that she spoke and asked Bernadette if she would like to meet her every day for two weeks. Bernadette enthusiastically agreed, and word of her visitations soon spread throughout the entire village. Crowds gathered to observe the girl and hear what messages she would relay from the lady. The apparition insisted again and again that priests must build a chapel in the grotto and that Bernadette was to drink from the spring there. Since there was no spring in sight, Bernadette began to scrape at the muddy ground until a spring bubbled forth with waters which were immediately believed to contain curative powers. Water from that same spring is still piped to a bathing house where pilgrims gather to receive its healing blessings.

Upset by the disturbances that she was causing in the town, the local police and civil authorities interrogated Bernadette, but they could not dissuade her from continuing her meetings by the grotto. The local parish priest, Father Peyramale, also did his best to convince Bernadette that she was only imagining the visions. Then, on March 25, after her sixteenth visit, the lady revealed her name to Bernadette, who, when questioned by the skeptical priest, relayed the lady's identity as "The Immaculate Conception." Because that title had been applied to Mother Mary by Catholic theologians only four years before and was only known to the clergy, Father Peyramale thought it highly unlikely that a teenaged girl who could not read or

A statuette of Saint Bernadette, who many believe spoke with the Virgin Mary in 1858.

write and spoke only a crude, provincial form of French would know the phrase used to define the doctrine that declared Mary free from the taint of original sin.

With the official endorsement of the clergy, the grotto at the edge of the river would soon support a healing chapel and begin to attract pilgrims from great distances. After 1866, when a railway line was completed to Lourdes, many thousands of those afflicted with various illnesses began to arrive in the little French town. In that same year, 22-year-old Bernadette Soubrious left for a convent in Nevers, hundreds of miles to the north. She died there in 1879.

Since the 1860s, thousands of pilgrims have left their crutches and canes at the shrine. Thousands more claim to have been cured of advanced cancers. Although there are thousands of cures and healings claimed by men and women who have immersed themselves in the cold spring waters of the shrine, the Lourdes Medical Bureau has established certain criteria that must be met before they will certify a cure as miraculous:

- The affliction must be a serious disease. If it is not classified as incurable, it must be diagnosed as extremely difficult to cure.
- There must be no improvement in the patient's condition prior to the visit to the Lourdes shrine.

The Sanctuary of the Virgin Mary of Lourdes in France.

- Medication that may have been used must have been judged ineffective.
- The cure must be totally complete.
- The cure must be unquestionably definitive and free of all doubt.

Such stringent requirements set by members of the medical profession in order to qualify as a miraculous healing do little to deter the five million visitors each year who travel to the small town in the foothills of the Pyrenees in search of their own miracle.

Since the Lourdes Medical Bureau was established in 1883, they have noted over 2,500 cases which they considered truly remarkable, but which fell short of their strict criteria of a miracle. Since 1958, the Church has acknowledged only six miracles occurring at Lourdes.

Miracle at Lourdes: Man Walks after 16 Years of Paralysis

The most recent Lourdes healing to be accredited as a miracle occurred to mill worker Jean-Claude Bely from western France, who had been stricken with multiple sclerosis in 1977. The disease left him almost completely paralyzed, unable to walk, and nearly as helpless as an infant. He had to have someone help him shave, get dressed, and perform daily hygienic tasks.

Bely was taken to Lourdes in 1987, and one morning before he was to be taken to the shrine, he prayed to the Blessed Mother to grant him a healing. Then, to his complete astonishment, in the next moment she appeared to him and told him to get up and walk.

As he later described the apparition to others, Mother Mary had blue eyes and was smiling at him. She was very young and beautiful, dressed all in white, but barefoot. She commanded him to stand, but Bely confessed that he was so in awe to be in the presence of the Blessed Mother that he could not move.

Later, after his son had helped him bathe in the waters before the shrine, Bely was deeply disappointed when nothing happened to alleviate his condition. He remained paralyzed, unable to stand. Perhaps, he reasoned, he had offended Mother Mary by not obeying her command to stand when she appeared before him.

The next day, however, when he was resting on his hospital bed, he suddenly felt an icy chill move through his body. Then, in the very next moment, a fiery heat came over him. At first the sensation of heat was mild, then it became difficult for Jean-Claude to endure.

It was then that he comprehended that he had been healed. He swung his legs over the side of the bed and stood up without assistance. He stretched both his arms and his legs to be certain that he had been cured—and took his first steps in years.

As he moved forward, feeling very much like a child learning to walk, he began to weep for joy, crying and hugging his wife. With tears streaming down both of their faces, Jean-Claude and his wife thanked God and the Blessed Mother for his miracle.

A representative from the Lourdes International Medical Bureau agreed that there was no scientific explanation for Jean-Claude Bely's healing and decreed it to be a true miracle. Some of the most accredited multiple sclerosis specialists in Europe agreed that Bely's healing was much more than a remission—which, they acknowledged, could occur, usually over several months. Bely's recovery had occurred literally overnight, which was inexplicable.

After 16 years of almost complete paralysis, Jean-Claude was able to walk with his wife, carry groceries home from the market, ride his bicycle, and visit the sick to inspire them with hope for their conditions.

The priest who had organized Bely's pilgrimage to Lourdes expressed his opinion that there was no medical explanation for such a miraculous cure. In 1999, the Church officially recognized the healing of Jean-Claude Bely as the first true miracle at Lourdes in a decade.

Mecca, Saudi Arabia

Mecca, known to the Muslim faithful as *Umm al-Qura*, the Mother of Cities, is the holiest place in the Islamic world. It was here that Muhammad the Prophet, the Messenger of God, the founder of the Muslim faith, was born in 570, and it is here within the Great Mosque that the Ka'aba, the most sacred shrine of Islam, awaits the Muslim pilgrim. Throughout the world, wherever they may be, all devout Muslims pray five times a day, each time bowing down to face Mecca. All able-bodied Muslims who have sufficient financial means and whose absence from their families would not create a hardship must undertake a pilgrimage, a *hajj*, to Mecca once in their lifetime during the Muslim month of Dhu-al-Hijah (the twelfth lunar month).

Physically, Mecca is located about 45 miles east of the Red Sea port of Jedda, a city surrounded by the Sirat Mountains. The experience of visiting the sacred city and worshipping at the mosque containing the Ka'aba is strictly limited to those who follow the Islamic faith. There is an area of several miles around Mecca that is considered to be *haram* (restricted), and non-Muslims are forbidden to enter this sacred zone. Those Muslims who travel into this area as they progress toward the Mother of Cities must profess their having undergone a state of ritual purity and consecration. It is at this point that they set aside the clothes in which they have traveled and don a special article of clothing consisting of two seamless white sheets.

The hajj begins with a procession called the *tawaf*, which takes the pilgrim around the Ka'aba seven times. The Ka'aba is a cube-shaped structure that stands about 43 feet high,

Every year, Muslims from all over the world make a pilgrimage to Mecca, the holiest city to those who follow Islam.

with regular sides from 36 to 43 feet. The building is draped in a black cloth that bears a band of sacred verses embroidered in gold and silver thread. In the southeastern corner of the Ka'aba is the sacred Black Stone, an ancient holy relic about 11 inches wide and 15 inches high that has been mounted in silver. Muslims believe that the Black Stone was sent from heaven by Allah. It is the fortunate pilgrim who manages to break free from the press of the crowd and kiss the Black Stone. Because of the great mass of humanity crowding into the Ka'aba at any given moment, it has been decreed centuries ago that the gesture of a kiss toward the stone will suffice and merit a great blessing.

The second element of the hajj is to run seven times between two small hills, al-Safwa and al-Marwa, which are enclosed and connected with a walkway immediately adjoining the mosque courtyard. The third aspect of the pilgrimage involves walking about five miles to the town of Mina, then onward to the plain of Arafat, 10 miles farther to the east. The time of the journey is spent in prayer and meditation. As the pilgrims walk back toward Mina, they stop to throw small stones at three pillars, an act which symbolically recalls the three occasions when Abraham threw stones at Satan, who was tempting him to disobey God's command to sacrifice his son. After they walk the five miles back to Mecca, the final stage of the hajj is achieved with a festival in which a sheep, goat, cow, or camel is sacrificed to commemorate the moment when God rescinded the command to Abraham to sacrifice his son and permitted him to slay a ram and offer its blood in Ishmael's stead. The hajj concludes with a final procession around the Ka'aba. The hajj generally lasts about 13 days, but when as many as two million pilgrims crowd in Mecca to observe the annual event, it may last a day or two longer to accommodate the vast numbers of the faithful.

Medjugorje, Bosnia and Herzegovina

In 1981, six children saw Mother Mary holding the infant Jesus near the village. The holy figure appeared on an almost daily basis for five months, leaving behind a continuing legacy of miraculous healings.

In 1985, 31-year-old nurse Heather Duncan severely injured her back while trying to lift a heavy patient at the hospital in Aberdeen, Scotland, where she was employed. The disks in her lower spine were severely damaged, and she was in constant pain. After she had undergone several operations, she was informed that she would be confined to a wheelchair forever.

Heather found it difficult to accept such a negative prescription for the remainder of her life. She had heard that there had been as many as 400 authenticated reports of healing miracles at the shrine near the small village of Medjugorje, where a group of children had seen Mother Mary standing on a cloud in 1981. In October 1990, after she had been paralyzed from the waist down for five years, Heather decided to act upon her faith in God rather than in conventional medical diagnoses, and she set out on a pilgrimage to Medjugorje in Bosnia and Herzegovina.

As she attended a prayer service in a graveyard near the shrine, Father Peter Rookey, a Roman Catholic priest from Chicago, laid hands on her head, then ran them down her arms and legs. Father Rookey laid his hands on Heather a second time, and asked her if she believed that Jesus could heal her.

It was then that Heather had the visionary experience that would lead to her healing miracle. She saw Jesus, not as his image appeared on a crucifix, but as he might appear as if he were standing there before her, ministering to her paralyzed legs.

Father Rookey asked again if she believed that Jesus could heal her. Heather answered in the affirmative, and a voice in the back of her head told her to stand up and walk. To the cheers and joyful applause of the other pilgrims who attended the prayer service, Heather walked around the graveyard.

When she returned home to Scotland, she surprised her husband, Brian, by walking unaided into their home and asking how he had been doing at work. Although he could scarcely believe his eyes, he simply replied that it was wonderful to see her walking again.

The former nurse is convinced that her recovery was a miracle. Her longtime physician, Dr. Catherine Legg, admitted that she had no medical explanation for the sud-

On a hill near Medjugorje, Bosnia and Herzegovina, six children claimed in 1981 that they saw the Virgin Mary.

den healing of Heather's back. The parish office in Medjugorje, which documents all healings which occur at the shrine, also confirmed that Heather Duncan had been healed of a crippling back injury.

A *Tale of Medjugorje: Wheelchair-bound Teenager Stands and Walks*

Thirteen-year-old Nicola Pacini, who lived with his family near Florence, Italy, had been confined to a wheelchair for five years with muscular dystrophy when his parents decided to take him to visit the Virgin Mary shrine in Medjugorje in December 1991.

In spite of the popularity of Medjugorje as a healing shrine, Nicola did not want to go, he told his parents that he would rather have them save the money that such a trip would cost. Nicola thought that it would be useless to go, and that the pilgrimage would only bring all three of them additional heartache and disappointment.

Nicola argued that he was but one of millions of handicapped people in the world, and he would be but one of thousands of pilgrims who would be crowding around the statue of Mother Mary at Medjugorje praying for a healing.

But at last after much discussion and prayer, Nicola agreed to accompany his parents to the holy place where Mother Mary had appeared wearing a crown of twelve stars.

The bus trip was exhausting, but when the Pacini family arrived at the shrine on December 8, Nicola's mother wasted no time in pushing his wheelchair directly in front of Mary's life-size statue. Perhaps more to please his parents than to get a miracle, Nicola began to pray.

Then, to his astonishment and his parents' great joy, he felt his paralyzed right hand slowly open.

Encouraged by such a marvelous sign of divine energy, Nicola was eager to return to the shrine the next morning. In his prayers, however, he asked that his healing not be done for his sake alone, but also for his parents.

And, then, Nicola simply felt like getting up and walking—for the first time in five years.

It was the strangest feeling, Nicola said later. It was as if something was moving inside him, and he had an overwhelming urge to get up and walk. An irresistible force seemed to be lifting him up from the wheelchair. Although he thought that it was impossible, he found himself standing upright and walking!

After he had taken the first few steps, he called out to his mother and heard her cry of joy that a miracle had occurred. Mrs. Pacini instinctively rushed to her son's side to help him, but Nicola asked her to leave him alone. He knew that he could walk on his own.

The Pacini family will always remember how the hundreds of pilgrims who were gathered around the shrine burst into applause when Nicola kept walking.

The boy's mind was filled with the wonder of it all. Mother Mary had heard his prayers and those of his parents.

When the Pacinis returned to Florence, Dr. Rosella Mengonzi, their physician, was shocked when she saw Nicola standing and walking. Dr. Mengonzi had been certain that Nicola would be forced to spend his life in a wheelchair. After a thorough examination, Dr. Mengonzi told journalist Silvio Piersanti that somehow Nicola Pacini had completely recovered from an incurable disease in a manner that she could not medically explain. It seemed a healing miracle had been performed.

Zeitoun, Egypt

As many as a million witnesses may have glimpsed the figure of the glowing Madonna standing, kneeling, or praying beside a cross on the roof of St. Mary's Coptic Church. Miraculous cures manifested among the pilgrims from 1968 to 1971.

Spirits Who Came Back to Help

Spirit of Pope John XXIII Heals Dying Nun

Early in 1967 the *Irish Independent* of Dublin carried the account of a miracle healing that had brought a dying nun "from death's door to a healthy normal life" after the spirit of Pope John XXIII, who had died in 1963, appeared and spoke to her.

Sister Caterina Capitani, a nun of the Sisters of Charity of St. Vincent de Paul, suffered from varicose veins of the esophagus, a condition thought to be incurable and surgically inoperable. However, because the unfortunate sister endured continual hemorrhages, physicians decided to attempt an operation at Medical Missionaries of Mary of the Clinica Mediterranea in Naples, Italy. Two surgeries were performed, but they were unsuccessful; and when the incision on her stomach opened, Sister Caterina's condition steadily worsened to the point where she collapsed. Desperate to attempt any new therapy, her doctors sent the nun south for a change of air, but she was soon returned to Naples when it was decided that she was dying and had only a brief time to live.

Sister Caterina lay in her room alone. She had turned on her side when she felt someone place a hand on her stomach. Summoning all her strength, she turned to see Pope John standing beside her bed. He was not attired in his papal robes, but she easily recognized him. In a quiet, yet authoritative voice, the ethereal image of Pope John

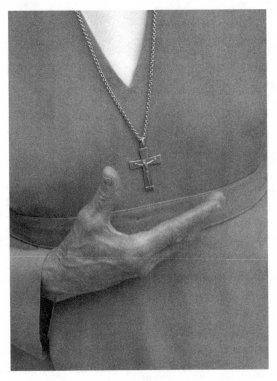

After two unsuccessful surgeries, a nun received help from the spirit of the late Pope John XXIII.

XXIII, who had died on June 3, 1963, spoke words of great comfort: "Sister, you have called to me so many times ... that you have torn out of my heart this miracle. Do not fear. You are healed."

The spirit of Pope John then told Sister Caterina to call in the sisters and the doctors so that a test could be made. But before she did so, he assured her once again that no trace of her illness would remain. Just before the image vanished, he told Sister Caterina to come to Rome and pray at his tomb.

The moment the spirit of the deceased pope disappeared, Sister Caterina rose from her bed and was elated that she felt no pain. When she summoned the sisters and doctors into her room, they were astonished to find that the scar on her abdomen, which had been open and bleeding, was now completely healed. There was no longer any other physical sign to indicate that moments before there had been a gaping wound. The sisters declared the healing a miracle. Sister Caterina had not been expected to survive the day, yet that evening she was up and eating her supper with the community.

According to the *Irish Independent*, ever since her miracle healing by the apparition of Pope John XXIII Sister Caterina lived a normal, healthy life in every way. "This is a phenomenon that cannot be explained in a human way," the account concluded.

Mother's Prayer Opens a Door between Two Worlds

In September 1981 little Geraldine O'Rourke suddenly fell ill at the isolated rural home in which the family had recently moved. Helpless to prevent her condition from worsening, the O'Rourkes were dismayed when Geraldine's fever soon reached 101 degrees.

To make matters worse, the area was beset by a torrential downfall of rain, which prevented their taking her to a hospital, and their telephone was out of order, making a call for help impossible.

Just when the desperate parents' hopes were fast sinking in despair and they felt their fervent prayers were going unanswered, Mrs. O'Rourke heard a peculiar rustling sound and looked up from her prayers to behold the figure of a man looking down at Geraldine on the bed.

The mother felt no fear at the appearance of the phantom, and she immediately regarded the entity as one sent by God in answer to prayer. Somehow she knew that their prayers had been somehow able to unlock the doors between worlds and summon assistance for their little girl.

The ghostly form led the amazed O'Rourkes to a hidden cache of medicines behind a panel in their living room. Trusting that the spirit entity had been sent by God to help them, they carefully followed the ghost's instructions regarding the proper administration of the medicines to their daughter.

As the astonished O'Rourkes watched, Geraldine became still and peaceful. The entity joined their vigil until dawn, then disappeared.

> *The mother felt no fear at the appearance of the phantom, and she immediately regarded the entity as one sent by God.*

Later, after little Geraldine had fully recovered, the O'Rourkes did a bit of investigation and learned that their house had formerly been occupied by a doctor. Fearing that burglars would steal his drugs, he must have hidden them in a secret compartment. Apparently, he had died so suddenly that he hadn't had time to leave instruction for their disposal.

The O'Rourkes will be forever grateful that the secret cache remained for the doctor's spirit to dispense to their daughter on that grim and stormy night. According to Colin Parsons in his book *Encounters with the Unknown*, they have made a kind of shrine out of the compartment in which their helping hand from beyond had kept the medicines that saved Geraldine's life.

Ghost of His Mother Moved Him Out of Torpedo's Path

During World War II, Victor Lasater of Omaha, Nebraska, had the misfortune to be temporarily stranded on a freighter in the middle of the Atlantic Ocean.

"Our engine had broken down about seven days out of port, and even though we were part of a convoy headed for Italy, the crucial war schedule demanded that the rest of the ships leave us behind while they went on," he remembered.

"In the period from 1942 to 1943 the waters of the Atlantic were thick with Nazi submarines, and they all had commanders eager to sink a ship for Adolf Hitler, *der Führer*. We were all tense and nervous, expecting at any minute to see two or three of those terrible metal 'fish' streaking toward our helpless vessel."

By the third day of bobbing in the water like a sitting duck during hunting season, the crew was becoming really jumpy and tense.

"We had a few guns on deck," Lasater said, "but we all knew that they would be of little use against submarines unless the U-boat surfaced. And it was hardly likely that any Nazi commander, no matter how fanatical, was going to waste all that time and effort to surface in order to engage us in an old-fashioned sea battle when launching a couple of torpedoes at our ship from the safety of Neptune's domain would do the trick"

In late afternoon of the third day, Lasater lay in his bunk, trying to get some rest before his next watch. He was alone in the quarters.

"I was awakened by the sensation that a warm hand was nudging my shoulder. I grunted and tried to shrug off the touch that was interfering with my sleep. But then,

A German U-boat had fired a torpedo at Victor Lasater's ship, but his mother's ghost woke him in time to save his life.

strangely enough, there seemed something very familiar about that particular style of nudging."

Lasater opened his eyes to see the image of his mother standing next to his bunk. She was still pushing at his shoulder, and when his eyes widened in astonishment at her presence, she smiled at him.

"Vic, honey," she told him in her softly pleasant voice, "you had better get up now. It is time to get up."

Before Lasater could respond, the form of his mother disappeared.

"Mom had been dead for eight years," he said. "I thought for a minute or so that maybe I had been dreaming, perhaps reliving a day in my childhood when my mother had been waking me to get ready to go to school.

"But the more I thought about the apparition, the more I began to feel so damn uneasy that I wanted to get dressed and get out of the bunk room as quickly as I could."

Since he did not wish to be alone and still had a couple of hours before he was to report to his watch, Victor Lasater decided to go down to the engine room and talk with the engineers who were working on the repairs.

"I had no more than nodded hello at one of the firemen who was a good buddy of mine when a tremendous explosion shook the entire freighter and knocked us all off kilter," Lasater said. "I went down on one knee, and a couple of the men fell flat on their backsides.

"No one had to tell us that we had been hit by a Nazi torpedo. One of Hitler's mighty U-boat commanders couldn't resist slamming one into a helpless freighter that was sitting dead in the water."

Within a matter of moments all of the crew members were crowded into lifeboats and rowing away from the sinking ship. Fortunately there were no casualties.

"But as I looked back at the slowly sinking freighter, I saw clearly that there would have been one fatality if the ghost of my mother had not awakened me when she did," Lasater said.

"From my position in the lifeboat I could see a massive hole that had been blasted in the starboard side where the torpedo had slammed us midship. Directly above that scorched and tangled mass of steel was the exact spot where I had been sleeping only moments before the torpedo had struck. My mother had somehow managed to go on recess from heaven so that she would be able to wake me up just in time."

The "Mexican Mauler" Returns to Lift Vehicle off Teenager

Estelle Santos cried out to God in an anguished prayer that awful day in 1985: "Oh, God, help us! Send us a miracle and help us lift the station wagon off Ray before he dies!"

With that heaven-sent supplication, two women and a girl sought to lift a 3,500-pound station wagon off the unconscious teenaged boy being crushed underneath its unrelenting bulk.

Ray Santos, 17, had been repairing the transmission of his 1978 Chevrolet in the yard of his home in Las Cruces, New Mexico, when the car slipped off a jack and pinned him.

A steel cross brace under the steering column pressed heavily, agonizingly against his chest. The pain was unbearable.

Ray tried to take a deep breath, but couldn't. He had the grim realization that if he didn't get the pressure off him, he would be crushed to death. Every time he shouted for help, he let air out of his lungs, and the deadly weight on his chest increased. He feared that any second he would hear the awful sounds of his ribs cracking. The last thing he remembered before passing out was asking God to forgive his sins.

> *There was something about him that was fierce and wild, but his brown eyes were kind.*

Felicita Madrid, 66, heard Ray's faint, frantic shouting. When she looked out of her window and saw a pair of shoes sticking out from under the station wagon, she knew that someone was in deep trouble. Mrs. Madrid's cries for help summoned Ray's mother, Estelle, their neighbor Roberta Gavarette, and her 11-year-old daughter, Rita.

The two women and the girl grabbed hold of the station wagon's bumper, and tried with all of their strength to lift it. The bumper rose up, but the wheels would not leave the ground.

Estelle prayed aloud for God's help before they tried once again to lift the car off Ray.

"That's when the man ran up to us," Estelle recalled. "He was not a very tall man, but he was stocky and powerfully built. His nose was crooked, like it had been broken. There was something about him that was fierce and wild, but his brown eyes were kind. He said that he would give us a hand.

"We figured that he was some stranger who just happened by and saw our trouble, and we were grateful for any help that we could get.

"I counted to three again; and when we lifted the bumper, the big man's muscles bulged—and the car rose completely off the ground. The station wagon now seemed no heavier than a feather."

The powerful man told Felicita and Rita to pull Ray out from under the car while he and the two women held the car up off his pinned chest.

"Somehow in all the excitement of the ambulance arriving to rush Ray off to the hospital, the stranger disappeared," Estelle said. "Ray was very lucky. He was treated at a hospital, but miraculously suffered no broken bones or internal injuries. Ray was thankful to God for letting him stay around a while longer, but he was upset with us that we didn't get the stranger's name so he could thank him for saving his life."

That night, Felicita Madrid startled the others when she told them that she knew the identity of the man who had appeared so fortuitously at such a desperate moment. At first, she said, she had not been certain, but after she had thought more about it, she was positive of the stranger's identity.

She explained that 20 years before, when she and her late husband, Ramon, had first moved to the neighborhood, the Santos home had been occupied by a man named Emilio Sanchez, a powerfully built man who had wrestled professionally under the ring alias of the Mexican Mauler. Felicita remembered vividly having watched the wrestler working out with barbells in the back yard, and she recalled the night he had been killed in an automobile accident.

"Emilio was a gentle giant," Mrs. Madrid said. "He loved people, children and young people especially, and I have often felt that I have glimpsed him in the neighborhood. He was always there to help when he was needed."

Although Felicita Madrid's explanation for the sudden appearance—and disappearance of the stranger with the strength of a Samson—seemed eerie at first, Estelle Santos summed up the feelings of everyone when she said, "God heard our prayers and spared my son Ray's life. He granted us a miracle. Who can say that God did not send us a spirit to give us a helping hand from beyond?"

A Nurse Appeared to Bring Little Buddy the Medicine He Needed

On a cold January night in 1988, Julia Cantrell, 13, of southern Missouri sat vigil with her mother, Ida, as Buddy, Julia's four-year-old brother, lay in a coma. The doctors at Memorial Hospital had told them it was unlikely that Buddy would live through the night.

"Sister," her mother said in a voice that was warped with emotion, "I have been praying for your little brother's life for hours now. You've got to join me in prayer, and we just have to pray him through this terrible time. Doctors aren't always right. And God can always work a miracle."

"I have been praying, Momma," Julia assured her mother. "I've asked God to please forgive anything wicked or nasty that I have ever done and to please, please not punish little Buddy for anything that I did."

For the first time that evening Julia saw a flicker of a smile tug at her mother's lips. "Child, what wicked or nasty thing have you ever done? You're a good girl, and your prayers are going to touch God's heart."

"I just wish Daddy was here to pray with us," Julia said. "He can make such big, powerful prayers."

"You know that he is praying himself hoarse in that big old truck of his," her mother told her. "And you know that he will be here just as fast as that old rig will carry him. Come now, let us bend our knees, bow our heads, and pray together for little Buddy."

The two of them got down on their knees beside Buddy's hospital bed and folded their hands. Ida Cantrell led them in the Lord's Prayer, and Twenty-third Psalm, and then began an earnest, heartfelt, personal prayer of supplication.

About 4:45 A.M., a tall nurse with a warm smile walked into the hospital room, removed Buddy's covers, gave him an injection, then gently stroked his face.

As the nurse turned to walk away, she touched Julia softly on the shoulder and told her not to give up hope. She reached into a pocket and gave Julia a handkerchief to dry her tears.

Miraculously, a short time later, Buddy began to cry. He had emerged safely from his coma.

"Praise the Lord, the angels, and all the saints in heaven!" Ida offered her thanks through her tears of joy.

A smiling nurse seemed to appear from nowhere, gave the boy an injection, and mysteriously disappeared.

Lonnie Cantrell, hollow-eyed from lack of sleep and from pushing his rig far more miles a day than he should have, arrived just in time to join his wife and daughter in fervent prayers of thanksgiving.

The doctors were amazed at the child's subsequent rapid recovery, and three days later Buddy was discharged.

As the family was leaving the hospital, Julia wished to thank the kind nurse and return the handkerchief that she had loaned her.

The soft linen bore the monogram "MAT," but the head nurse said that none of the nursing staff had such initials.

And when they checked Buddy's records, there was no indication that any nurse had visited him at 4:45 A.M.—and no injection of any kind had been authorized by the doctors.

The Cantrell family's confusion was resolved when a cleaning lady overheard their questions and informed them that a young nurse named Mary Ann Taggert had been killed in a car wreck as she left the hospital many years ago. Mary Ann had dreamed of becoming a doctor, and many of the older members of the hospital staff believed that her spirit lived on by helping very sick children.

"I can't swear that I know the whole truth of what happened," Julia Cantrell said. "But my folks and I like to believe that our prayers touched God's heart. We like to think that maybe He permitted the spirit of Mary Ann, the loving, caring nurse, to come back and help Buddy pull through. Momma always says that prayer really can move mountains."

His Loyalty to His Friends Brought His Spirit Back to Guide Them

In the summer of 1991 three fishermen—Tabwai Mikaie, Nweiti Tekamangu, and Arenta Tebeitabu—set out on a fishing trip from their South Pacific island of Kiribati, in the Republic of Kiribate.

Not far from land, off a coral atoll called Nikunau, they were suddenly pummeled by a powerful, unexpected cyclone that capsized their 12-foot boat and tossed them into the sea.

Although the men lost their outboard motor, they managed to climb safely back into the boat. However, since they were no longer able to power the tiny vessel, they began to drift farther and farther out into deeper waters, thus commencing a voyage that at times must have seemed endless.

> *On numerous occasions razor-jawed sharks circled their boat, sizing them up for dinner.*

Incredibly the three men remained adrift for 175 days, floating for nearly 1,000 miles.

By using a spear and a fishing line, they were able to survive on fish. From time to time they achieved some variety in their diet when they were able to snare a coconut floating by. To supplement their meager water supply, they collected rainwater.

On numerous occasions razor-jawed sharks circled their boat, sizing them up for dinner, but the fishermen turned the tables on the monsters and caught and ate no fewer than 10 of the voracious predators during their six months adrift.

Tabwai Mikaie, 24, said that they prayed to God four times a day, asking for his tender mercies to save them.

Tragically, after a seeming eternity of helpless drifting, Nweiti Tekamangu, 47, died when they were at last in sight of land.

Although his friends wept and pleaded with him to hold on for just a few days longer, Tekamangu's heart simply gave out after such a strenuous ordeal, and his sorrowful companions had no choice other than to cast his body overboard.

The survivors, Tabwai Mikaie and Arenta Tebeitabu, were now terrified by the thought of the formidable ordeal that lay before them. Since they were now only a few days from the mountainous island of Upolu in Western Samoa, they would soon have to maneuver their little 12-foot boat through some of the most treacherous reefs in the South Pacific. In their weakened condition, the task seemed impossible.

Tekamangu, the oldest of their tiny crew, had also been the most experienced and by far the most accomplished navigator. If he were still alive, they cried out to each other in their anguish, he would have had the necessary skills to guide them to a safe harbor.

Mikaie and Tebeitabu began to resign themselves to what appeared to be their certain destiny: They, too, would perish before they reached land.

Just as it seemed certain that the boat would be shattered into a thousand pieces of driftwood, the two men were astonished to see the spirit of their dead friend rise from the depths of the turbulent sea.

"Just listen to me, and you will be safe," the ghost of Tekamangu told them authoritatively.

Although there were sharp and treacherous reefs on each side of their weather-beaten and sea-battered boat, Mikaie and Tebeitabu placed their complete confidence in the commands of their ghostly comrade, who masterfully guided them through the murderous offshore rocks to the safety of the beach on Upolu.

Soon the two skeletal, half-dead fishermen were being lifted from their little boat and taken to a hospital.

Later, while authorities and journalists decreed the feat of their having survived six months adrift at sea as a miracle, Tebeitabu and Mikaie testified that only the supernatural presence of their friend had allowed them to live.

In their fervent statements to the authorities they declared that if Tekamangu's love and loyalty had not sent his spirit back to help them, they would surely have been dashed to splinters on the reefs of Upolu. After six months adrift at sea, they, too, would have perished just a few miles from land.

INDEX

A

Abma, Pam and Fred, 137–38

Abraham, 254, 255

Adams, Chanta, 42–43

Adamsville, Quebec, 65

Adhan, 239

Adirondack Mountains, New York, 115

airline crashes

 car seat saves granddaughter, 53–54

 man took wrong seat and survived, 54–55

 positive attitude helps survivor of homebuilt plane crash, 51–53

 teenager survives two-mile fall and ten days in rainforest, 49–51

 twelve-year-old sole survivor saved by falling luggage, 55–57

Alabama, 88, 155

Alaska, 118

Alberta, 8, 53, 163, 186

Albuquerque, New Mexico, 132

Alderton, Kevin, 213–14

Aleita, Jeremy, 99–100

Alexander, Charles, 166

Allahabad, India, 250

Allegany, Oregon, 107

Allen, Alicia, 185

alligators, 121–23

Alma, Nebraska, 159

Alps, 231–33

Amato, Joseph, 180

amazing recoveries

 car crash ends twenty-two years of paralysis, 205

 handshake reveals serious condition to doctor, 208

 man's eyesight returns after punch to head, 205–6

 spinal treatment restores sight in eye after twelve years, 207

 walking into pole restores sight in eye, 206

 woman regains sight through childbirth, 206–7

Amos, Wendy, 173–74

Anaheim, California, 95

Anderson, California, 167

Anderson, Doris, 9–10

Anderson, Fred, 235–38

G

H

I

J

M

N